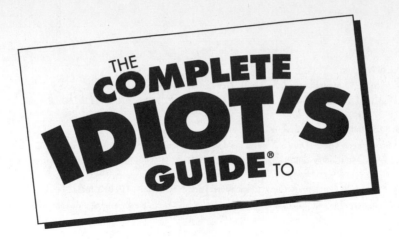

THE COMPLETE IDIOT'S GUIDE® TO

# Common Household Disasters

by Paul Hayman and Sonia Weiss

ALPHA

A member of Penguin Group (USA) Inc.

## ALPHA BOOKS

Published by the Penguin Group

Penguin Group (USA) Inc., 375 Hudson Street, New York, New York 10014, U.S.A.

Penguin Group (Canada), 10 Alcorn Avenue, Toronto, Ontario, Canada M4V 3B2 (a division of Pearson Penguin Canada Inc.)

Penguin Books Ltd, 80 Strand, London WC2R 0RL, England

Penguin Ireland, 25 St Stephen's Green, Dublin 2, Ireland (a division of Penguin Books Ltd)

Penguin Group (Australia), 250 Camberwell Road, Camberwell, Victoria 3124, Australia (a division of Pearson Australia Group Pty Ltd)

Penguin Books India Pvt Ltd, 11 Community Centre, Panchsheel Park, New Delhi—110 017, India

Penguin Group (NZ), cnr Airborne and Rosedale Roads, Albany, Auckland 1310, New Zealand (a division of Pearson New Zealand Ltd)

Penguin Books (South Africa) (Pty) Ltd, 24 Sturdee Avenue, Rosebank, Johannesburg 2196, South Africa

Penguin Books Ltd, Registered Offices: 80 Strand, London WC2R 0RL, England



International Standard Book Number: 1-59257-348-7

Library of Congress Catalog Card Number: 2004115796

07 06 05 8 7 6 5 4 3 2 1

Interpretation of the printing code: The rightmost number of the first series of numbers is the year of the book's printing; the rightmost number of the second series of numbers is the number of the book's printing. For example, a printing code of 05-1 shows that the first printing occurred in 2005.

*Printed in the United States of America*



**Publisher:** *Marie Butler-Knight*
**Product Manager:** *Phil Kitchel*
**Senior Managing Editor:** *Jennifer Bowles*
**Senior Acquisitions Editor:** *Paul Dinas*
**Development Editor:** *Ginny Bess Munroe*
**Production Editor:** *Janette Lynn*
**Copy Editor:** *Amy Borrelli*
**Cartoonist:** *Shannon Wheeler*
**Cover/Book Designer:** *Trina Wurst*
**Indexer:** *Angie Bess*
**Layout:** *Ayanna Lacey*
**Proofreading:** *Donna Martin*

# Contents at a Glance


**Part 1: Water, Water Everywhere** 1

1 My Roof's Got a Hole in It 3
*What causes roof damage, how you can find it, and repairs you can make.*

2 My Pipe Has a Break in It 15
*What you can do to keep household plumbing in good shape and running at full strength.*

3 My Sewer Backed Up 23
*No one likes to come home to smelly water in their basement. Want to avoid the problem? You'll learn how in this chapter.*

4 My Septic System Is Clogged 35
*If you live in the country or a similarly sparsely populated area, chances are good there's a private sewer system lurking under your yard somewhere. Here's what you need to know if it acts up, and what you need to know to keep it from acting up.*

5 My Basement Is Flooded 47
*Lots of things can cause water to come into a basement. This chapter covers some of the most common causes of wet basements and what you can do to mitigate them.*

6 My Walls Are Wet 59
*Wet walls indicate two things: water where it shouldn't be and indoor humidity levels that are higher than they should be. This chapter discusses the various causes behind both problems and remedies for them.*

7 Drying Things Out 73
*Everything you need to know about drying your home out after a water-related disaster, including battling mold.*

**Part 2: House on Fire!** 87

8 Heat in the Kitchen 89
*Food left to cook unattended—especially on a stovetop—is the number-one cause of kitchen fires. This chapter tells you what you need to know to avoid these fires, and what you should do if one erupts.*

9 Heat in the Chimney 97
*There's nothing that beats the warmth of a good fire—that is, when it's burning where it's supposed to be.*

10 Burning the House Down 111
*Many house fires are avoidable and preventable. For those that aren't, all you can do is know how to respond to them. You'll learn more about both types in this chapter.*

11 After the Fire 125
*It can be difficult to know where to begin and who to call after the fire is out. This chapter will tell you what to do.*

**Part 3: Rock Solid? Maybe Not! 133**

12 My Foundation Has a Crack in It 135
*Foundation cracks happen to the best houses. Some aren't cause for concern. Others are.*

13 My House Has a Hole in It 143
*The materials on the outside of homes are chosen for their ability to protect what's inside. For the most part, they do their job extremely well, but sometimes they don't.*

14 My House Is Rotting Away 155
*All about wood rot, and what you can do to keep it from happening in and around your home.*

15 Something's Eating My House 167
*Termites cause an estimated $2.5 billion worth of damage to homes and businesses every year. Want to keep your house from becoming part of this statistic? Here's how.*

**Part 4: Uninvited Guests 185**

16 There's a Mouse (or a Rat) in My House 187
*The pitter-patter of tiny feet can be a welcome sound. But not if there's a rodent attached to them.*

17 Other Furry (and Not) Intruders 205
*Other unwanted animal guests, including squirrels, opossums, raccoons, and skunks, are also common household visitors. Some are solo travelers and just drop in for a spell. Others take up residence with their families. None of them are welcome guests. In this chapter, you'll learn how to get rid of them.*

18 Ants, Cockroaches, and Other Creepy Crawlies 217
*Bug experts have identified some 1 million species of insects, so it stands to reason that you're going to share your home with a certain number of creepy crawlies. But you definitely can control how many you have to live with.*

19 Things That Go Bzzzz 239
*Inside or out, a couple of flies or a bee or two typically aren't much cause for alarm. Hundreds of them are.*

20 Out, Out, Damn Flea! 257
*There are more than 2,000 species of fleas in the world—that we know about, anyway. Of them, only about a dozen or so cause problems for humans and their pets. But they can cause lots of problems. Just ask anyone who has ever had to deal with a flea infestation.*

21 Bats (and Birds) in the Belfry 269
*Winged things—birds and bats—can, and do, take up residence where they're least welcome: in attics, under eaves, and in other favorable nesting and roosting spots. If you're dealing with one winged intruder—or lots of them—this chapter is for you.*

**Part 5: Third-Party Issues: Insurance, Contractors, and Service People 283**

22 Finding, Hiring, and Working with Contractors, Repairpersons, and Service People 285
*There are plenty of good companies and people out there, and a whole lot of others that aren't. In this chapter, you'll learn how to tell the good from the bad, and how to work with the ones you hire.*

23 Covered or Not: Homeowner's Insurance and Home Warranties 297
*What you need to know about protecting your most valuable investment.*

**Appendixes**

A Glossary 309

B Annual House Checklist and Maintenance Schedule 317

C Resources 325

Index 329

# Contents


**Part 1: Water, Water, Everywhere** 1

**1 My Roof's Got a Hole In It** 3

Plugging the Leak ....4
*Storm-Related Leaks* ....4
*Ice-Dam–Related Leaks* ....5
Causes of Roof Problems ....6
Diagnosing the Problem ....8
*Reviewing the Situation: Outside* ....8
*Reviewing the Situation: Inside* ....9
Fixing the Problem ....10
*Temporary Roof Relief* ....10
*Permanent Roof Relief* ....11

**2 My Pipe Has a Break in It** 15

Stopping the Flow ....15
*Calling for Help* ....17
Why Pipe Breaks Happen ....17
Fixing the Problem ....18
Repairing the Problem ....19
Preventing Pipe Problems ....20
Mopping Up ....21

**3 My Sewer Backed Up** 23

Stopping Sewage Flow ....23
Understanding Sanitary Sewers ....25
*Blocked Up!* ....25
*Overflow!* ....26
*Breakdown!* ....27
Why It's a Problem ....27
Prevention ....27
*Keeping Things Clean* ....28
*De-Rooting* ....29
*Modify Internal Plumbing* ....30
*Keep Extra Water Out* ....32
Cleanup ....32

**4 My Septic System Is Clogged** **35**

Immediate Steps ... 36
The Skinny on Septic Systems ... 36
Causes of Septic Problems ... 38
*Overloading the System* ... *38*
*Excessive Water Usage* ... *39*
*Compaction* ... *40*
*Dumping the Wrong Things Down* ... *40*
Keeping Your Septic System Happy ... 41
*Inspect It* ... *41*
*Pump It* ... *42*
*Keep It Thirsty* ... *43*
*Keep It Healthy* ... *44*
Clean Up ... 44

**5 My Basement Is Flooded** **47**

Your House Against the Elements ... 47
River Deep, Water High ... 49
Maintaining a Good Grade ... 51
*Dirt Fixes* ... *52*
*Pavement Fixes* ... *52*
Gutter Problems ... 53
Draining Things Off ... 53
Pumping Things Out ... 54
Cracking Things Up ... 56
Window-Well Water ... 57

**6 My Walls Are Wet** **59**

Walls of Water ... 59
Visiting the Scene of the Crime ... 61
Cracked Pipes ... 62
Trouble with Toilets ... 62
Rub-A-Dub-Dub, There's a Leak in My Tub ... 65
Dishing It Out ... 67
Hello Dampness, My Old Friend ... 67
Repairing Water-Damaged Interiors ... 69
*Sagging Drywall* ... *70*
*Patching Plaster and Drywall* ... *70*
*Water Stains* ... *70*
*Water Damage to Woodwork* ... *71*

**7 Drying Things Out** **73**

Before You Bail ....74
Bailing Things Out ....76
Scrubbing Things Up ....78
*More on Walls* ....78
*More on Floors and Floorcoverings* ....79
Slimy, Grimy Mold ....80
*Putting Out the Mold Welcome Mat* ....81
*Keeping Mold at Arm's Length* ....81
Cleaning Possessions and Valuables ....84
*Books* ....84
*Photographs* ....85
*Furniture* ....86
*Artwork* ....86

**Part 2: House on Fire!** **87**

**8 Heat in the Kitchen** **89**

The Heat Is On ....89
Firing Things Up ....90
Smokey the Bear Redux ....92
*Home Economics Redux* ....93
*Taking Your Kitchen Up a Notch (with Apologies to Emeril)* ....94
*Fire-Fighting Equipment* ....95

**9 Heat in the Chimney** **97**

Fire in the Hole ....98
Dirty Business ....101
Fire-Building 101 ....104
*Starting a Fire* ....104
*Keeping It Going* ....105
*Putting It Out* ....106
*Cleaning It Up* ....106
A Clean Chimney Is a Happy Chimney ....107

**10 Burning the House Down** **111**

The Wide World of House Fires ....112
One Homeowner's Story ....113
Electrical Fires ....114
*Goings-On Behind the Walls* ....115
*Alternative Wiring Products* ....116

*Signs of Problems* .....117
*Other Causes of Electrical Fires* .....117
Combustion Gas Fires .....117
An Ounce of Prevention .....118
Savvy Saves .....119
Fire or Not Fire? .....120
*Light at the Top* .....120
*Room with a View* .....120
*Let the Light In* .....121
*Nice and Toasty* .....121
*Rays and Rainbows* .....121
*How Dry I Am* .....121
*Hubby's New Hobby* .....122
*Hot Rock* .....123
*Waffling Over an Iron* .....123

**11 After the Fire** **125**

Actions in the Aftermath .....126
In the Cinders .....127
Clearing the Smoke .....128
Getting Rid of the Smoke Smell .....131

**Part 3: Rock Solid? Maybe Not!** **133**

**12 My Foundation Has a Crack in It** **135**

Foundation Faults .....135
Small Crack, Big Problem? .....136
Why Cracks Happen .....137
*Settling Things Down* .....137
*Soils of Clay* .....137
Keeping Foundations Happy .....138
Patching Cracks .....139

**13 My House Has a Hole In It** **143**

Old Friend Water .....143
Finding the Break .....145
The Inside Scoop on Exterior Construction .....146
How the Brick Crumbles .....146
*Spalling* .....147
*Cracks* .....147

Fixing Brick ....................148
*Water Problems* ....................*148*
*Mitigating Mortar Problems* ....................*149*
*Special Problems with Brick Veneer* ....................*150*
Wood Siding ....................150
Stucco ....................151
Vinyl and Metal Siding ....................153

**14 My House Is Rotting Away** 155

Rot Repair ....................156
Something's Rotten ....................157
*Dry vs. Wet Rot* ....................*157*
*Rot vs. Mold* ....................*158*
Why Wood Goes to Rot ....................159
Rooting Out Rot ....................160
*How Dry Am I?* ....................*161*
Drying Things Out ....................162
Repairing Wood Rot ....................162
Fixing Minor Rot Damage ....................164

**15 Something's Eating My House** 167

Immediate Fix ....................168
Insect I.D. ....................169
The Trouble with Termites ....................169
*Subterranean Termites* ....................*170*
*Drywood Termites* ....................*171*
*Dampwood Termites* ....................*171*
Preventing Termite Infestations ....................172
*Eliminating Wood-Ground Connections* ....................*173*
*Keeping Things Dry* ....................*173*
*Keeping Things Screened and Sealed* ....................*174*
Taking on Termites ....................174
Going with the Pros ....................175
*All About Warranties* ....................*176*
Treatment Options ....................177
*Soil Barriers* ....................*177*
*Colony Elimination* ....................*177*
*Wood Treatment* ....................*178*
*Approaches for Drywood Termites* ....................*178*
Repairing the Damage ....................179

Other Wood Lovers: Carpenter Ants ....................................180
*Diagnosing Carpenter Ants* ....................................*180*
*Preventing Carpenter Ant Infestations* ....................................*181*
*Controlling Carpenter Ants* ....................................*181*
*Repairing Carpenter Ant Damage* ....................................*182*

**Part 4: Uninvited Guests** **185**

**16 There's a Mouse (or a Rat) in My House** **187**

Getting Past "Eek!" ....................................188
Meet the Enemy ....................................188
*The House Mouse*....................................*189*
*The Rat on Rats*....................................*189*
Why They Come Inside ....................................190
Why They're a Problem ....................................190
Recognizing Rodent Infestations ....................................191
Getting Rid of Rodents....................................194
Sanitizing Your Home....................................195
*Food Sanitation* ....................................*195*
*Outdoor Sanitation* ....................................*196*
*Indoor Sanitation*....................................*196*
*Rodent Repellents* ....................................*197*
Rodent-Proofing ....................................198
Reducing Their Numbers....................................199
*Trapping* ....................................*199*
*Poison Control* ....................................*201*
*Zap 'Em* ....................................*202*
*Fumigating* ....................................*202*
Disposing of Your Guests ....................................203

**17 Other Furry (and Not) Intruders** **205**

Animal in the Room ....................................206
*Overriding the Panic Button* ....................................*206*
*Say Buh-Bye!*....................................*206*
*No, No, I Won't Go* ....................................*207*
Next Steps ....................................208
Why They Come In ....................................208
Why They're a Problem ....................................209

Removing the Nuisance ....................209
*Can't Touch Me!* ....................209
*Why Can't We Be Friends?* ....................210
*Animals in the Chimney* ....................210
*A Family Affair* ....................211
*Animals in Crawl Spaces and Attics* ....................212
*Animals Under the Porch* ....................213
Keeping Them Away ....................214

**18 Ants, Cockroaches, and Other Creepy Crawlies 217**

Under Siege! ....................218
Living the Bug-Free Life ....................218
Taking Control Over Bugs ....................218
Name and Number Please! ....................220
Ladybugs ....................221
*IPM Controls* ....................222
*Chemical Control* ....................222
Ground Beetles ....................222
*IPM Controls* ....................223
*Chemical Controls* ....................223
Spiders ....................223
*IPM Controls* ....................224
*Chemical Controls* ....................224
Annoying Ants ....................224
*IPM for Ants* ....................225
*Chemical Controls* ....................225
Pantry Pests ....................226
*Treating Suspect Food* ....................227
*IPM for Pantry Pests* ....................227
*Chemical Controls* ....................228
Bedbugs ....................228
*IPM Controls* ....................229
*Chemical Controls* ....................230
Carpet Beetles ....................230
*IPM Controls* ....................231
*Chemical Controls* ....................232
Clothes Moths ....................232
*IPM Controls* ....................232

Wood-Destroying Beetles ....232
*IPM Controls* ....233
*Chemical Controls* ....234
Cockroaches ....234
*IPM Controls* ....234
*Chemical Controls* ....235
Silverfish and Firebrats ....235
*IPM Controls* ....236
*Chemical Controls* ....236

**19 Things That Go Bzzzz 239**

Flying Things in the House ....240
*Trapping* ....240
*Quick Kill Via Insecticide* ....240
Calling in IPM ....241
Stinging Things ....241
*Risk Factors* ....241
*Should They Go or Should They Stay?* ....242
Bald-Faced Hornets ....242
*DIY Hornet Nest Removal* ....243
Yellow Jackets ....244
*Playing "Keep Away"* ....245
*IPM for Yellow Jackets* ....245
*Hitting Them Where They Nest* ....246
*Yellow Jackets in Walls* ....247
Paper Wasps ....247
No-Worry Wasps ....247
Hard-to-Hate Honeybees ....248
*Going on the Defensive* ....248
*Chemical Control* ....249
*Bees in the House* ....249
On the Fly ....249
IPM for Flies ....251
*Sanitation* ....252
*Inspection* ....252
*Exclusion* ....253
*Mechanical Controls* ....253
*Chemical Controls* ....254

**20 Out, Out, Damn Flea! 257**

Flea-Bitten? ....257
Quick to the Kill ....258
*Spot-On Insecticides* ....259
*Insect Growth Regulators* ....260
*Insect Development Inhibitors* ....260
*Washing the Problem* ....260
Treating Your Environs ....261
*Cleaning Up* ....261
*Insecticide Control* ....262
*Outdoor Control* ....263
Meet the Flea ....263
*Scratching the Itch* ....264
*More Serious Health Concerns* ....264
Why Fleas Happen ....265
Defensive Measures ....266
Questionable Control Measures ....266

**21 Bats (and Birds) in the Belfry 269**

Solo Intruders ....270
*Corralling a Bird* ....270
*Birds in the Chimney* ....271
*Battling a Bat* ....272
Bats—Good and Bad ....273
Bat-Proofing Your Cave ....274
Ruling the Roost ....275
*Caulk It Up* ....277
*Screen Shots* ....277
*Lights, Camera, Action!* ....277
*Gimme Shelter* ....278
Battling Bunches of Birds ....278
Banishing Birds ....279
*Saying Boo!* ....280
*Barriers for Birds* ....281

**Part 5: Third-Party Issues: Insurance, Contractors, and Service People 283**

**22 Finding, Hiring, and Working with Contractors, Repairpersons and Service People 285**

Finding the Talent ....286
*Word of Mouth* ....287
*Let Your Fingers Do the Walking* ....287
*Chambers of Commerce* ....287
*Professional Organizations* ....287
Special Considerations—Disasters ....288
Hiring the Talent ....288
The Skinny on "Underground" Contractors ....291
More on Estimates ....292
Getting It in Writing ....293
Mechanic's Liens ....295
Working with Contractors ....295
When the Job Is Done ....296

**23 Covered Or Not: Homeowner's Insurance and Home Warranties 297**

Protection from the Unexpected ....298
Property Protection ....298
Protection from Peril ....299
*Levels of Protection* ....300
*Homeowner's Insurance, Texas Style* ....301
What's Not Covered ....301
Understanding Loss and Recovery ....302
Living Away from Home ....303
Liability Coverage ....304
Buying the Right Policy ....304
Upholding Your End of the Deal ....305
Existing Home Warranties ....306
New Home Warranties ....306

**Appendixes**

**A Glossary 309**

**B Annual House Checklist and Maintenance Schedule 317**

**C Resources 325**

**Index 329**

# Foreword

Home ownership can be found at the heart of the American economy and the American dream. It is the engine that drives our business expansion and creates the single best investment opportunity for the average middle-class family. I have pursued a successful 30-year career designing several products that can be found in all of our homes. Whether it is new construction, professional remodeling, or a weekend do-it-yourself project, I am familiar with what it takes to survive in the home environment.

It was with this smug sense of insider entitlement that I recently purchased a beautifully situated and modified Cape Cod–style house. Built in 1948, this house was created using a level of professional skills and quality materials that I haven't seen in years. I just knew from my design experience that I could handle any problem that I encountered. I was such a fool.

Within weeks of moving in, the first of my household crises began to emerge. I quickly realized how vital a survival manual like *The Complete Idiot's Guide to Household Disasters* can be. In only three months, I have experienced emergency situations that can be found in Chapters 1, 5, 7, 13, 16, 19, and 23.

First came the panicked realization that my beautiful backyard was, in reality, an invertebrate war zone featuring battling hornets and wasps. Chapter 19 taught me that I not only needed to eliminate the winged critters, but more importantly, eliminate their habitats. Within weeks came the rainstorm and consequent flooding that kicked in the need for Chapters 1, 5, 7, and 13. Being so unprepared not only cost me money, but also time, sleep, and a certain amount of my sanity.

Using my new fireplace for the first time led me to Chapter 16 and the discovery of a mouse. The poor little guy was living in the house before I was—warm and snug in the flu, apparently—and he was even more horrified than I at our first meeting. Finally, I encountered the most frightening homeowner experience of them all—acquiring homeowner's insurance (discussed in Chapter 23). Dealing with insurance agents and contractors requires just as much know-how, if not more, than dealing with the aforementioned animal pests and household hazards.

I can only assume that I will encounter a need for the knowledge and skill in the balance of the chapters in the months and years ahead. This book is my one shot at being ready. Personally experiencing household emergencies is not simply a matter of if these emergencies happen, but how soon. *The Complete Idiot's Guide to Household Disasters* offers the best chance at peace of mind for today's homeowner. I do love my new home. I do believe it is a good investment. However, the goal now is to be prepared and to not take the needs of my house for granted anymore.

Gary Uhl
director of product design
American Standard, Porcher, and Jado brand products

# Introduction

We depend on our homes for many things. We rely on them to keep us safe, to protect us from the elements, and to provide a comfortable and enjoyable place to live. For the most part, they deliver. But sometimes things go wrong. Sometimes they go very wrong.

Any kind of disaster can turn your life around. Disasters that involve the structures that shelter us are no exception. Recovering from them can be a challenge on many levels—physically, emotionally, and financially. Sadly, the aftermath of some disasters can affect your life for a long, long time.

Unless you're Superman, it isn't possible to reverse a disaster after the fact. But it is possible to keep many household disasters from happening in the first place. And knowing how to respond to them can go a long way toward lessening the damage when they do happen. That's what this book is all about.

Houses are inanimate objects, but in their own way they are living, breathing things. As such, things can happen to them just like they do to people. They can get hurt; they can develop diseases and illnesses. Their occupants are typically the first line of defense when something happens. When the occupant is you, it's your responsibility to know what to do when things go wrong.

## How This Book Is Organized

To help you be the best "first responder" you can be, we've organized *The Complete Idiot's Guide to Household Disasters* by the types of disasters homeowners are most likely to encounter:

In **Part 1, "Water, Water Everywhere,"** you'll learn how to deal with disasters created by roof damage, plumbing problems, sewer backups, and more.

**Part 2, "House on Fire!,"** details the most common causes of fires in and around the home.

In **Part 3, "Rock Solid? Maybe Not!,"** we cover structural problems ranging from faulty foundations to crumbling brick.

**Part 4, "Uninvited Guests,"** will tell you what you need to know to rid your home of mice, birds, insects, and other animal intruders and keep them from coming back in.

**Part 5, "Third-Party Issues: Insurance, Contractors, and Service People,"** offers solid advice on the protection you should have for your home as well as hiring people to work on it.

We also included a glossary and two appendixes containing the terms used in this book, resources, and a home maintenance checklist and schedule.

## Bonus Information

In addition to the main narrative of *The Complete Idiot's Guide to Household Disasters*, you'll find other types of useful information. Here's how to recognize these features:

**In the Nick of Time**

Ways to make dealing with household disasters a little easier.

**A Fine Mess**

Situations to avoid.

**Tool Chest**

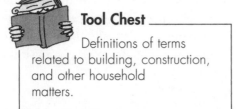

Definitions of terms related to building, construction, and other household matters.

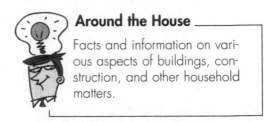

**Around the House**

Facts and information on various aspects of buildings, construction, and other household matters.

## Acknowledgments

We extend our sincerest thanks to Will Bond, who provided invaluable research assistance on many chapters, and Curt Stonecipher, D.V.M., for his assistance on the chapter on fleas.

Thanks also go to Paul Dinas for his superb editorial guidance throughout the development and writing of this book; Ginny Bess for her outstanding work shaping this book's final form; Janette Lynn, our production editor; Donna Martin, our proofreader; and Ayanna Lacey, our layout tech.

## Special Thanks to the Technical Reviewer

*The Complete Idiot's Guide to Common Household Disasters* was reviewed by an expert who double-checked the accuracy of what you'll learn here, to help us ensure that this book gives you everything you need to know about household disasters. Special thanks are extended to tech editor Johanna Harden for her extensive wisdom on most, if not all, household pests.

## Trademarks

All terms mentioned in this book that are known to be or are suspected of being trademarks or service marks have been appropriately capitalized. Alpha Books and Penguin Group (USA) Inc. cannot attest to the accuracy of this information. Use of a term in this book should not be regarded as affecting the validity of any trademark or service mark.

# Part 1

# Water, Water, Everywhere

The structures we live in are designed to do many things. Managing water—the essence of life—is one of them. We have plumbing systems that bring fresh water into our homes and take used water out of them. Roofs, gutters, sump pumps, drain tile, and other devices keep unwanted water out and protect the people and belongings within.

In well-built, well-maintained homes, water isn't much of a concern. It comes in and goes out as it should. But lots of things can happen to disrupt this balanced flow. When they do, you either have unwanted water in your house or none at all.

Water leakage and damage are the most common insurance claims, costing homeowners and insurance companies millions of dollars every year. In this part, you learn how to minimize water-related damage and losses and what you can do to avoid them in the future.

Chapter 1

# My Roof's Got a Hole In It

## In This Chapter

- Causes of roof leaks
- Finding the source
- Breaking up ice dams
- Preventing future problems

Even if you aren't a child of the '50s (or even the '60s), you've probably heard a song with the chorus, "Oh no, don't let the rain come down, my roof's got a hole in it and I might drown." (For you trivia buffs, it was recorded in 1964 by the Serendipity Singers.)

No matter what kind of house you're in—old or new—or the kind of roof that tops it, odds are that some time during your stay there, you'll have to deal with some sort of roof problem. If that time is now—your roof has a hole in it and the rain (or whatever) is coming down—this chapter is for you.

# Plugging the Leak

We'll get into what roof leaks are all about and how you find, fix, and prevent them in a moment. Right now, if there's water coming into your house, you've got an immediate problem to contend with, so let's look at what you need to do now.

## Storm-Related Leaks

Hail, wind, and torrential downpours can all cause roof leaks, either from the elements themselves or what they do to other things, such as causing tree limbs to fall. If the storm is still raging, your goal is to minimize interior damage while you're waiting for the storm to end. Your plan of attack will depend on how much damage you see:

- If you notice brown or reddish-tinged discoloration on the ceiling or walls that you haven't seen before, keep on eye on things. If the discoloration starts to bulge, it means that water is gathering behind the plaster, wallboard, or ceiling tiles. To minimize damage, locate the center of the bulge and break it open by driving a nail or an awl into the center of the stain area. Place a bucket under the leak. (For tips on how to repair discoloration and water damage from roof leaks, turn to Chapter 6.)
- If water is coming into your house from a specific spot in the ceiling, place a bucket under the leak. Keep an eye on things, and empty the bucket as necessary.
- If water is coming in from lots of places, position containers under as many spots as possible. Or cover the area where the leaks are dripping with a plastic tarp. If you don't have a tarp, garbage or leaf bags will work in a pinch.
- If a ceiling is beginning to sag or a wall is starting to buckle inward, significant structural damage is a possibility. There's nothing you can do about it until the storm is over. If it's in

**Around the House**

Roof leaks can be deceiving as water can run quite a distance from the actual leak. For this reason, it doesn't do you much good to try to find a leak during a storm. Nor is it the safest approach. Wait until after the storm passes or the snow melts.

**In the Nick of Time**

Water that comes through your ceiling and flows down toward a wall can be hard to contain. You can divert it by nailing a small block of wood flat against the ceiling in the water trickle. This will direct the water into a bucket.

a part of your house that poses a threat to you and your family, find somewhere else to stay until the storm passes, at which time you can have an expert (an inspector or contractor) come to assess the damage.

## Ice-Dam–Related Leaks

If you live in a cold, snowy area, an ice dam might be causing the leak. Ice dams happen when snow on a roof melts from sunlight or heat from the house. The melted snow runs off the roof down into the gutter, which may be at below-freezing temperatures, where it freezes. The ice builds up and works its way under the tarpaper under the shingles where it can again melt and enter the house.

Ice dams usually form on the north side of the house or on a sheltered side and can become several feet thick, building back from the gutter. Many houses at high elevations (where this is common) lack gutters to prevent the formation of ice dams.

Ice dams don't necessarily make holes in your roof, although they can loosen shingles. They prevent the water caused by melting snow and ice from going where it should—off the roof and into gutters or onto the ground. Instead, the water goes under the roofing material and seeps into your home.

> **In the Nick of Time**
>
> An adhesive underlayment, sometimes called a snow and ice shield, can be applied under shingles at the time the roof is installed to minimize leakage from ice dams.

If an ice dam is causing the leak, follow the measures outlined in the previous section for water that's coming inside your home. Outside, try the following:

- Remove snow with a snow roof rake. This is a long-handled tool with a rectangular head, specially designed for the job it does. Many come with telescoping attachments for reaching high, out-of-the-way spots. You'll find them in just about any hardware, home supply, or building products store.
- Call a professional to thaw and remove ice dams using steam equipment.
- Melt a channel through the ice by pouring hot water on it. This will let the water flow off the roof before it freezes. This typically involves climbing up on a ladder, and can be a bit risky. It's also usually very temporary. If the temperature of the gutter isn't above freezing, the hot water will quickly freeze in the gutter.

There is one more emergency fix you can try on an ice dam. Opinions vary on it, as it uses a chemical that can damage your roof and nearby vegetation, but it's one that a lot of people use. And if it looks like the ice dam is going to cause significant damage in your house, it probably can't hurt.

CAUTION

**A Fine Mess**

Do not chop ice off shingles or use a blowtorch to remove an ice dam. Doing so could cause more damage to your roof.

Cut one leg off an old pair of panty hose. Tie a knot in one end of the leg, and fill it with calcium chloride or another ice-melting substance. Lay it vertically across the ice dam. You might need a roof rake or another long-handled implement for this. The chemical inside the stocking will cut through the ice and open a channel through which the backed-up water can flow.

*Icicles cascading off a roof like the ones here are pretty, but they also indicate an ice buildup that can lead to an ice dam.*

# Causes of Roof Problems

Now that you've got the immediate problem under control, let's take a look at why your roof sprung a leak.

The main reason why leaky roofs are so common is because roofs are constantly exposed to the elements. As such, the materials that cover them—shingles, tiles, sheathing, etc.—are under attack 24/7 from moisture, wind, and debris. Even certain types of seeds from trees can damage roofing material.

Almost all roofs are protected from leaks by the tarpaper beneath the shingles. The purpose of the shingles, whether they are wood, fiberglass, or concrete, is to protect the tarpaper.

Damaged or worn roofing materials—especially shingles and *flashings*—are the most common causes of roof damage. In cold climates, ice dams are another major cause of roof leaks.

**Around the House**

Bad weather often exposes subtle roof leaks that have been going on for a long time. Damage from these leaks often remains invisible to the eye unless you look for it. As damage accumulates, it's only a matter of time before something happens. When it does, what was once a small, easily remedied problem turns into a disaster.

**Tool Chest**

**Flashings** are materials that connect roofing materials to other building materials. They're used wherever there's an interruption in the roofing, such as around dormers, skylights, chimneys, etc., and to waterproof areas like roof valleys, hips, and the angles between chimneys and roofs. Metal is a common flashing material; granular asphalt sheets are also used.

Other causes of leaky roofs include …

- Defective or incorrectly installed roofing material. Flashings are a chief culprit here.
- Clogged gutter downspouts and eaves. Leaves, bird nests, and other materials can clog gutters and cause water to back up under shingles.
- Age-related wear and tear. All roofing material—even the most impervious—has a life span. As the materials age, they become more susceptible to damage from the elements.
- Animal damage. Roosting birds and other small animals can damage roofs. Animals like roof rats can even chew through them. For more on this, turn to Chapters 16 and 17.

- Tree damage. Falling trees and limbs are the most common form of damage. As mentioned, some trees bear seeds containing substances that can damage roofing material.
- Poor workmanship. Some roofs simply aren't installed correctly.

The good news is that all of these problems can be solved. Some of the fixes, such as keeping gutters clear of debris and keeping trees trimmed back, are easy to do and should be a part of your annual home maintenance checklist. You'll find more on this checklist in Appendix B.

Other roof issues, such as defective roofing material or materials that have simply exceeded their lifespan, aren't easy fixes, nor are they cheap. But they definitely can be remedied.

> CAUTION
>
> **A Fine Mess**
>
> Wait for dry weather before examining exterior roofing. If you can't wait, don't risk serious injury by clamoring up on the roof during a storm. Use a pair of binoculars for a close-up look.

## Diagnosing the Problem

Knowing what to do about your leaky roof requires determining the cause of the leak. There are two ways to do this assessment: from the outside and on the inside.

The physical causes of roof damage, such as toppled antennas or tree limbs poking through shingles, are pretty obvious. But this isn't always the case. The things that cause roof damage can be very subtle. They can also vary quite a bit depending on the type of roof you have.

### Reviewing the Situation: Outside

There are two ways to view roof damage from the outside—up close and personal, which means climbing up on a ladder, or at arm's length via binoculars. You'll get a better picture of what's going on if you can get on the roof, but it isn't always necessary. Also, you don't have to do it yourself. You can hire an expert, such as a roofing contractor, to do it for you.

If you decide to climb up on your roof, be sure to use a solid ladder and don't go it alone. Station someone at the foot of the ladder in case you need assistance.

Here's what you might see when you go up on your roof:

- Uplifting or splitting of the roofing membrane (the material that covers the roof) or decking on flat roofs.
- Punctures in the roof caused by debris hitting it.
- Cracking or other age-related deterioration. This is typically most apparent on southern exposures, and especially on wood or composition shingles.
- Damaged roof-mounted vents or air-conditioning equipment.
- Stripped ridge tiles, or missing or broken tiles on concrete or clay roofs.
- Pitting or pock marking on asphalt shingles or membranes. This can be caused by hail or from toxic substances in seedpods.
- Stripped or torn shingles on asphalt, fiberglass, or cedar roofs.
- Algae growth from poor drainage.
- Previous roof repairs.
- Rotted or rusted decking.
- Worn or rusted flashings.
- Wrinkled roofing membrane.
- Holes from missing shingles or other roofing materials.

If you find the exact area of damage, poke a stick or piece of wire through the hole so you can see it from the inside.

## Reviewing the Situation: Inside

This inspection is typically a lot easier to do and something that most homeowners don't mind doing. Here's what to look for:

- Holes and cracks through which you can see outside.
- Wetness or signs of water damage, such as watermarks, rot, or mold, on beams, rafters, sheathing, walls, floors, etc.

If your house has a chimney, pay special attention to the area where the roof meets the chimney. Water seepage or drainage in this area is usually a sure sign of a flashing problem.

**In the Nick of Time**

Even if there's no apparent water damage after a severe storm, it's a good idea to inspect roofs and attics for it. Storms can cause damage that might not show up as interior leaks for months afterwards. It's always better to catch problems before they cause bigger ones. If you suspect storm damage but you don't know what to look for, hire a roofing contractor to check things out.

Keep in mind that water travels down to its lowest point before it drips. For this reason, wet spots can be a bit misleading as they often aren't directly under the damaged area. To get the fullest picture, look for drip trails on rafters and sheathing. When you find what appears to be the source of the leak, mark it with a nail, wire, stick, or similar object that's long enough to see from the outside.

# Fixing the Problem

There are two types of roof fixes: temporary and permanent. A temporary fix not only minimizes additional water damage inside your home, it's also important from an insurance perspective. Here's why: It's your responsibility as a homeowner to protect your house and belongings from further damage. If you don't take the appropriate steps to do so, your homeowner's policy might not cover this damage.

## Temporary Roof Relief

As mentioned, all you're going to do for a temporary fix is prevent additional water damage inside your house.

Temporary fixes are appropriate if …

- You can see obvious damage to your roof, such as holes, missing shingles, mangled flashing, etc.
- Water is still coming into your home.
- An appropriate repairperson, such as a roofing contractor, is unavailable.

Be sure you, or the person who is going to do the repairs, is physically able to do them. Here's what you'll need:

- Ladder
- Plywood boards, tarp, or plastic sheeting
- Strips of wood, if you're using a tarp or plastic sheeting
- Hammer and nails or duct tape

And here's what you'll do:

1. Climb onto your roof.
2. If you're using plywood sheets, nail them into place.
3. If you're using plastic sheets or trash bags, nail strips of wood over them or secure with duct tape. If the holes are large, you might have to support the plastic in the middle to keep it from tearing if additional water collects in it.

Only attempt these repairs if your roof isn't sagging. If it is, leave everything alone as it's too dangerous for you to be up there. Call a contractor, and describe the problem. These areas need bracing to prevent further damage, and this needs to happen sooner rather than later.

**Around the House**

Homeowner's insurance pays for emergency repairs. Be sure to keep all your receipts so you can file them along with your claim.

## Permanent Roof Relief

Always notify your insurance company before making permanent repairs. Claims can be denied if repairs are done before an adjuster can assess the damage.

Unless you've worked on roofs before, it's strongly recommended that you hire a professional roofer. What's more, your insurance company might insist on it. Remember, how materials are installed can make or break a roof. Shoddy workmanship is a major cause of roof problems.

**In the Nick of Time**

It's a good idea to be home when an insurance adjuster arrives. Your knowledge of what happened can be important to the amount of recovery you receive. Plus, you might be able to point out things that the adjuster might overlook.

It's also not a bad idea to get an estimate from a roofing contractor before the adjuster arrives, or even have a contractor there when he does. Differences of opinion on roof damage are common. Insurance companies pay out big time on roof damage claims. As such, they tend to err on the conservative side when it comes to assessing the extent of the damage.

That said, it's not that tough to replace a loose or missing shingle or two, especially if you're handy, you feel comfortable on ladders, and your roof isn't too steeply pitched. Here's what you'll need:

- Something to kneel on, such as a moving pad, if you're going to climb onto the roof to do the repairs
- Hammer
- Pry bar
- Shingles that match the existing color as closely as possible
- Galvanized roofing nails
- Roofing sealant

If you're going to be working on the roof itself, rather than from a ladder, you should also wear a safety harness and line. This will keep you from tumbling off the roof. Safety glasses and gloves are also highly recommended. If you work from a ladder, station someone at the foot of it in case you need help.

Finally, think twice about doing these repairs if your house is taller than a single story or if the roof is steeply pitched.

Here's what you'll do:

1. If you're working on the roof, put on the safety harness and secure the rope to your harness. Put the pad under your knees.
2. Use the pry bar to lift up just enough of the shingles to expose the heads of the roofing nails. Pry the nails out and remove the damaged shingles.

3. Slide new shingles into place. Line them up with existing shingles.
4. Secure shingles with roofing nails. Dab roofing sealant over the nails for a watertight finish.
5. Press shingles down flat. Heat from the sun will activate the adhesive part of the shingles and seal them into position.

Homeowner's policies provide coverage for direct losses from things like tornadoes, windstorms, hail, and so on. Be sure to check your policy for specific coverage terms. If you live in an area where windstorms or hailstorms are prevalent, there might be specific deductibles for these perils.

## The Least You Need to Know

- No matter what kind of house you're in, you'll probably have to deal with some sort of roof problem sooner or later.
- Damaged or worn roofing materials are the most common causes of roof damage.
- Never assume that a big storm hasn't caused damage. Visually inspect your roof both inside and out after any major rain, hail, or windstorm.
- The best way to prevent roof problems is to repair small problems before they become big ones. Inspect attics, crawl spaces, and roofs for signs of damage on a regular basis, and fix all problems when you find them.

Chapter 2

# My Pipe Has a Break in It

## In This Chapter

- Causes of pipe breaks
- Thawing things out
- Fixing leaks and cracks
- Preventing future breaks

Most people find the sound of running water peaceful and soothing, which is why resorts and spas typically have an abundance of it by way of fountains, streams, pools, jetted tubs, and other water features.

However, hearing running water inside your house, especially when you don't have a faucet turned on or you're not running an appliance like a dishwasher, can be far from a tranquil experience.

It means you have a broken pipe inside your house.

## Stopping the Flow

Plumbing systems have two components: a clean-water supply system and a wastewater system. A burst pipe is a problem with the clean-water supply inside your house. For wastewater problems, turn to Chapter 3.

**Tool Chest**

An **angle stop** is a valve that shuts off water to appliances, faucets, washing machines, toilets, and so on.

Before you do anything else, you need to stop the water from coursing through the break. There are two ways of doing this. If you can see where the break is, and there's an *angle stop*—a valve in the line that feeds the pipe—open the faucet at the end of the pipe, then turn the valve until the water flow stops.

But not all pipelines have valves, and walls can hide breaks. If either is the case, you'll have to shut off the water to the entire house. To do this, you need to know where your main shutoff valve is.

There are two types of main water valves. Gate valves have round handles that must be turned a number of times to close the valve. Ball valves have a single handle. When the water is on, the handle will be in line with the pipe it's located on. Give the handle a quarter (90-degree) turn, so it's perpendicular to the pipe, and the water is off.

These devices are typically located in one of the following places if your home is connected to a municipal water system:

- Basement or utility room. Both are typical locations in cold climates, as placing valves indoors protects them from the cold. The valve is usually sited near the wall where the service pipe enters.
- Garage.
- Outdoors by the foundation. A common location is near the front hose faucet.

If you have a private well, look for the valve on the supply line coming out of the pressurized storage tank.

**In the Nick of Time**

It's a good idea to identify your home's main water supply before you have an emergency. Make sure it's in working order by turning the handle. Identify it with a tag, and tell all household members where it is.

If your home doesn't have a main water shutoff valve—and not all do—consider having a plumber install one.

## Calling for Help

If you can't find the shutoff valve, or there's another reason why you can't shut off the water, you have two options:

- If you're on municipal water, call the public works department where you live. They'll shut off the water at the main. Some mains can be shut off at the curb if you have a key to the cover and a device called a t-handle, which you can buy at a home improvement store.
- If you're on a private well, turn off the electricity to the pump.

If you're on municipal water, be aware that it might take some time for department personnel to reach you. Remember that if you're having problems, others might be in the same boat. This is just one reason why it's a good idea to do what you can to prevent water breaks from happening.

# Why Pipe Breaks Happen

Freezing weather is the leading cause of pipe breaks. As temperatures plummet, water expands. As it does, it causes localized pressure that normal metal pipes can't handle. This can cause one of the following:

- A pinhole leak
- A hairline break
- A big crack

**In the Nick of Time**

Sometimes pipes freeze but don't break. This also causes problems, as the frozen water blocks water to faucets and appliances. If this happens, thaw the blockage before it breaks the pipe and creates further damage. To do so, you'll have to locate the blockage. Leave the blocked faucets or valves turned on to equalize pressure as much as possible, then trace the pipes back from there, feeling along the pipes for the coldest spot. Pay particular attention to exterior walls and unheated areas, which are common locations for pipe breaks.

# Fixing the Problem

Thawing is the immediate fix for frozen pipes. Find the coldest part of the pipe with your hands. That's where the block is, and where you want to apply heat. Use any of the following, but don't heat the pipes too quickly. Doing so might make the water in the pipe boil, which can burst it. If you're warming plastic pipe, be extra careful, as too much heat can cause even bigger problems, and follow the specific recommendations below:

- **Heat gun.** Set the gun on low, and keep the nozzle moving near the frozen section but not right on it. If there are flammable materials nearby, be careful about overheating them. Heat guns typically come with shields. If yours did, use it. You can use a heat gun on plastic pipe, but keep the gun a good distance away from the pipe.
- **Hair dryer.** This will take longer, as hair dryers can't reach the temperatures that heat guns do, but it's a good approach (and a safer one in general) if you don't own the former. Again, be sure to keep the nozzle of the dryer moving to minimize heat buildup, and be careful around flammable materials. This is a better method than heat guns for plastic pipes.
- **Electric space heater.** Same cautions as above.
- **Heat lamp.** Same cautions as above.
- **Electric blanket.** Probably one of the safest methods, although it can take a while. Simply wrap the blanket around the pipe and turn it on.
- **Electric heat tape.** Also known as heat cable, this is plastic-coated wire that's wrapped around a surface to keep it from freezing. Be careful with this stuff; the U.S. Consumer Product Safety Commission has issued a safety advisory on electric heat tape, as it can cause fires if not installed correctly or if it's allowed to deteriorate. There are different kinds of heat tape, so be sure to buy the right kind for the type of water pipe you need to treat and read the instructions before installing.
- **Light bulb.** Take the shade off a lamp and place it near the pipe.

CAUTION

**A Fine Mess**

Never thaw frozen pipes with an open flame. Doing so could start a fire, regardless of the type of pipe. And be careful when using an electrical appliance for thawing. Should the pipe burst and spray water, you run the risk of electrocution. Finally, never use electrical tools or appliances to heat a pipe if you're wet or there's standing water about.

You can also thaw frozen pipes by wrapping them in rags or towels and pouring hot water over them. Whichever method you use, keep doing it until the water flows.

As the ice thaws, you should see water start to drip out of the faucet. If there's a break in the pipe, you should also see drips of water where the break is.

## Repairing the Problem

As mentioned, pipe breaks typically fall into three categories: pinhole leaks, hairline cracks, and big breaks. Of these, pinhole leaks and hairline cracks are breaks that many do-it-yourselfers feel confident about fixing. Most experts recommend hiring a plumber to fix anything larger than a hairline crack.

Electrician's tape or duct tape is a quick fix for pinhole leaks. All you have to do is wrap it firmly around the pipe where the leak is. Be sure to dry the pipe off thoroughly before you do to give the tape the best chance for sticking in place. This type of repair won't last very long, due to the amount of pressure in the pipe, but it should last until you can make a more permanent repair.

You can repair hairline cracks with a pipe clamp repair kit or fiberglass-resin tape. Pipe clamp kits come in different configurations, but typically consist of a rubber or neoprene sleeve and a couple of clamps that fit together and hold the sleeve in place. Fiberglass-resin tape is available pre-packaged in pipe repair kits. Some tapes have to be mixed with epoxy before they're applied; others come impregnated with the epoxy, which is activated by soaking it in water. This product can also be used as a permanent fix for pinhole leaks.

For either fix, first make sure the line has no pressure in it by turning off the water and opening a faucet or release valve. Next, clean the area around the break with a scrub pad. If the pipe is corroded, remove the corrosion with sandpaper, steel wool, or a wire brush. You want a smooth, clean surface for the best fix.

If you're using a pipe clamp kit, you'll need a screwdriver to install it. Place the sleeve around the break. If it has a seam, locate it on the opposite side of the pipe, away from the break. Then, cinch the clamps around the sleeve and tighten them firmly.

If you're using fiberglass-resin tape, follow the package instructions. You'll have to work fast, as the epoxy in the tape sets up fast. Start wrapping at least 1" away from the break. Wrap the tape back and forth around the pipe to at least 1" on the other side of the tape. Wrap snugly and smooth it with your hands as you go for a tight seal and to keep air bubbles from getting caught between layers.

When the repair is complete, open the water back up and check for leaks. Wait about 30 to 40 minutes before doing so if you used fiberglass-resin tape so it can cure completely.

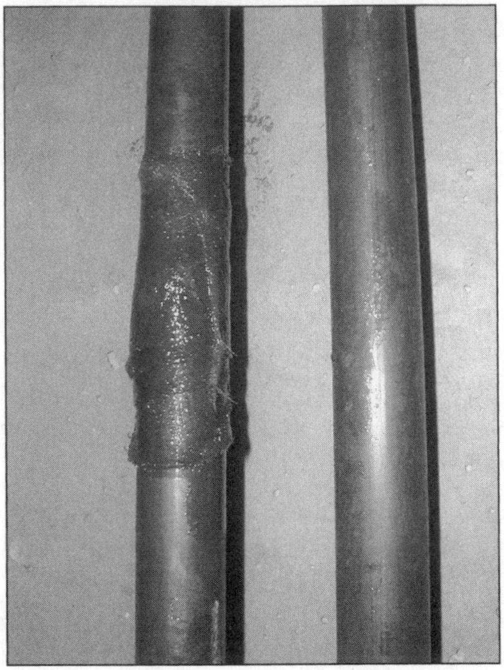

*Fiberglass-resin tape was used as an emergency fix on this copper pipe. For the best seal, make sure the tape extends at least 1" beyond the leak on both sides.*

As mentioned previously, anything larger than a hairline crack typically requires replacing the damaged section of pipe. If it's a very large crack necessitating a major repair, it's best to hire a plumber.

## Preventing Pipe Problems

The best way to deal with frozen pipes is to keep them from freezing in the first place. Going through the following list and implementing necessary fixes should keep your pipes free of cracks, even in the severest weather:

- Insulate outdoor faucets, pipes in unheated garages, and pipes in crawl spaces with materials such as rags or newspapers. Cover the materials with plastic and secure everything with string or wire. This is a quick fix, as there are better products for insulating and protecting your pipes, but a good one if a sudden cold snap catches you off guard.

- Wrap foam pipe insulation around pipes. You can find this material precut to match the diameter of your pipe at hardware and home stores. Installing it is super easy: Just slip it around the pipe and seal the seams with duct tape.
- Install electric heat tape. As previously discussed, be sure to buy the appropriate product for the type of pipes you need to protect, and follow installation instructions closely.
- Seal up all small cracks and holes around doors and windows with caulk to keep cold air out. Choose a high-quality product that will last a while.
- Remove all hoses from outside faucets. Drain and shut off the water supply to these fixtures.
- Shut off and drain all underground irrigation systems. Depending on how your system was installed, you can probably shut it off yourself, but this won't drain it, as the water must be pumped out. You'll need to call a sprinkler installation and maintenance company for the latter.
- During extremely cold weather, protect pipes by opening the highest faucet in your house and keeping a trickle of water running from it. This might seem wasteful, but the trickle doesn't need to be any bigger than a pencil lead. Why does this work? Running water has a lower freezing point than static water.
- Let warm air caress cold pipes by opening cabinet doors below sinks located against an outside wall.

If you leave your house empty for long periods of time during cold-winter months, consider installing a leak-detection system. These devices do what their name implies—they monitor your plumbing for leaks.

# Mopping Up

If caught early enough, cleaning up after a pipe break can necessitate nothing more than mopping or vacuuming up some water. However, broken pipes can cause bigger problems, such as standing water; water damage to ceilings, walls, and belongings; mold growth; and more. For detailed information on returning your home to normal after a water pipe break, turn to Chapter 7.

Homeowner's insurance generally covers water damage if the damage is "sudden and accidental," which typically covers burst pipes. That said, filing a water-damage claim can be a warning sign to insurers, and can result in higher premiums. If the damage isn't extensive, you might want to think twice about filing one.

Shoddy construction or inadequate insulation on exterior walls can cause pipe breaks. If you feel that one of these conditions exist and your home is under warranty, contact your builder or the company that issued the policy.

## The Least You Need to Know

- Cold weather is the enemy of water pipes.
- Never use an open flame to thaw a frozen pipe.
- Pinhole breaks, hairline breaks, and small cracks are easy-to-fix problems for most homeowners. Anything else usually requires the services of a licensed plumber.
- Following a simple maintenance schedule can avert most pipe breaks.

Chapter 3

# My Sewer Backed Up

## In This Chapter

- Main line vs. lateral line problems
- Getting to the root of the problem
- Keeping lines clear
- Other preventative measures

As you learned in Chapter 2, plumbing systems have two components: clean water and wastewater.

A sewer backup is a wastewater problem. If you've got one going on, you'll know it right away. There will be water in your basement. And it will smell.

The problem might be your fault. Then again, it might not.

## Stopping Sewage Flow

First off, let's make sure you're dealing with a sewer line. Chances are good that you are if sewage is flowing into your home, which happens in most backup situations. However, not all homes are serviced by municipal wastewater systems. If your home has a private septic field, it, too, can have sewage backup problems, but these usually manifest differently. Turn to Chapter 4 for what to do.

If sewage is coming into your home, you need to stop the flow as quickly as possible. To do so, call the officials in charge of your city's sanitary sewer system. This is typically a division of the public works department. Many municipalities put this information on their websites, or you can look it up in the phone book in the government section.

While you're waiting for help to come, don't use anything that needs water. Don't flush toilets, run dishwashers or clothes washers, or run water into drains.

**In the Nick of Time**

Lateral lines—the lines from the city's main system to individual residences—are often equipped with clean-outs, which are usually located somewhere near the houses. Taking the cap off the clean-out could slow down the flow of sewage into your home. If you don't know where your clean-out is, look for a round or square plate marked sewer. Depending on where the sewer main runs, it could be in a variety of places, but it most likely will be near the street or sidewalk in front of your house. Open the lid and you should see the top of the pipe leading to your lateral line. Some pipes have caps that can be unscrewed; others have sewer-relief caps with spring-loaded tops that pop up to allow water and materials to escape.

When the city crews arrive, one of two things will most likely happen:

- If a main sewer line is causing the problem, they'll fix it. If this problem is causing problems in the line from the city's main system to your house, they'll typically fix that, too.
- If the problem is in the line from the city's main system to your house, and the city's sewer system is not the cause, it's your responsibility to fix it, as property owners are responsible for the care and maintenance of lateral lines. You'll need to call a licensed plumber, drain cleaning service, or drain layer to clear it, typically by *rodding* it, and if need be, fix any cracks that are found.

**Tool Chest**

**Rodding** a sewer line is pretty much what the name implies—inserting a long rod through it to clean any clogs that might be present.

These fixes, no matter where they happen, are beyond the scope of do-it-yourself repairs. However, depending on what caused the problem, there are things you can do to minimize the chances of it happening again.

**Around the House**

In many cases, cities will rod a sewer line if a plumber can't clear it. You'll typically need to provide a receipt from the plumber to verify the previous attempt to clear the line.

# Understanding Sanitary Sewers

Community sewer systems channel liquids and human wastes through underground pipes to sewage treatment plants.

Sewer systems typically have two lines:

- **Main lines,** which run along streets and interconnect to one another. These drain to the sewage treatment plant.
- **Lateral lines,** which carry waste from the household plumbing to the main sewer line. Everything you pour down your sink drains or flush down the toilet goes through these lines to the main sewer, and ultimately to the treatment plant.

**Around the House**

Like pipe breaks, sewer-line damage causes millions of dollars of losses each year. If you have sewer backup insurance, you should be covered for damage caused by the backup.

Sewers are open systems. All sorts of things can flow into them, and do. And because they're open systems, they're shared by many people. As such, a sewer problem at your house can cause problems in other houses on the same line.

## Blocked Up!

Blockages are the most common sewer problems, and can happen in both main lines and lateral lines. When they occur, wastewater behind the blockage flows backwards to the first available outlet. Most of the time, this outlet is a manhole. However, it can also be your home. If it is, your drains and toilets will back up, or even overflow.

Blockages in sewer mains are caused by …

- Pipes becoming filled with debris. Heavy storms can cause more than the usual amount of leaves, twigs, and sludge to flow into sewer systems, which can clog sewer mains in a hurry.
- Tree roots growing into pipes. Roots inside pipes are believed to cause more than 50 percent of all sewer blockages.
- Dumping large objects, such as tree branches or rocks, into manholes.

Lateral line blockages are commonly caused by …

- Pouring grease and other waste into sinks.
- Tree-root intrusions.

## Overflow!

Sewers can also back up when more water is trying to flow into the main line than it can hold. When the main can't handle all the water coming into it, the water can back up to the lateral lines. When this happens, sewage can come up through floor drains, toilets, and sinks located on the lowest level of houses. If your house has a plumbing fixture—a toilet or a shower, washing machine or floor drain—that's located lower than the nearest manhole lid, it's especially susceptible to a sewer main backup.

Contributors to overflow situations include downspouts, footing drains, and sump pumps illegally connected to a sewer line.

**Around the House**

In the early 1970s, the Environmental Protection Agency recognized the health problems that sewer backups cause and outlawed storm-water connections into sanitary sewer systems. Since then, it's been against the law to connect any rain- or groundwater lines to a city sewer. That said, sump pumps that are illegally connected to sewer lines are still one of the most common causes of overcapacity flooding. During a storm, just 10 sump pumps can overfill an average residential sewer main.

Overflow problems can happen anywhere, but they're a particular concern in areas that are susceptible to flooding. If you don't know whether your house is at risk for flooding, talk to your local floodplain manager, building official, city engineer, or planning and zoning administrator. They can tell you if you're in a flood hazard area. If you are, think seriously about buying flood insurance if you don't already have it. You can find out more about it in Chapter 23.

### Breakdown!

Both main sanitary lines and lateral lines can collapse, typically due to age, poor maintenance, or tree-root growth. When they do, they can cause your yard or the street in front of your house to cave in as well.

Old lateral lines were often made of clay and joined together with cement mortar joints. Over time, pipes often shift out of place and joints crack or separate. Not only does this let tree roots in, it also allows raw sewage to seep into the ground. Groundwater and rainwater can also seep into old lateral lines and overload them.

> **In the Nick of Time**
>
> To keep sewer systems in good working order, many municipalities offer financial assistance to property owners who need to repair or replace old lateral lines. Contact your local public works department to see if such a program is available where you live, and what you need to do to qualify for it if there is one.

## Why It's a Problem

Sewer backups are problems for the obvious reasons. Sanitary sewage is a health hazard, and contact with it can cause infectious diseases such as hepatitis and salmonella.

A sewer backup can also cause significant damage to your home and property. If the backup is in the lateral line and it's your fault, repairing it can put a big dent in your wallet. And we mean big. There are lots of variables to consider, but a $3,000 bill for repairing a lateral line is not unheard of. Replacing one can cost significantly more.

## Prevention

Since repairs can be costly, it's a good idea to do everything you can to keep sewer problems from happening in the first place. Fortunately, there is a lot you can do.

Your options vary in complexity and cost, ranging from simple maintenance to making some physical changes to your house and property. Many you can do yourself. Others require complicated or large-scale changes to your house and/or its plumbing that must be done by a licensed professional who can ensure that the work is done correctly and according to all applicable codes.

## Keeping Things Clean

This is the easiest way to prevent sewer problems, and it boils down to one main effort: not putting things down your pipes that shouldn't go down them. This includes …

- **Cooking grease and oil.** Bacon grease, fat from browning hamburger meat … you name it. Keep it out of your drains. Put it in a carton, let harden if necessary, and put it out with your garbage. Another approach is to let it cool and pour it into old newspapers. Again, throw it away in your trash.
- **Paper products,** such as paper towels, moist towelettes, handy wipes, disposable towels, diapers, napkins, and tampons. The only truly flushable paper product is toilet paper. Other products might say they're flushable, but why take the chance?
- **Kitchen solids,** such as watermelon rinds, potato peels, corn kernels, eggshells, and chicken bones. It's also not a good idea to put them down a garbage disposal, as they don't break down finely enough to easily pass through lateral lines. If you have a garbage disposal, avoid using it to excess. Disposals shred solid materials into finer pieces, but they don't liquefy them. Nor do they keep grease out of plumbing systems. Don't put anything down a disposal that is too hard or large to be thoroughly ground up.
- **Other oils, greases, cleaning fluids, antifreeze, thinners, paints, solvents, and similar chemicals.** If your community has a hazardous waste disposal program, check with officials there for disposal recommendations. If it doesn't, throwing it away might be your best bet. Check with your waste hauler first to see what they'll accept.

CAUTION

**A Fine Mess**

Avoid using anything that claims to keep plumbing lines clear by dissolving grease. This includes commercial drain cleaners as well as such fixes as pouring vinegar and baking soda down drains. Oftentimes, these products merely dislodge grease clogs and move them to other areas where they can cause the same problems. Your best bet for preventing clogs is to keep materials that cause them out of your pipes.

All sink, tub, and floor drains should be fitted with baskets or strainers to catch debris. Inspect them often, and clear them regularly.

In the bathroom, keep sinks with pop-up stoppers clog-free by routinely cleaning out the hair and other material that collects in them. Long tweezers or hemostats—you can find them at most hardware and hobby stores—work well for this. What comes out of bathroom sink drains can be pretty obnoxious, especially if you haven't cleaned them before, so you might want to wear latex or plastic gloves, and even a face mask if you're particularly squeamish. To prevent buildup, lift stoppers out of drains periodically and rinse them off.

## De-Rooting

As mentioned, trees are believed to be the root (pardon the pun) of more than 50 percent of all sewer line clogs. Simply put, roots love sewer lines, and will readily grow toward them, especially lines with openings caused by deterioration and movement.

Once inside a pipe, roots continue growing. If not disturbed, they'll eventually fill the pipe with hairlike root masses wherever they enter. These masses are what grease, tissue paper, and other debris get caught in.

Because root growth in sewer pipes is such a common problem, it's a good idea to have your lateral line cleaned on a regular basis, either by mechanical means or by using products that kill the roots inside pipes without harming trees.

Experts recommend visually inspecting lateral lines to determine the extent of the damage before treating them. This is done by snaking a small video camera into the line. Check your yellow pages under the sewer contractor heading for companies that do these inspections.

**In the Nick of Time**

The first signs of root clogs and other sewer clogs include slow-flowing drains, toilets that make gurgling noises when flushed, and wet areas around floor drains that appear after you do the laundry. If you take action when you see these signs, you might be able to avoid a complete sewer-line blockage.

Finally, don't plant trees and shrubs with shallow, spreading root systems anywhere near lateral sewer lines. If you don't know where your lateral line is, check the survey documents you received when you bought your home. If you don't have them, your city planning or public works department might have a copy.

Sewer laterals usually run in straight lines, so it's fairly easy to get a general idea of their location. Simply find the clean-out. If it's near your house, draw a straight line from the clean-out to the street. If it's near the street, do the same thing in reverse.

## Modify Internal Plumbing

Making some changes in the plumbing inside your house can significantly reduce the chance of basement floods caused by wastewater backups.

The following chart shows the most common fixes, with their advantages and disadvantages. Before implementing any of them, talk to a plumber about the most appropriate approach for your situation.

| Fix | Advantages | Disadvantages |
|---|---|---|
| Floor drain plug | Cheap and easy | Water pressure can force plug out. Screw-in plug can cause pipe break due to pressure buildup, allowing sewage seepage through foundation cracks. |
| Floor drain standpipe | Inexpensive, easy to install, can be left in if floor drain isn't needed | Flooding can still occur, as water will seek next higher opening. If not correctly installed, could leak at connection. Drain can't be used until standpipe is removed. |
| Backup flow valve | Blocks drain pipes temporarily, prevents flow into house | More expensive, effectiveness depends on type of valve. |
| Overhead sewer protection | Most reliable | Expensive, needs alternate power source to run during power outage. |

### Floor Drain Plug

Floor drain plugs, which are placed into the floor drain below the grate, stop sewer backups where they first occur. One type of plug operates by tightening bolts on the metal end pieces. This causes a rubber gasket to expand and seal the plug in the drain, but it also stops water from flowing in either direction. If something overflows in your basement, the water will stay there unless you remove the plug.

Other plugs have floats that allow water to drain out of the basement. When the sewer backs up, the float rises and plugs the drain.

### Standpipe

Standpipes are common alternatives to floor drain plugs. They consist of an open-ended pipe that fits into a metal and rubber gasket placed into the floor drain. When the sewer backs up, the water stays in the pipe instead of flooding your basement.

One advantage that standpipes have over floor drain plugs is that the overflow pipe acts as a safety valve. As such, it equalizes water pressure, which reduces the chances of pipe breaks. However, having a pipe sticking up from a drain presents a safety hazard, and water pressure can build up enough to blow a standpipe out of a floor drain. Backups can also be deep enough to overflow the standpipe.

### Backup-Flow Valves

Backup-flow valves come in various configurations. Most common are flap, or check, valves, which open automatically to allow flow out of the house and close when the flow reverses. Mechanical, or gate, valves do basically the same thing, but must be operated by hand. Of the two, gate valves provide a stronger seal. Some valves incorporate the advantages of both types.

Backup-flow valves can be installed on a lateral line. This approach typically requires a plumbing permit and digging up your basement floor. They can also be installed on each plumbing fixture. This approach is easier and cheaper; however, these valves typically don't work as well.

Local codes and/or building requirements generally specify the type of backup-flow device you can install. Check with local officials before installing them.

Depending on where you live, your city might pay a portion of the cost for installing a backup-flow valve on a lateral line.

### Overhead Sewers

Overhead sewers, which run along basement ceilings, are the most effective way to prevent sewer backups as they eliminate the connection between the main sewer system and the basement. With these systems, all above-ground sewage flows by gravity into the lateral line. Below-grade sewage is collected in an ejection pit. From here, it's pumped up to the house sewer line.

These systems are costly to install, but they're a good choice for homes with finished basements. However, they need electricity to operate. If there's a power outage, and there's no alternative power source to operate the pump, basement plumbing fixtures can't be used.

## Keep Extra Water Out

As mentioned, illegal connections to sanitary sewers, such as footing tiles, downspouts, and sump pumps, can overload sewer systems. In addition, defective lateral lines can collect groundwater.

If your house has a sump pump to handle groundwater buildup, it should discharge through a pipe in your foundation wall to the outside of your home. Downspouts and footing tiles should discharge to a ditch or storm sewer. If you can't tell where they're discharging, contact your public works department and see if they'll do an inspection. If necessary, they'll run a dye test to track drain discharge.

# Cleanup

If the backup was caused by problems in the sewer main, cleanup assistance might be provided by the city. Be sure to ask.

For cleanup tips, turn to Chapter 7.

## The Least You Need to Know

- Clogs are the cause of most sewer problems. Humans cause about half of them; nature, via tree roots, is responsible for the rest.
- Many cities with older sewer systems offer financial assistance to homeowners needing to replace lateral lines.

- You can prevent lateral-line problems by keeping substances that shouldn't be in your plumbing out of it.
- Installing a backup-flow valve is one approach for keeping sewage from flowing into your house.

Chapter 4

# My Septic System Is Clogged

## In This Chapter

- Understanding private sewer systems
- Why systems fail
- Using water wisely
- Keeping systems healthy

Are gray or black liquids surfacing in your yard or coming through the fixtures in your house? Are you smelling the unmistakable odor of sewage? Are your toilets not working properly, possibly even flushing backwards?

If so, you've got a big problem. Your septic field is overflowing. What's more, if you're seeing (and smelling) these signs, the problem is very likely at an advanced stage.

You didn't know you had a septic field? Surprisingly, lots of homeowners don't. And many who do don't realize these private sewage treatment systems need ongoing maintenance to keep them running right.

## Immediate Steps

Like sewer system backups, septic-tank problems are also wastewater problems, but of a very different nature. However, your immediate goal with them, just like with sewer problems, is to keep additional water from entering the system. Don't flush toilets or run water anywhere in your house. Better yet, shut off your water supply at the main valve. For more information on how to do this, turn to Chapter 2.

Next, call a septic-system expert. This individual will inspect your system and tell you what needs to happen to restore it to health. If you're lucky, all you'll have to do is have the septic tank pumped or a blockage removed.

If you're not lucky, you might be looking at costly repairs running into the thousands of dollars. And that's really sad, because there's so much you could have done to keep the problem from happening.

## The Skinny on Septic Systems

Septic systems are common in rural areas that aren't serviced by municipal sewers and in areas where the costs of running a sewer line are prohibitive.

They consist of the following:

- **A septic tank.** This is a large, watertight container made of concrete, steel, fiberglass, or polyethylene. A septic tank is always placed underground and can be rectangular or cylindrical. It is connected to your home's sewer line and collects all water and waste from it. Heavy and solid materials settle to the bottom of the tank as *sludge* while lighter solids, such as hair, soap suds, fat, and grease, also called *scum* or *buoyant waste*, float to the top. In the middle is a layer of wastewater. Baffles inside the tank prevent scum from leaving the tank. Pumps are sometimes used to move wastewater out of holding tanks, especially if the tank is lower than the drain field.
- **A drainage system.** This consists of an outflow pipe, a distribution box, a network of perforated pipes, and an absorption (also called leach or drain) field or mound. When liquids inside the tank get high enough, they flow out of the tank into the outflow pipe, which connects to the distribution box. The distribution box channels wastewater into the perforated pipes. The pipes distribute the waste through the absorption field, where bacteria and other organisms in the

ground provide additional waste treatment. Some septic systems are designed with two or more smaller drain fields instead of one large one. A diversion valve switches flow between the fields. Instead of septic fields or mounds, some systems have seepage pits, also known as dry wells. They work in much the same way.

**Tool Chest**

**Sludge** is the layer of solid waste that accumulates at the bottom of a septic tank. **Scum** or **buoyant waste** are technical terms for the lighter solids that float to the top of the tank.

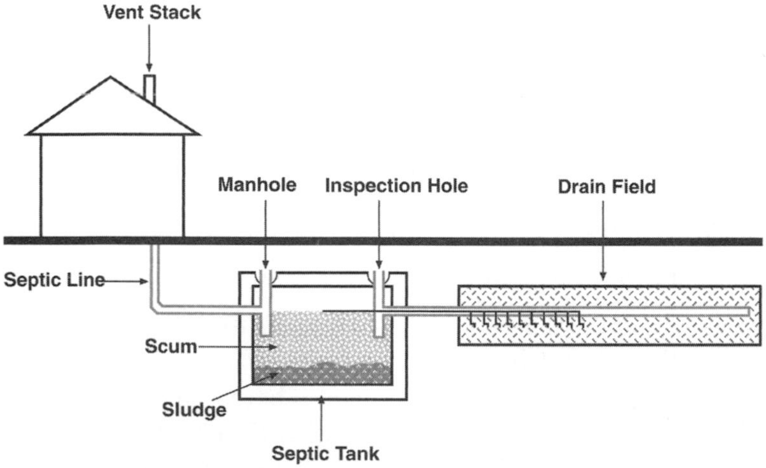


*A typical septic-system layout, showing tank, pipes, and leach or absorption field. Some septic systems use mounds instead of fields.*

A well-built, well-maintained septic system can do an excellent job of treating household wastewater for a long time. If maintained properly, they can last between 25 to 35 years. However, it's easy to forget there's a private sewer system under your turf. And that's when problems set in.

There are lots of things that can happen to keep septic systems from doing their job well. Unfortunately, the majority of them are brought about by neglectful homeowners.

When they happen, you've got trouble.

**In the Nick of Time**

Early signs of septic-field problems include patches of bright green grass; turf that feels spongy when you walk on it; toilets, showers, and sinks that take too long to drain; sewage and/or smelly liquid near the leach field; and sewage odors after a rainfall. If you notice any of these signs, have your septic system inspected right away.

# Causes of Septic Problems

Septic tanks, by their nature, accumulate solid material over time. About 50 percent of this material will decompose, thanks to the bacteria that are naturally present in all septic systems. The rest has to be pumped out on a regular basis. If too much of it accumulates, it can cause several problems.

First, the solids take up too much space in the tank, which greatly reduces the tank's treatment volume. In other words, it can't hold household wastewater long enough to adequately treat it. As a result, the tank has to release partially treated wastewater into the septic field. Over time, these wastes can clog the field and reduce its disposal capacity. In other words, the field simply won't work as well.

Solids can also reach the outlet level and flow into the leaching bed, where they plug the pipes or the bed. The result: a clogged septic field. If the tank's baffles are working properly, they'll prevent this, but baffles can disintegrate or collapse, especially in older tanks that have seen many years of service.

Both scenarios can be hazardous to the environment and your health, as they can contaminate drinking water supplies. They can also have a significant effect on your property values. Finally, they can create a big hole in your wallet, as repairing a septic system can mean digging out the old system and relocating the drain field. Depending on where you live, you might be required to replace the entire system and any damaged landscape.

**CAUTION**

**A Fine Mess**

If you plant trees and shrubs too closely to septic drain fields, you could be asking for trouble. Tree and shrub roots can clog and even block the pipes running through the area. Keep plantings away from septic fields if at possible. If you have to plant something, choose slow-growing varieties with root systems that don't spread out too widely.

## Overloading the System

Inadequate size is another common septic-tank problem that results in poor treatment and overloaded drain fields. Septic tanks are sized to accommodate the number of bedrooms in the homes they serve. This number gives installers a rough idea of how many people occupy the home and how much waste the system has to treat.

The following chart shows the relationship between septic-tank size and the number of bedrooms:

| No. of Bedrooms | Tank Capacity in Gallons |
|---|---|
| 2 or fewer | 750 |
| 3 | 900 |
| 4 | 1,000 |

If you've added family members or added onto your home, your septic tank might be too small to handle the additional load. Drain fields are also sized by the number of bedrooms in a house, with a typical rate being 50 linear feet per bedroom. Adding on can also make them inadequate. Depending on the field's location and construction, it might be possible to improve or expand it.

**Around the House**

Building another absorption field is sometimes the only cure for septic fields that have lost their efficiency. Resting a field for a year can restore it to near original capacity. Having two fields can extend the life of a septic system, and is often the best approach in areas where the ground contains a significant amount of clay.

Another type of septic-system overload can occur during the spring when water tables are high. When this happens, saturated soils slow down and sometimes halt system operations.

Homes sited on flat lots with poor surface drainage are especially susceptible to groundwater problems. Depending on the severity or the problem, it may be necessary to lower the water table by installing drain tile. The tile should discharge to a surface ditch or a larger drain system located away from the drain field.

## Excessive Water Usage

As mentioned, septic systems are slow-moving devices. They need to work slowly because bacteria and other organisms in septic systems aren't real speedy when it comes to breaking down household waste, and they can only handle a certain amount at a time. Plus, it simply takes time to separate liquids from solids.

**Around the House**

Washing machines are a leading cause of septic-system failure. A typical wash cycle can use up to 62 gallons of water. Doing more than a couple of loads in a day can easily overload a small septic tank or one that's full of sludge.

The less water you pour into your septic system, the more time it has to do its work well. Push too much fluid through the system too quickly, and untreated solid material can flow into the drain field, again causing clogs.

## Compaction

Driving or parking cars and other heavy machinery over your septic system can compact the septic field, diminish its absorption ability, and even crush the drainpipes. If this happens, replacing them is your only alternative.

## Dumping the Wrong Things Down

Certain chemicals and substances can cause real problems in a septic system. Flushing even minute amounts of things like paint, solvents, or nail polish remover down toilets or pouring them down sinks can poison the system and kill its microorganisms.

Other no-no's for septic fields include

- Excessive amounts of laundry bleach, toilet bowl cleaners, and caustic drain openers. These products can impair and even halt microorganism breakdown. If this happens, sewage will flow into the drain field before it's adequately treated. However, normal use of these products and other household cleaning products shouldn't harm the system.
- Oils, grease, and fat. As is the case with municipal sewer systems, these substances are notorious for clogging septic systems.
- Garbage disposals. Yes, they're convenient, but they can easily overburden septic fields, especially when used to excess, as they can significantly increase the amount of suspended solids that enter the tank.
- Paper products, including tampons, paper towels, facial tissue, and many supposedly "disposable" products such as diapers, towelettes, and what not. These products can clog drain lines.
- Other potentially harmful solid materials include cigarette or cigar butts, coffee grounds, and cat litter.

CAUTION

**A Fine Mess**

Septic fields can be improperly installed. If this has been diagnosed as the cause, and you have a home warranty, check your policy regarding coverage.

It's also a good idea to keep nonbiodegradable materials out of septic systems. This includes plastic or foil wrappers, tampon holders, and condoms.

# Keeping Your Septic System Happy

Even on a proper diet, septic systems still need regular attention. Get yours on a schedule of checkups and cleanouts, and it will serve you well for a long, long time.

## Inspect It

Septic tanks should be inspected on a regular basis. Every two years is the minimum, with an annual inspection being ideal. You'll want to hire a licensed septic-field inspector for this. The tank may not need to be pumped out this often, but this schedule will also help diagnose other problems, such as worn or damaged baffles, clogged pipes, or damage to the drain field.

**In the Nick of Time**

If you have a new septic system, it's a good idea to check sludge and scum levels annually. Not only will this tell you how rapidly solids are accumulating in the tank, it will indicate how well (or poorly) you're treating your system, and give you time to remediate any usage problems.

Sludge and scum levels are measured during inspections, but this is also something you can do yourself. All you need is an 8-foot length of lumber—a 2 × 2 works well—and an old white towel or a large rag.

First, find the tank. Typically, it will be located about 10 feet from where the sewer drain exits your house. There will be a manhole and possibly an observation pipe. Open one or the other. Wrap the towel or rag around the bottom 5 feet of the board. Lower it into the tank until it touches bottom. As you do, you should be able to determine the thickness of the scum as the board penetrates it. Hold it there for a couple of minutes. Then raise the board and inspect the towel. The discolored portion will indicate the depth of the sludge layer. If it's greater than 24 inches deep, have the tank cleaned out.

**A Fine Mess**

Never lean into or over a septic tank. The fumes generated in these tanks are deadly, and can rapidly cause poisoning or asphyxiation. They're also flammable, so smoking around a tank or using any other type of flame is also verboten.

## Pump It

As mentioned, all septic tanks, no matter how large, need to be pumped out on a regular basis. How often depends on the following:

- Tank size
- Number of people in the household
- Volume of solids in the wastewater
- Garbage disposal use

You'll want to call a licensed septic pumper and hauler for this. Many people simply schedule a pump-out every three to five years or so. However, if you have a small tank and a large family, you'll definitely need to do it more often. As an example, a 1,000-gallon tank might be able to go for almost six years between pump-outs if only two people are using it. In a six-person home, it might need annual pumping.

### Suggested Pumping Frequency In Years for Year-Round Residences

| Tank Size | Household Size | | | | | |
|---|---|---|---|---|---|---|
| Gallons | 1 | 2 | 3 | 4 | 5 | 6 |
| 500 | 5.8 | 2.6 | 1.3 | 1.0 | 0.7 | 0.4 |
| 750 | 9.1 | 4.2 | 2.6 | 1.8 | 1.3 | 1.0 |
| 900 | 11.0 | 5.2 | 3.3 | 2.3 | 1.7 | 1.3 |
| 1,000 | 12.4 | 5.9 | 3.7 | 2.6 | 2.0 | 1.3 |
| 1,250 | 15.6 | 7.5 | 4.8 | 3.4 | 2.6 | 2.0 |
| 1,500 | 18.9 | 9.1 | 5.9 | 4.2 | 3.3 | 2.6 |
| 1,750 | 22.1 | 10.7 | 6.9 | 5.0 | 3.9 | 3.1 |
| 2,000 | 25.4 | 12.4 | 8.0 | 5.9 | 4.5 | 3.7 |
| 2,250 | 28.6 | 14.0 | 9.1 | 6.7 | 5.2 | 4.2 |
| 2,500 | 31.9 | 15.6 | 10.2 | 7.5 | 5.9 | 4.8 |

*Source: Montana State University Extension Service*

If you use a garbage disposal, plan on pumping your tank more often, too. The age of the system and how well it has been maintained will also determine pumping frequency.

Depending on where you live, you might be required to pump your system on a regular basis. Check with your local planning and zoning department to see what regulations, if any, are in effect.

It's a good idea to keep a maintenance record on your septic system, including who serviced the system, what was done, the date, and a brief description of the system's health.

## Keep It Thirsty

One of the best things you can do to keep your septic system healthy is to minimize the amount of water that flows into it in general, and not overload it at any one time. Here's how:

- Space out wash loads over a week instead of running numerous loads in one day.
- Don't let the tap run when washing vegetables, dishes, shaving, brushing teeth, and so on. Fill the sink with water instead.
- Take short showers.
- Load dishwashers and clothes washers as full as possible before running. Select cycles with the shortest and lowest number of rinses.
- Buy water-wise appliances, such as low-flow toilets, showerheads, and faucets. You can also insert water-saver dams in toilet tanks to limit water use.
- Fix all dripping faucets, running toilets, and so on.
- Don't use a sprinkler to water the grass over the drain field. Do it by hand instead.

Finally, keep runoff from foot drains, basement pumps, drain tile systems, and so on out of septic systems.

**In the Nick of Time**

Think your toilet is running on, or leaking, but you're not sure? Put a couple of drops of food coloring in the tank. The darker the water in the bowl, the faster the water is leaking from the tank.

## Keep It Healthy

It's not that difficult to keep a septic system healthy, but it might require educating and training family members on how to do it. Here are the basics:

- Keep garbage disposal use to a minimum. If you use it regularly, plan on pumping your tank more often. Composting is a good option, and your plants will thank you for it, too.
- Consider using biodegradable products for cleaning your home, including vinegar, baking soda, borax, and oxidized bleaches.
- Don't put disinfectants, pesticides, medicine, solvents, acids, or other bacteria-killing substances down your drains. Normal amounts of household chemicals are okay.
- Use high-quality toilet paper that breaks down easily when wet.
- Consider installing an outlet filter on the tank if it doesn't have one. These devices keep such field-clogging solids as diapers and other paper products in the tank, and will catch most grease. However, they don't filter harmful chemicals. They should be cleaned when the tanks are pumped. Some filters even trigger an alarm when service is needed.

Some people swear by septic-tank additives. These products purport to improve septic-system performance, but there is no proof that they do, or that they'll prevent system failure. What's more, they don't eliminate the need for pumping out tanks on a regular basis. And, they can contaminate soil.

# Clean Up

There's nothing fun about cleaning up sewage. Keep your septic system in good health, and you'll reduce the chances of ever having to do it.

However, if you need to do it now, turn to Chapter 7 for the procedures to follow.

## The Least You Need to Know

- Septic systems are a common way of treating and disposing household wastes for homes that aren't served by municipal sewer systems.
- Septic tanks need to be pumped out on a regular basis. Doing so will keep the system happy and keep sewage out of your home.
- Don't waste the money on septic-system additives. They haven't been proven to be effective, and they can cost more than having the tank pumped regularly.
- Prolong the life of your septic system by keeping household water usage as low as you can.

Chapter 5

# My Basement Is Flooded

- Rivers of water
- Downspouts and drains
- Sloping away
- Pumping it up (and out)

Water in the basement is the bane of almost every homeowner. Ask around; chances are pretty good you'll find more people who have had to deal with this problem than not. It's so common, in fact, that the term "dry basement" is really a contradiction in terms.

Lots of things can cause water problems in basements. We've already covered two of the leading causes in previous chapters. In this chapter, we'll take a look at some other reasons for basement floods, what you can do to prevent them, and what you can do if they happen.

## Your House Against the Elements

When you think about how houses are built, and all the different elements of a home that are designed to keep water out of them, it's pretty easy to understand why wet basements are so common. In a perfect world, all of these elements would be 100 percent effective at keeping structures dry. But it's not a perfect world. The best we can hope for, in fact, is about 95 percent effectiveness, and even that's on the high end of the hopeful scale.

This is the case regardless of how old your home is. While it's true that modern construction practices employ more waterproofing techniques than older ones did, there isn't a home on this planet that isn't susceptible to some sort of water problem. Why? Because water always seeks the path of least resistance. Foundations almost always develop little cracks and fissures. When groundwater builds up, for any reason, the water's increased pressure forces it to seek an outlet.

If that outlet is a crack or fissure in your basement … well, what happens from there is pretty obvious. If the crack is big enough, and there's lots of water looking for a place to escape to, you could end up with a basement that looks more like a subterranean grotto.

**Around the House**

Lots of people who own older homes put up with leaky basements because they figure they're part and parcel of an old house. There's some truth to that, but conditions for a leaky basement can happen even with new construction. Regardless of a house's age, when excessive water accumulates around the foundation of a structure, water can seep into a basement through basement floors and walls.

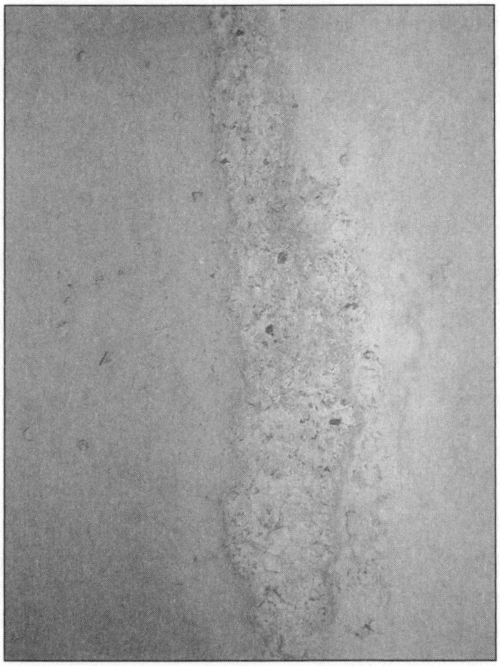

*Crack and water leak in new construction.*

Damp basements can happen in the newest homes. In the preceding figure, surface water is seeping through seams in the foundation of a home that's less than two years old. Note the crumbling filler in the seam and the stains from water seepage. This is caused by the salts in the concrete leaching out to the surface. The seepage is minor at this point; however, if allowed to continue, it could result in foundation damage and a wet basement.

# River Deep, Water High

Typically, it's not one single thing that causes a basement flood. Instead, it's a set of existing problems that are exacerbated by something else, say a spring thaw or a heavy rainstorm.

By way of illustration, let's take a look at one homeowner's story. As you read through it, note the various problems and compare them to similar ones that might exist around your house. We'll offer solutions to them throughout this chapter.

> I bought an older home—actually, a very old home, built in 1904. I always wanted to work on an older home. Little did I realize there was so much work involved.
>
> The house checked out okay when I had it inspected prior to purchase. There were a few problems, but the roof was newer, the wood beams and supports in the basement looked good, and the exterior in general seemed to be in good condition.
>
> We did find evidence of water problems in the basement—in particular, one very nasty-looking foundation crack that had clearly been repaired more than once. The owners disclosed this, and said they had made several repairs. They also said that the problems were old, and that the repairs seemed to fix them. This was confirmed by the inspector, who said the repairs were several years old and found no evidence of moisture.
>
> About a month after I moved into the house, one of the worst thunderstorms I'd ever been in hit. In addition to high winds, it dumped a ton of hail and water in a very short time. After the storm passed, I heard what sounded like water running. I figured the water had overflowed the gutters, so I wasn't that worried.
>
> Then I remembered there had been water problems in the basement, so I went to the top of the stairs and looked down. Much to my dismay, I found about 6 inches of water in the basement. It was coming in through the foundation crack, where the repairs were made.

> I had a wet/dry vac down there, so I bailed out the basement in a hurry, turned on the air-conditioner, and opened all the windows and doors to get air moving through the house. Things dried out pretty quickly. I patched the crack in the foundation where the water came through, and filled in a low spot in the ground outside near the foundation wall where water had pooled after the storm.
>
> I figured maybe the flooding was a fluke occurrence, caused by what was the most torrential downpour anyone could remember in recent years, so I didn't think much more of it.
>
> We had another bad storm about a month later. Not as bad as the first, but the basement flooded again. This time, however, the water didn't come through the crack. Not much, anyway. So that fix seemed okay. Instead, it seeped through the adjoining wall, and it seemed to be coming in from everywhere there.
>
> I had the inspector come out and take a look at things. He found a few things that needed fixing, such as the grading around the house that had flattened out over the years. He also recommended fitting the house with new gutters, extending the gutter downspouts farther away from the house, and installing window well covers.
>
> The water table in the area was also a problem, I was told. He said there were remnants of an underground stream running between my house and the one next door. A torrential rain would be enough to raise the water high enough to flood my basement.

Most of the issues that caused flooding in this basement are easily fixed. What's more, most of these fixes are things that just about anyone can do. Ground and surface water levels can't be controlled, but there are things you can do to keep them from entering your house. Let's take a closer look at all of them.

**In the Nick of Time**

Grading and gutter problems are two of the highest suspects on the list of things that cause wet basements. Inspecting and fixing them should always come first when dealing with wet basements. Not only are these problems fairly easy and relatively inexpensive to solve, fixing them will take the burden off of things like drainage systems, which can be incredibly expensive to repair or replace.

# Maintaining a Good Grade

How your house is sited—where it sits on its lot and how the land slopes around it—is important in keeping basements dry. Improper grading—that is, ground that doesn't correctly slope away from the foundation—can allow excessive amounts of groundwater to collect in the soil around basement walls.

The ground should slope away from the foundation of your house for several feet at a grade of at least 1 inch per foot. It is improperly sloped if it is level or angles toward the house. Unfortunately, all of the following can easily affect grade:

- **Incorrectly installed landscaping.** Foundation beds should follow the original grade of site, not slope toward the house.
- **Soil compaction.** The soil used to back-fill around foundations settles over the years. As it does, grading can flatten or even begin to slope toward the foundation.
- **Soil erosion.** Wind and water can cause soil erosion, also resulting in flat or negative grades.

It's easy to check the grade around your house. You'll need a *level* and a flat, straight piece of thin plywood or metal that won't sag. Here's what you do:

1. Put the piece of wood or metal on the ground next to the house. Remove any decorative rock or mulch—you want to take the measurement on bare ground, as water flows right through rock or mulch.
2. Place the level on the wood or metal, perpendicular to the house. Raise the lower end of the level until the bubble centers on the indicator.
3. Measure the height between the end of the level furthest from the house and the ground. This will tell you how many inches of drop there is from the house.

As mentioned, the ground should slope away from the house for several feet at a grade of at least 1 inch per foot. As an example, if you're using a 3-foot level, there should be a 3-inch difference between the two ends of the level. This may not seem like much, but it's all you need to keep water away from your house.

**Tool Chest**

A **level** (or spirit level) is used to determine whether a surface is flat or at an angle. It contains a sealed, liquid-filled tube with an air bubble. The bubble moves to the center of the tube when the instrument is on an even plane.

## Dirt Fixes

If you come up with anything less than an inch of drop per foot, you'll need to fix the grade around your house. This can be as simple as filling a few small depressions, but it can also call for more extensive work. If it's just a few depressions, you can fill them yourself if you have enough soil.

It will probably take more than a few bags of dirt from the home and garden store, so you might want to call a nursery or landscaping supply house and order a delivery of clean fill. When it arrives, shovel it into the holes until they're slightly more than full. If you're expecting rain, simply leave them alone. If you're not, water them down. Check back in a few days. If the holes are still lower than the surrounding ground, add more fill.

More extensive work will require some earth-moving equipment at a minimum. You might have to consult with an excavation contractor or a landscape company that does grading. For more information on finding and hiring a contractor, turn to Chapter 22.

## Pavement Fixes

If there's pavement such as a sidewalk or driveway right next to your house, it also has to slope correctly. If it doesn't, you'll need to correct the grade. There are several ways to do this:

- Replace the pavement. This is the most expensive alternative, but one to consider if sidewalks and/or driveways are in poor condition.
- Mud-jacking. This process is pretty much what the name implies. It involves drilling holes every few feet into the pavement and injecting grout (mud) through them at high pressure so that the concrete plate can be lifted and releveled. This can only be done by a professional.
- Add another layer of pavement next to the house to reverse the slope. Make sure the new layer is at least 2 inches thick (3 is preferable). Anything less will crack fairly quickly.

If you choose the last approach, be sure to seal all joints and cracks in both surfaces—old and new. If you don't, water could penetrate them and end up where you don't want it—in your basement.

## Gutter Problems

As previously noted, gutters are a leading culprit when it comes to basement leaks. Older gutters sometimes connect to house drains or sewers via their downspouts. If the connections crack or break, or the drain line gets clogged, water will enter your basement instead of the drain line. This is an easy fix—just disconnect the downspouts and let them discharge onto the ground. Install gutter extenders to direct the water flow well away from your house.

Leaky gutters, saggy gutters, gutters that are incorrectly sized, and gutters that don't have downspouts are also big problems. If your gutters fall into any of these categories, have them fixed or replaced.

**A Fine Mess**

Splashguards, which are sometimes placed at the bottom of downspouts that don't have extenders, are largely ineffective at keeping water out of basements. Don't waste your money on them. You can buy plastic gutter extenders that easily attach to existing downspouts for as much or even less than splashguards cost, and they do a much better job.

**Around the House**

To best handle rainwater runoff, gutters should be properly sized, attached solidly to the house, and should have one downspout for every 50 linear feet of roof eave. Extensions should discharge water at least 4 feet beyond the foundation of the house. Downspouts without extenders are worse than having no downspouts at all, as they dump lots of water onto one specific spot. Over time, this will both saturate the soil and erode it.

## Draining Things Off

If your house has a basement or crawl space, and was built in the last 20 to 30 years, it probably has a subsurface drainage system around its foundation. These typically consist of …

- A *footing drain* or *drain tiles* that collect groundwater.
- A *sump tank*, which fills with groundwater collected from the drain tile. It's usually located at the lowest point of the basement.

**Tool Chest**

**Footing drains** or **drain tiles** are a pipe or piping system intended to capture and redirect water that collects around a foundation. **Sump pumps** are either electric or water-driven. When groundwater reaches a certain level, they turn on and pump excess water to a drain or pipe for removal. Sump tanks capture the water collected from drain tile.

- A *sump pump*. This device, as the name implies, pumps water. It's activated by a float or another switching device inside the tank, and turns on when the water level in the sump tank reaches a certain level.
- An outlet drain or discharge pipe, which carries water away from the foundation of the house.

In newer homes, drain systems are typically connected to sump pumps or storm sewers. In older homes, they were commonly connected to the house's sanitary sewer. No matter how they're connected, water will collect around the foundation of the house, instead of draining away from it, if these systems aren't working properly.

Most of the time, drain systems work like they should. But they can develop problems. Sump pumps, in particular, need a little TLC to make sure they run like they should. Drain tiles can break or get blocked from sediment deposits or tree roots growing into them.

There are a couple of different solutions for drain tile problems, including cleaning, repairing, or replacing the tile and redirecting older systems that empty into sanitary sewer lines to sump pumps or storm sewer lines. Typically, these fixes involve digging down to where the tiles are located, which can be costly and is best done by an expert, such as a plumber or a basement-waterproofing contractor. However, you might not have a choice in the matter if your basement is flooding on a regular basis.

## Pumping Things Out

As mentioned, sump pumps need some care and attention from time to time to keep them in good working order. This includes …

- **Checking the pump.** Every so often, take the cover off the tank. Slowly pour water into it. This will make the float rise and trigger the pump. If it's working properly, the water level will quickly go down and the pump will shut off.
- **Cleaning the tank.** It's kind of a groady job, but it needs to be done. To do so, you'll need to scoop out any debris that has collected in the tank. Hose off the tank.

- **Cleaning the pump.** Sump pumps draw water in through a filter trap. This trap also needs to be cleaned on a regular basis. To clean the trap, you'll need to pull the pump out of the tank. Disconnect it from its power source and the piping, then pull it out of the tank.

Pumps can and do malfunction or break. Fortunately, replacing them is pretty easy. All you have to do is disconnect the old one and put in the new one. However, you do need to consider the following factors when choosing a new pump:

- **Pumping capacity.** This is measured by gallons per minute (GPM) or gallons per hour (GPH). It indicates both the pump's efficiency and how well it moves water from the bottom of the sump to the highest discharge point (expressed as "the head").
- **Horsepower (HP).** Horsepower for sumps range from $1/6$ to $1/2$ HP. The higher the horsepower, the more expensive the pump. A $1/3$ HP pump is considered standard for most houses.
- **Construction.** Parts and housings should be made of corrosion-resistant or corrosion-proof substances like stainless steel, cast bronze, and epoxy-coated cast iron.
- **Cord length.** It's not a good idea to hook sump pumps to extension cords. Buy a pump with a cord long enough to reach its power source.
- **Type of switch.** The switch is what triggers the pump to swing into action. There are several types, and they can be manually or automatically controlled. Automatic switches are the best bet as you don't have to be home to turn it on when it's needed.

**A Fine Mess**

Always disconnect your sump pump from its power source when you're working on it. Failing to do so could result in a nasty shock.

You'll also have to decide which kind of pump you want to use. There are two different kinds of sump pumps: pedestal and submersible. Typically, homeowners stick with the style they're replacing, but you do have a choice.

Submersible sump pumps are completely concealed in their tanks. They sit in the water and are quieter. However, they don't last as long—typically about 5 to 15 years, depending on how much they have to run and the conditions in which they're running. If they aren't maintained well and have to pump a lot of grit and sediment, they won't last very long.

Pedestal pumps have a column that sticks up through the top of their tanks. The motor that drives these pumps is attached to the column. This makes them noisier and more obtrusive and a bit of a hazard if small children are around. But they last longer than submersible pumps do—often as much as 15 years longer. They're also easier to repair.

## Cracking Things Up

As previously mentioned, foundation cracks happen. Either your house has them, or it will have them. For houses, they're a fact of life, kind of like getting wrinkles.

Hairline cracks aren't a problem. If they get bigger than that, they can be.

*This old masonry wall crack shows evidence of earlier repairs but water is clearly still coming through. To remedy this problem, a drainage system around the foundation of the home and resloping the ground away from the foundation is in order.*

Good drainage will keep water away from cracks, but it's usually a good idea to repair any that are more than just hairline. For more on repairs, turn to Chapter 12.

## Window-Well Water

Window wells, if not built properly, can literally siphon water right into your basement.

The top rim of a window well should be above grade, and the ground around it should slope away from it. The well should also be much deeper than the window sill. If it isn't, it will easily overflow.

Fitting plastic bubble covers over window wells kind of defeats the purpose of the wells, but it will help keep water out of them. There are also window-well liners that can be placed inside existing wells to extend them above grade.

### The Least You Need to Know

- The term "dry basement" is really a contradiction in terms.
- Gutter and grading problems are the most common causes of wet basements.
- Sump pumps should be checked and cleaned on a regular basis to make sure they work properly.
- Water will always seek the path of least resistance. If there's a crack or hole in your foundation, chances are good that there are water problems waiting to happen.

# Chapter 6

# My Walls Are Wet

## In This Chapter

- Causes of wet walls
- When good toilets go bad
- Tub troubles
- Mitigating household moisture

By now, you've probably heard the message loud and clear: Water is an ever-present issue in houses. Or, perhaps better put, water is an issue when it's in places where it shouldn't be, like inches deep in your basement or dripping through a recessed lighting fixture in your ceiling.

Walls are also prime targets for water problems, and there are lots of things that can make them wet. Some are pretty obvious. Others aren't. In this chapter, we explore some things that can cause wet walls—ceilings and floors, too—and talk about how to remedy them.

## Walls of Water

Wet walls, no matter the cause, indicate two things: uncontrolled or misplaced water and too much moisture in your home. Both are conditions that should be addressed as soon as you see them. Allow either to continue

> **Around the House**
>
> Estimates place the amount of time the average person spends indoors at 90 percent. If indoor air quality isn't good—if it's full of mold spores, for example—all that indoor time can easily lead to asthma and respiratory problems.

and you might be looking at some hefty repair bills and exposing yourself and your family to some significant health risks due to mold and mildew formation. (For more on mold and mildew and associated health risks, turn to Chapter 7.)

Not only are some of the causes of wet walls fairly obvious, the problem itself usually manifests in a very visual way. In other words, you'll see water in places where it shouldn't be or signs of water damage on things like wallboard or wood.

But water damage doesn't always show up right away. Nor is it always apparent. In fact, it can go on for years without being detected. More than one homeowner has tackled a bathroom remodel only to find the walls behind the shower and tub enclosures rotted away or covered in mold or found the subfloor under a toilet ready to cave in.

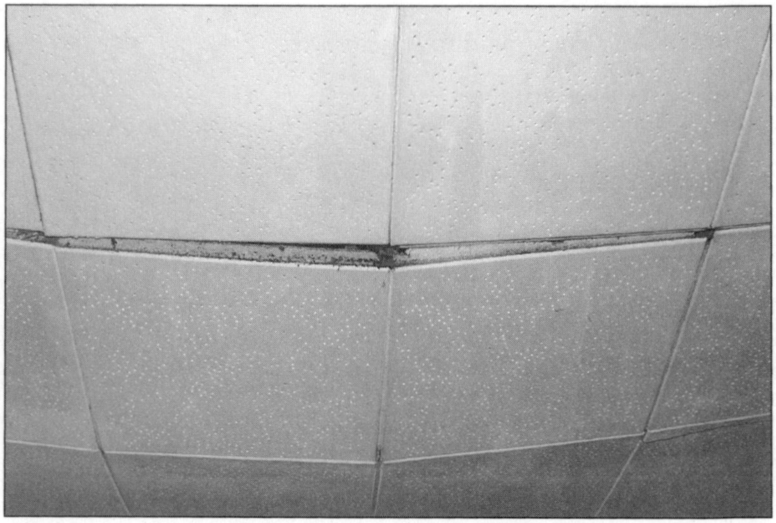

*An undetected plumbing leak under the sink in the bathroom located above these ceiling tiles has rotted the subfloor and damaged the tiles. Note the mold growth under the tiles—evidence of long-term moisture damage. The owners of this home lived there for almost 10 years before the tiles dropped.*

Finding a wet wall in your home calls for immediate action. And your first goal is to find out what's causing the problem.

# Visiting the Scene of the Crime

The fastest way to troubleshoot a wet wall is to trace the problem back to its roots. Doing so might take some sleuthing, so it's a good idea to bring a flashlight along for peering into dark spaces.

As mentioned, the things that cause wet walls are often fairly apparent. The following are the more obvious culprits, and they'll be the things that we'll cover in this chapter:

- Pipe cracks. Check under every sink for signs of drips.
- Leaky toilets. Suspect this if you see water pooling around the base of a toilet or water damage on a ceiling beneath a bathroom.
- Leaky bathtubs/showers. Another suspect if you see water damage on the ceiling beneath a bathroom or on a wall outside of a bathroom.
- Leaky plumbing or hose connections/fittings. A likely suspect if you spot water damage on walls, floors, or ceilings where dishwashers or washing machines are installed.
- *Condensation.* This is caused by high *relative humidity* levels. Indications are wet windows, brown marks on walls, mold growth, and water pooling on window sills.

If none of the above seems to be causing the problem, you're probably dealing with water that's coming through from the exterior surface of your home. If so, turn to Chapter 13 for what to do.

If any of the first four culprits on this list are the cause of the problem, you'll want to shut off water to the area until repairs can be made. You might be able to do this right where the problem is if there's a shutoff valve in the area. If not, you'll need to figure out which line is the source of the problem, and turn off the water there.

**Tool Chest**

**Condensation** is the change of a gas to a liquid, or when water vapor changes to liquid water. **Relative humidity** is the amount of water vapor present in the air divided by the amount of water vapor the air can hold. It's expressed as a percentage. For indoor spaces, a good relative humidity range is between 30 and 50 percent, with 45 percent being ideal.

# Cracked Pipes

Pipe cracks are covered in detail in Chapter 2. The crack repairs detailed there will cover many of the problems you might encounter. Remember that these are often temporary fixes. Unless you're somewhat experienced with plumbing problems and have the right tools on hand, you'll need to call a plumber for a permanent fix.

# Trouble with Toilets

Toilets are pretty durable things, but they can spring leaks. The good news is that toilet leaks are fairly easy to fix, and are definitely within the skill range of many, if not most, homeowners. The bad news is that toilet leaks can cause big problems if they go undetected, which many of them do.

Failures in the wax seals that help secure toilets to floors are at the root of most toilet leaks.

**In the Nick of Time**

If there's water pooling around the base of your toilet, chances are good that you're dealing with a seal failure.

If you're not sure, here's how you can tell: Mop up the water and dry off the toilet. Watch for more water. If it seeps out from under the toilet, it's a pretty good bet that the wax seal is shot.

Sometimes fixing a leak just takes tightening up the bolts—they're called closet bolts—that anchor the toilet to the floor. This is a good place to start. Simply use a slotted (flat-head) screwdriver or putty knife and pry off the decorative caps that cover the bolts. Next, tighten each bolt a little at a time with a wrench. Don't tighten one bolt completely, and then move on to the other bolt. This can make things worse. Instead, tighten one a little bit, then switch to the other one. Keep switching back and forth until they both feel tight and secure.

**A Fine Mess**

A little bit goes a long way with closet bolts. Don't tighten them down too firmly. Doing so can crack the base of the toilet. If this happens, you'll have to buy a new one.

If tightening the bolts doesn't stop the leak, you'll have to replace the wax gasket. This also isn't that tough to do, but it might warrant calling in a plumber if you're not handy. You'll probably need help moving the toilet around. Also, it requires pulling the toilet off the floor, which can expose you to some sights and smells you may not want to encounter. Again, not a bad reason for calling in someone else.

If you decide to do this fix yourself, you'll need to buy a few things. Here's your shopping list:

- A wax gasket. This is a simple, ring-shaped piece of wax. A newer design incorporates urethane foam and wax for a tighter fit. The choice is up to you as far as which one you want to use.
- Mounting bolts. You might end up having to hacksaw through the other ones. Might as well have new ones on hand, just in case.
- Mineral spirits or rubbing alcohol, if you don't have any on hand.
- Small putty knife.

You should be able to find all of the above at any hardware store. You'll also need a basic tool kit that contains such things as pliers, wrenches, and screwdrivers.

Before you start, put some old towels down on the floor around the toilet. If there's carpeting in the area, pull it back so it won't get wet.

Here's what you'll do:

1. Locate the shutoff valve. You'll probably find it behind the toilet, but it can also be in the basement or crawl space directly beneath it. Turn off the water to the toilet.
2. Flush the toilet. Hold the handle down through the entire cycle. This will drain out as much water as possible. Take the tank lid off and remove any remaining water, either by bailing or sponging it up. If there's any water left in the bowl, use a plunger to push it through.
3. Remove the nut connecting the water supply—the tube that runs from the shut-off valve to the toilet—from the shut-off valve.
4. Remove the caps from the closet bolts, and remove the nuts from the bolts. They might be rusted in place; if so, spray on a penetrating lubricant (WD-40 or something similar). If this doesn't work, you might have to cut the bolts off

with a hack saw. If there's a caulk seal around the bottom of the toilet base where it connects to the floor, you'll have to cut through it all the way around in order to move the toilet.

5. Now you're ready to remove the toilet. Do so by putting your hands on either side of the bowl. Gently rock it back and forth. This will break the wax seal.
6. Lift the toilet up off its bolts. Put it down on something—not directly on the floor. An old towel, blanket, a sheet of plastic, even a piece of cardboard will work. Stuff the drain opening with some rags or an old towel to keep the sewer gases where they should be, not in your bathroom where you can inhale them.

CAUTION

**A Fine Mess**

If you see rotten subfloor when you pull the toilet off the flange, you've got bigger problems on your hands than just a leaky toilet. Stop what you're doing and call a plumber for expert advice, and be aware that this might not be the last call for help you'll need to make. Depending on the level of damage, you might also have to call in a contractor to repair or replace the subfloor.

7. Inspect the flange—also called a closet flange, this is the piece that the toilet bolts to—for signs of damage, including cracks or bends. If it's damaged, you'll probably want to call a plumber to replace it. If it isn't, go to the next step.
8. Clean the old wax off the base of the toilet. Clean off the flange as well. A small putty knife works well for this. When you're done, clean the surfaces with rubbing alcohol or mineral spirits; all surfaces should be squeaky clean for the best seal.
9. Put the new wax gasket in place on top of the flange. Be sure it's sitting exactly centered on the flange. If it's off-center, it could impede flow from the toilet. Some people find it easier to put the gasket on the toilet's discharge outlet. If you go this route, be sure to press it into place as it can fall off when you pick the toilet up.
10. Place the new mounting bolts into the slots on the flange. Tighten a quarter turn.
11. Now it's time to put the toilet back into place. Use the closet bolts as a guide. When the toilet is in place, slip the washers and nuts on the bolts. Press down hard on the toilet with one hand on each side of the bowl. Really put your weight behind it. Or, just sit on the toilet seat. This will compress the gasket and firmly seat the toilet into position.

12. Check to make sure the tank is parallel to the floor. When it is, tighten each nut by hand until they feel snug. Press down hard again, and tighten the nuts a little more. This time, it's okay to use a wrench, but be sure to not over-tighten the nuts. Keep pressing and tightening until the base of the bowl is snug to the floor.

13. Reconnect the water supply line, and tighten the compression nut. Now, open the valve. Water should fill the tank of the toilet. Flush the toilet several times. If water is still leaking out, push down on the bowl and tighten the nuts a little more. Test again.

> **In the Nick of Time**
>
> Getting the toilet down and evenly footed in the right spot can be difficult to do. If possible, get someone to help you do this. Have this person sit on the floor by the toilet so he or she can really see how things are progressing. If the toilet wobbles when it's in place, be ready to prop up the low side with shims.

When you have the toilet seated as well as you can get it, go ahead and use it for a couple of days. Check the bolts again to make sure they're tight. If they aren't, tighten them down again.

If there was caulk around the base, this would be the time to replace it. The next section has tips on how to do this.

## Rub-A-Dub-Dub, There's a Leak in My Tub

Cracks in caulking around a bathtub or shower base can allow water to leak out of tub and shower enclosures, where it can then seep into adjoining walls or floors. When this happens, it can cause substantial and extensive damage to walls as well as plywood subfloors, which can only hold so much water. As seepage continues, the wood rots and the floor on top of it sags. Eventually, the whole thing could give way.

How to know if you have a bathtub or shower leak? Water pooling around a shower or tub enclosure is an obvious sign. So are the following:

- Water stains or mold growing on walls adjoining the bathroom or the ceiling under the bathroom.
- Stains or leaks on plywood subfloor under the bathroom.
- Cracks and/or gaps in the caulking around your tub or shower where it meets the wall. Don't assume that since there's no apparent water damage that none is

**Around the House**

Caulking isn't designed to last forever. How fast it breaks down depends on a lot of things—how often the fixture is used, how well it's maintained, the humidity levels in the bathroom, and so on.

occurring. When there are gaps, water can, and typically will, go through them. It's as simple as that.

You should fix any caulking problems as soon as you see them. Doing so is easy and fast. All you need is good-quality caulk. Ask someone at the hardware store to recommend a product if you don't know what to pick.

Here's how to do it:

1. Use a flat-head screwdriver, putty knife, or awl to remove all the old, dried-out caulk.
2. Clean all surfaces in the area with rubbing alcohol on a rag or sponge. You want to remove all soap scum and grease as caulk won't stick to it. Let everything dry for a few minutes.
3. Cut the tip off the caulk tube, and run a thick bead of caulk around the joint. Run the bead as evenly as possible.
4. Wet your finger and smooth the bead.

Follow the package instructions for how long you need to wait for the caulk to set and dry. Don't use the shower or tub until the caulk is completely cured. Doing so might interfere with the curing process, and could deposit more water behind the walls.

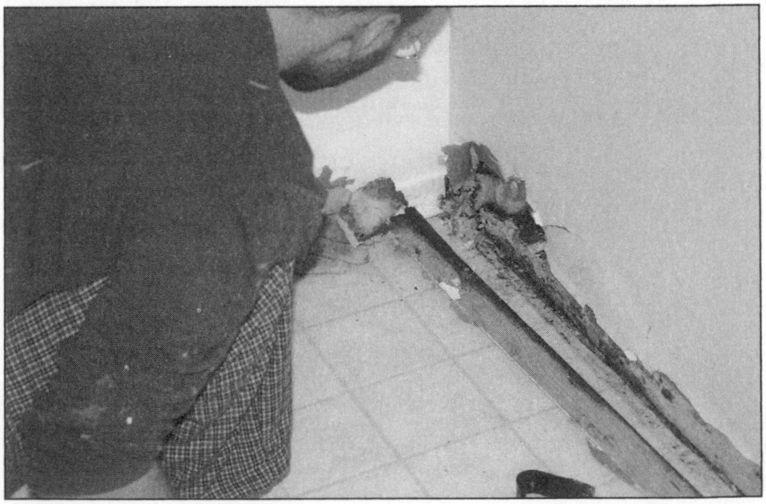

*Water seepage from shower stalls or tubs can damage adjoining walls, as is the case in this home. The homeowners noticed brown stains running along the baseboard of the wall, which led them to further exploration. When they pried off the baseboard, they found mold growth underneath.*

# Dishing It Out

Dishwasher leaks are fairly common. Sometimes they'll show up as puddles in front of the machine, but they can also simply seep into the floor or surrounding walls. There are several things that can cause leaking, including:

- Loose drain-hose and water-inlet fittings. Checking these requires removing the service panel on the front of the machine and poking around to find the drain-hose connection and the water-inlet valve. If you can find them, check the fittings that hold them in place to see if they're tight. If they're not, tighten them with a screwdriver (for the drain hose, which will be held in place with a clamp), or adjustable wrench (for the compression fitting on the water-inlet valve). It can be hard to reach these pieces; if you can't or if problems continue after you've tightened things up, call a repairman.
- Leaks around the door. These are caused by a door gasket that's not fitted properly or that's cracked or hardened with age. These aren't too hard to work with; your service manual might have directions on how to remove and replace them.
- Leveling problems. Dishwashers are fitted with small feet on the bottom to keep them level. If they're not, water can slosh out during the wash cycle.

# Hello Dampness, My Old Friend

One of the reasons moisture problems in homes are so common is because there is always a certain amount of water in the air, put there by water that evaporates from bodies of water and the water vapor that plants give off. You add to it every time you run a bath or shower, cook, do laundry, and even when you breathe.

Humidity that's too low—below 30 percent—can cause lots of problems for both people and the houses they live in. For people, skin and mucous membranes dry out. In homes, too little water will cause cracks in drywall, wood trim, and hardwood flooring, among other things.

Humidity that's too high—above 50 percent—can produce enough condensation to cause water stains on walls and ceilings. It can also cause wallpaper to peel and paint to crack.

Condensation is often thought of as a summer/winter issue, but it really can be a problem year round. It's getting to be more and more of a concern, especially in new, more energy-efficient homes. Just like people, houses need to breathe. They do so by continually absorbing and releasing moisture. Things like increased insulation, weather stripping, and caulking are great for energy conservation, but they also trap moisture inside homes. If the areas in which water gets trapped—typically ceilings and walls that are not properly ventilated—water has nowhere to go and will accumulate.

> **Around the House**
>
> Skylights, particularly in bathrooms, will produce condensation under the best of circumstances. When the moisture-laden warm air of the bathroom rises and hits the cold surface of the skylight window pane, water will condense and there is absolutely no way to prevent it. Many people will assume that their skylight is leaking when is it not.

Certain spots inside a house are more prone to condensation problems. These are areas where interior moisture comes into contact with cool surfaces, such as …

- Inadequately weatherized and insulated windows.
- Inadequately insulated exterior walls and ceilings.
- Masonry and/or concrete surfaces.
- Cold water pipes.
- Toilet tanks.

> **In the Nick of Time**
>
> Indoor hygrometers, which measure humidity levels, are an easy and inexpensive way to keep an eye on the relative humidity inside your house. Buy a couple, and put one where humidity builds up, such as in a bathroom or the kitchen. Place the other one in a common area, such as a living or family room.

If you're seeing condensation or evidence of water damage on any of these surfaces, you need to reduce the humidity level inside your home. Here's how:

- Run the air-conditioning during the summer. Yes, air-conditioners keep the air cold, but they also remove humidity from it, hence the conditioning name.
- Improve air movement through your home with ventilating fans or louvers.
- Use a dehumidifier. These devices take humidity out of the air.
- Always use exhaust fans or vents when showering, bathing, and cooking. If your home isn't equipped with them, consider having them installed. They should vent to the outside of your house instead of the attic or another interior space.

- Clothes dryers should always vent outside. If yours doesn't, have the venting rerouted.
- Install vents in the crawl space or attic.
- Install a humidistat-controlled attic fan. Humidistats measure relative humidity. When it rises above where it should be, the fan will kick in. This can prevent moisture buildup in your attic, which can cause structural damage and/or mold growth.
- Regularly inspect oil or gas heating appliances to make sure they're operating correctly. If they're not, they can cause excess moisture.
- Add insulation to cool surfaces such as wall cavities, ceilings, and basement walls.
- Install waterproof insulation inside toilet tanks or add hot water to the tank's water supply by installing a mixing valve.
- Wrap water pipes with insulation.
- If there's a humidifier connected to your heating system, disconnect it.
- Waterproof your basement from the outside. Doing so tackles the problem where it exists—on the outside—rather than where it manifests—on the inside. For more on this, turn to Chapter 12.

**Around the House**

Evaporative coolers, which cool things off by blowing air over water-soaked pads, can keep things cool inside your home, but they also add lots of humidity to the air. Some coolers can increase indoor relative humidity levels to 80 percent—far above where they should be. If you're having trouble with excess water inside your home and you use an evaporative cooler, be sure to provide adequate ventilation or consider switching to air-conditioning.

# Repairing Water-Damaged Interiors

Water leaks typically cause some interior damage, ranging from stains to structural problems. Some repairs are fairly easy to do. Others, especially if damage is extensive, are best left to experts.

> **A Fine Mess**
>
> It can take a house weeks to thoroughly dry out from water damage, especially if water has collected in wall cavities, in ceilings, or under floors. Repairs could cause mold problems if water becomes trapped behind them. Be sure to wait until your house is completely dry before proceeding.

As detailed in Chapter 7, mold is often a concern when there's water damage. Mold can be cleaned off some surfaces. However, if there's extensive mold growth inside of walls and other materials, it's best to remove these materials and rebuild these areas.

### Sagging Drywall

Sagging drywall is damaged drywall. You can remove and replace it, or install new sheets in front of the sagging panels. Unless you've worked with drywall before, this is best left to the experts. If you're concerned about mold, or you've spotted mold growth, have the drywall removed and replaced.

## Patching Plaster and Drywall

Water can make these materials swell and crumble. If the damage isn't extensive—you're seeing small holes and cracks—patching is fairly easy to do. Ready-mixed spackling compounds, which come in small tubs, work well for this. Use a putty knife to apply the material to all damaged areas. Wipe away the excess with a damp rag or sponge and let dry. If the product shrinks when it dries, apply another coat. For larger holes or cracks, it might be necessary to patch first with a layer of fiberglass mesh tape to provide support. Apply the patch over the tape.

Larger repairs typically require some structural work, and are often more than homeowners want to tackle on their own. If you're in this category, you'll want to call a drywall contractor or handyman. If you want to do these repairs yourself, you'll find several sources for step-by-step instructions in the resources appendix.

## Water Stains

Water damage typically causes streaks and blotches on walls and ceilings that range in color from dark yellow to brown. They're caused by substances in the drywall or plaster that have leached to the surface. If the surfaces themselves aren't damaged, you can paint over these stains. But you'll need to seal the area first to prevent further leaching.

Wash the area with either a detergent solution or a product designed for cleaning paint. Trisodium phosphate or TSP works well. (For more on TSP, turn to Chapter 7.) Try to remove as much of the stain as you can without soaking the surface. Let the area dry for a couple of days. Next, apply a stain-blocker primer or sealer. You can find it at paint, hardware, and home improvement stores. When it's dry, go ahead and paint.

## Water Damage to Woodwork

If painted surfaces are blistered or peeling, you might have to remove the paint with a paint stripper. Follow label directions carefully. If they're just dulled or stained, sand them lightly and apply an enamel undercoat. Let it dry thoroughly, then sand the area again. Wipe the area clean, and then paint.

Minor damage to varnished wood can often be repaired by lightly sanding the area and applying a new coat of varnish. If the damage is extensive, you might have to remove the varnish, sand the wood down to smooth out the damage, and refinish.

## The Least You Need to Know

- Water—either too much of it or where it shouldn't be—can damage walls, floors, and ceilings.
- Fixture leaks in bathrooms can lead to rotten subfloors, which can be expensive to replace.
- Most toilet leaks are the result of a wax gasket failure.
- The ideal indoor relative humidity level is between 30 and 50 percent.

# Chapter 7

# Drying Things Out

## In This Chapter

- Quick tips for fast dry-outs
- Dealing with ooze and debris
- Slippery, slimy mold
- Handling with care

Sloshing around in icky, brackish water is no one's idea of fun, which makes cleaning up after many water-related disasters—especially those that involve your basement—a real challenge. Depending on the kind of break you're dealing with, it can be an obnoxious job, too. Sewage? Sludge? Unless you're like Ed Norton and work in a sewer, it's got to be high on your "yuck" meter.

It's important to get after all disaster cleanups as soon as you can, but it's especially important to attack water cleanup as soon as possible. The faster you do it, the better the chances will be of minimizing water damage and potentially dangerous mold growth.

## Before You Bail

Before we get started, a quick comment: For ease of discussion, we primarily address basement floods in this chapter. However, most of the information you'll read also applies to water remediation in other parts of the house.

One of the first things you need to decide is whether you want to tackle the problem yourself or hire experts to do it. There are certain things that just about anyone can do, including …

- Drying out walls, ceilings, and floors.
- Sorting through belongings.
- Cleaning the structure and its contents.

Other aftermath efforts are best left to professionals. These include …

- Structural repairs.
- Repairing damaged ceilings, walls, and floors.
- Cleaning upholstered furniture and carpets.
- Drying out and restoring fragile and/or valuable items such as antiques, documents, artwork, books, and so on.

There are also a few compromise positions to consider:

- You do the first level of cleanup, such as starting the drying process and sorting through belongings, then have the experts come in for a more thorough attack.
- Leave the big cleanup jobs to the pros, and tackle the other things—like documents, books, and so on—yourself.

How to decide what to do? Part of your decision should be based on your resources—that is, if you have the equipment and the time to do the job. If you don't have the equipment (it isn't super-complicated, but it typically includes a wet/dry vac or a similar device for making short work of removing standing water, plus something to get the air moving and keep it moving), how quickly can you get your hands on what you'll need?

**In the Nick of Time**

Also consider how you feel about tackling the cleanup. It's one thing if there's just a lot of water from a broken pipe around, or if you need to dry out a room that was damaged by a roof or shower stall leak. But if you have to deal with sewage backup and you're squeamish about that, or you're simply overwhelmed by what's ahead of you, you'll probably feel better hiring experts to do the job. Go with what's right for you. There are no medals of valor to be won here.

If you decide to hire help, talk to your insurance company to see what your coverage is and to ask if they have any recommendations for who to use. There are companies that specialize in water cleanup and restoration, and your insurer may want you to work with a particular firm. If not, you'll find them listed in the yellow pages under fire and water-damage restoration. If you can't find anyone there, check one of the restoration resources listed in Appendix C.

Regardless of your decision, you can do a couple of things right away to start the drying process:

- Get some air moving through your house by opening up all doors and windows (weather permitting).
- Increase air circulation by running window, ceiling, and/or floor fans. Rent or buy some if you don't own any.
- If you have air-conditioning, run it, too. Yes, it will make things cooler inside your house, which might be the last thing you want to do if it's cool out, but lower temperatures can keep down mold, mildew, and fungus growth. Don't run an air conditioner if it's less than 60 degrees out. Doing so can damage the compressor.

A dehumidifier is another helpful device. It will remove moisture from the air, which will speed up the drying process. Again, see if you can rent one of these from an equipment rental or restoration company if you don't need one on an ongoing basis.

**A Fine Mess**

If standing water is above electrical cords or outlets, the water could be electrically charged. Stay out of it until electricity is shut off to the circuits in the area. If the breaker or fuse panel is inaccessible, ask the power company to cut the main line to your house.

> **In the Nick of Time**
>
> Insurance adjusters need accurate descriptions of damage, but not lengthy ones. Be thorough, but keep your descriptions short and to the point.

Before you get started, be sure it's safe to enter the water-damaged areas. If you have any concerns, call in a structural engineer to do an assessment. Bowed walls and saggy ceilings not only look awful, they can be a safety risk as well. Be sure and be safe.

If it is safe to enter, take pictures of all affected areas before you start. A digital camera or video recorder is ideal for this. Make a list of everything that's damaged. Itemize the damage and how extensive it is.

After you're done documenting the damage, locate the most valuable items in your house and move them to a safe place. You'll find tips on how to handle things like books, papers, photographs, and other items later in this chapter. Be sure to read this information; it's easy to damage things when they're wet, and it's important to know how to handle them so this doesn't happen.

Don't take the time to clean everything you have now. It's more important to get things to a place where they won't incur further damage while you work on the rest of your house.

## Bailing Things Out

As mentioned, it's important to get the water out of your house as quickly as you can. If it isn't too deep, you might be able to mop it up. If it's lapping up past the soles of your shoes, whether in the basement or on another level of your house, a wet/dry vac is the better way to go. Plug it in far away from the water—if necessary, use a heavy-duty extension cord—to avoid getting a shock, and use a nozzle attached to a long hose to vacuum up the water. For the best protection, plug the vac into an outlet protected by a *ground-fault circuit interrupter*, or use an extension cord that has one.

> **Tool Chest**
>
> A **ground-fault circuit interrupter** is an electrical device that senses potential shock hazards caused by moisture or a damp floor. When it detects a problem, it shuts off power to the circuit in question.

If the water is really deep, you might have to use an electric- or gas-powered sump pump. If you use a gas pump, keep fumes out of your house by putting it outdoors and running the hose through a window or door.

While it's important to get the water out of your house as soon as possible, you don't want to pump it out too quickly if you're dealing with lots of water in your basement caused by groundwater or floodwater seepage.

These floods often cause little or no structural damage because the water pressure inside the basement usually equals that of the water in the ground outside. This stabilizes the walls and prevents cave-ins. Maintaining this equilibrium is necessary to prevent damage. If you pump all of the water out of the basement while the ground is still saturated, the outside water pressure could push in the walls or cause the floors to buckle and heave.

Pumping the water out gradually will keep pressure at an even keel inside and out and minimize damage risks. Here's how to do it:

1. Pump the water down about 2 to 3 feet. Mark the water level and leave everything as is for 24 hours. Do not pump out any additional water.
2. Check the water level the next day. If it hasn't gone up over the mark you made the previous day, it's safe to keep pumping. If it did, pumping out additional water may be unsafe. Wait another day, then pump out another 2 to 3 feet. Mark the new level and wait another 24 hours.
3. Check the water level again. If it hasn't gone back up, pump out another 2 to 3 feet and wait another day.

Repeat step 3 until you get all the water out of your basement.

As water levels go down, you might start seeing a certain amount of sludge, sewage, or other debris. It's all a health hazard, and you want to avoid touching it as much as possible. However, you don't want to vacuum it up as doing so can clog your vac. Instead, scoop or shovel as much of it as you can into a bucket.

CAUTION

### A Fine Mess

If you're dealing with sewage or septic backup, wear protective gloves, goggles, and boots, and consider wearing a mask, too. You don't know what you're going to come into contact with, and that's a risk that's best avoided. Always avoid touching raw materials, and protect all cuts and scrapes from contacting them, too. Wash out any that do come into contact with contaminated materials with soap and water.

# Scrubbing Things Up

When all standing water and debris have been removed, it's on to phase 2: cleaning and disinfecting. First, mix up a solution of cleaner in a large bucket. Any kind of general-purpose household cleaner will work.

Be sure to follow dilution instructions on the cleaner. Mop all hard-surface floors and wipe down all walls. Start at the top and work down. Let everything dry, dump the cleaning solution, and mix up a 1:10 solution of household bleach and water. Go over everything again. Have another bucket nearby for each step, and rinse your cleaning utensils often.

If there's hard-to-remove silt and dirt on concrete or masonry foundation walls, you might have to use a high-pressure hose or power washer to get it off. First, try scrubbing them with household detergent and a stiff-bristled brush. If they refuse to budge, call in the power washer.

## More on Walls

As you're working on the walls, you might notice some that appear to be weeping water. This means that the wallboard is soaked. If you leave it in place, it will eventually dry out. However, doing so can allow mold growth. If you're dealing with black water from a sewer problem, you're also facing contamination problems.

A better approach is to strip off the wallboard or paneling to a point above where the high water mark was. This will also help dry out wet wood and insulation.

If there's fiberglass batt insulation behind those walls, and it's muddy or contaminated, you should discard it. If it's just wet, it will dry out but it will take a long time. Cellulose insulation, which can lose some of its protective qualities when water-damaged, should also be removed and replaced.

**In the Nick of Time**

Water can also get trapped in wall cavities. If you think there's water trapped behind your walls, but you're not sure, take the baseboard off (if there is one), and tap a sharp object through the wallboard. Aim your tap about four inches or so off the floor. If water drips or pours out, make a bigger hole so water can drain out.

If there are vinyl wallcoverings on any affected walls, and water damage isn't too severe, see if you can pull the wallpaper up past the watermark. It's probably loose on the bottom from getting wet, so this should be pretty easy. If you can get it up, tape or otherwise anchor it in place and let it dry out, then clean and reapply it after everything is dry.

If the walls are soaked, pull this stuff completely off. Not only does it keep underlying wallboard from drying properly, the glue used to adhere it is a breeding ground for mold and mildew.

Walls with water-damage stains can be repaired and repainted. Wood surfaces, such as trim, doors, or paneling, can usually be refinished or repainted. For more information on how to do this, turn to Chapter 6.

Walls with extensive water damage might need to be replaced. It's typically best to hire a contractor to assess the damage and estimate repair costs. For tips on finding and hiring, turn to Chapter 22.

## More on Floors and Floorcoverings

Carpeted surfaces can be hard to dry out, especially if they're thoroughly soaked. Typically, your best bet will be to pull up the carpet and the pad after you've vacuumed up as much water as you can. This will help the wood subfloor dry faster. Training some fans on the area will help, too. It's important to get all trapped water out as quickly as possible. Failing to do so can both warp the subfloor and cause mildew.

After the carpets are dry, they can be reinstalled over new padding and steam-cleaned. However, if they were contaminated with sewage or dirty water, plan on replacing them. The same thing goes for upholstered furniture and, depending on the level of damage, possibly wood furniture too. In general, if you're in doubt about anything, throw it out.

Once the water is gone, hang wet throw rugs and other movable floor coverings outside over a clothesline or sawhorse so they can air out without mildewing.

It can take some time for a house to dry out. If you had to deal with a significant water problem, it could take weeks. During this time, you might start smelling a musty odor. This indicates mold and mildew growth.

# Slimy, Grimy Mold

As mentioned, mold and mildew growth are the some of the biggest reasons why it's important to start cleaning up water disasters right away. Mold and mildew are the same thing; mildew is just another common term for mold growth.

Mold has received a lot of media attention in recent years, as problems with it indoors are on the rise. Interestingly, it's more of a problem in newer homes than in old construction. Such things as the materials used and more airtight construction methods are believed to be the culprits.

Not all molds can cause serious problems. But some definitely can. One infamous example of mold gone rampant involved an 11,500-square-foot luxury home in Texas. In the late 1990s, the house developed several plumbing leaks. This led to the growth of a mold called Stachybotrys atra, an especially lethal strain that produces airborne toxins that can cause breathing difficulties, dizziness, flulike symptoms, bleeding in the lungs, and memory and hearing loss. Other, less potent molds can cause skin and eye irritation, asthma, and sinus problems.

**In the Nick of Time**

Mold is, to put it simply, fungi. Microscopic mold particles are always present both indoors and out and can be found in soil, plant matter, foods, and other items. Although molds typically get a bad rap, they are an essential part of the world around us as they help break down dead organic matter like fallen leaves and dead trees. Molds also produce spores, which are microscopic cells that can spread through the air. When mold spores land in the right conditions, they can form new mold growths or colonies. No one knows exactly how many types of mold there are; estimates range from tens of thousands to as many as 300,000 or so.

The family involved developed serious health problems, including difficulty breathing, stomach problems, brain seizures, and memory loss. They also had to abandon their dream home. They eventually won a $32 million judgment (it was later reduced to $4 million) against their insurance company.

Mold problems draw their share of controversy. While there's scientific evidence linking mold in homes and buildings to asthma symptoms and other respiratory problems, a 2004 report from the Institute of Medicine of the National Academies didn't find enough evidence to support the association between indoor dampness or mold and other health problems they reportedly cause. The panel, however, did warn that research was limited and that further studies were warranted.

## Putting Out the Mold Welcome Mat

As mentioned, mold spores are part and parcel of the world around us, both inside and outside our homes and other buildings. For the most part, they don't present too much of a problem. But they don't need much to become one. All it takes are the following:

- Nutrients. As mentioned, molds ingest organic materials. Different molds will attack different kinds of materials.
- A favorable place to grow. Most molds favor relative humidity levels above 60 percent and temperatures between 50 to 90 degrees F. They also like poorly ventilated areas with little air movement.
- Moisture. It's impossible to get rid of all indoor mold and mold spores since they travel through the air. However, mold can't grow without water. As such, controlling indoor moisture levels is the best way to keep mold in check.

## Keeping Mold at Arm's Length

You can be exposed to mold in one of three ways: by breathing spores (the most common), touching moldy surfaces, and eating it. For this reason, it's important to wear protection—at a minimum, a dust mask and gloves—when you're cleaning moldy surfaces and materials. For the best protection, experts recommend the following:

- Rubber gloves.
- Eye goggles.
- Pants with long legs and shirts with long sleeves.
- A medium- or high-efficiency filter dust mask or an N-95 respirator. You can find them at most hardware or home stores.

You also want to minimize the spread of mold spores and protect others from breathing in moldy air by doing the following:

- Isolate the area you're working in by draping plastic over door openings. Tape plastic over air vents and other openings.
- Put all moldy materials you're discarding into plastic bags, or wrap with plastic sheets, before carrying through the home. Better yet, put a large, lidded garbage pail in the area you're working in, and throw everything in it.
- Remove your clothing in the work area. Bag and dispose of it or wash it separately from your family's wash.

If you moved moldy objects to a dry area for cleaning, wash down the entire area you worked in after you're done.

If you're cleaning a basement from a sewer or other type of leak, what you've already done will go a long way to keep mold growth down.

If you're cleaning an area where there's been a water leak for quite some time, seeing and/or smelling mold may have been the first indication of a problem. While there might not be much water to clean up, there may be a good deal of mold-related damage to deal with. You might have to remove and throw away some mold-contaminated materials, including …

- Sheet rock.
- Plaster.
- Insulation.
- Ceiling tiles.
- Carpet and pad.
- Laminated wood products.

These are all porous materials, which means mold can grow on them and in them. If only the top painted surface is moldy, you should be able to clean it off. However, mold growing underneath paint or inside of materials is virtually impossible to eliminate, especially if colonies are well established.

Nonporous materials with mold growing on their surface can often be saved via a thorough cleaning and drying. These include …

- Concrete.
- Glass.
- Hard plastic.
- Metal.
- Solid wood.

Follow the previous procedures for cleaning these surfaces. Disinfecting with bleach is recommended, but is not essential if you're not cleaning up after a sewer or septic break. If you do disinfect, mix $\frac{1}{4}$ to $\frac{1}{2}$ cup of bleach per gallon of water and apply to all surfaces where mold was growing. A sponge or spray bottle works well for this. Don't rinse or wipe off the bleach solution. Instead, let it air dry. Collect any solution that runs off with a sponge, wet/dry vac, or mop.

> **A Fine Mess**
>
> Never apply a bleach solution to any surface on which you used an ammonia-based cleaner. Doing so can cause a toxic chlorine gas to form. Always use bleach in well-ventilated areas. Test it on a small spot or corner before use; bleach is corrosive and can mar or damage the finish on some surfaces.

After you're done cleaning up, keep an eye out for new mold growth. Pay particular attention to areas where mold has grown before. New growth in these areas may mean that moisture still isn't under control. If you see new mold growth, repeat the above cleaning steps and use a stronger cleaning solution such as trisodium phosphate (TSP). TSP is a caustic chemical commonly used as an all-purpose cleaning agent. It's a powerful degreaser and cleaner and makes short work of things like grease and soot. You can use TSP to clean clothing, walls, floors, and some furniture. You can also add bleach to this mixture at a ratio of one part bleach to four parts water.

> **A Fine Mess**
>
> TSP is a very strong cleaner. As such, it's important to follow dilution instructions carefully when using it. Always wear skin and eye protection when mixing and applying it, and be careful where you apply it. It can damage some metal and painted surfaces, especially if not properly mixed.

If mold growth continues, you might have to remove and discard the affected materials.

## Cleaning Possessions and Valuables

We won't go into how to clean every little thing here. There are websites that detail this information, and we'll direct you to some of them in the resources appendix. Instead, we'll discuss how you can rescue, and hopefully save, some of the things that are most likely to be damaged in a water-related disaster.

For best results, work in a cool space with low humidity and circulating air. This will help items dry out gradually and keep mold growth down. Use what is necessary to create these conditions: fans, open windows, dehumidifiers, air-conditioners.

### Books

First, go through what you have and decide what's worth keeping. Use both hands to pick up any books that were submerged. This will stabilize the spine and binding. Place the books in a ventilated, water-resistant container, such as a milk crate or a wire or plastic basket. Plastic clothes baskets also work well for this. Take the books to a dry area where you can work on them.

**Around the House**

Be sure to keep all soggy books closed until you're ready to work on them. Wet books are very fragile—you don't want to risk further damage by opening them up. The weight of the pages will also help keep them from curling.

**A Fine Mess**

Never speed-dry books—not any you care about, anyway. Using an oven, hair dryer, iron, or even a microwave can cause irreparable damage to delicate papers and bindings.

Lay the soaked books flat on a clean table or bench covered with absorbent material such as paper towels, towels, blotters, or newsprint (not newspapers; ink can stain the books).

Place sheets of absorbent material between small groups of pages. Don't use too many sheets—doing so might warp the binding. Change them when they get wet. Be careful with this—wet paper is very fragile. Each time you replace the sheets, put them in a new location. This will speed up the drying.

Coffee-table books and others printed on slick, coated paper are extremely difficult to save as the coating on the paper usually makes the pages stick together as they dry out. If you decide to try to save them, use the previous approach. Instead of blotters, put sheets of wax paper between the pages.

Books that are damp or partially wet can be dried by standing them on their driest edges with their pages fanned open. Keep the pages from drying out too fast by facing them away from fans if you're using them to keep air circulating. If necessary, place blotting material between groups of pages as before.

You want to get the books to the point where they're almost dry. If they feel cool to the touch, you're there. Close them up and place them flat on their sides. Weight them slightly, and leave them be. Check periodically for mold growth.

> **In the Nick of Time**
>
> If you have more books than you can get to within a day or so, freeze them. Wrap them in wax paper, then pack tightly in a sturdy container with their spines down.

## Photographs

Again, assess what you have and assign priorities for what you'll work on first. Set aside all photos that you think you can reprint from negatives. Focus on images that you don't have negatives for. It's important to work quickly here; as pictures dry, the emulsion on their surfaces will make them stick together. Once they do that, you might not be able to save them. Mold growth is also a problem as it can damage fragile emulsion.

Handle all wet photographs carefully and only by their edges as much as possible. If you have lots of them to work on, rinse them off with clean water and seal them up in a plastic garbage bag or a plastic bag with a zipper-type seal. If you have time, put pieces of wax paper between each picture. Freeze them until you can get to them. When you can, defrost, separate, and air dry.

If you can't freeze them or even refrigerate them, rinse them all in clean water. Dry face up in a single layer on a clean surface. Don't dry them in direct sunlight—this can scorch the paper and damage the emulsion. Don't worry if they curl as they dry; a photo restorer might be able to flatten them out when they're dry. If not, you should be able to have copy shots made of them.

## Furniture

Gently rinse off wood furniture with a hose sprayer set on fine, or sponge off. Blot surface water with cloth or paper towels.

> **A Fine Mess**
>
> Don't hose or sponge off painted furniture without checking it first. If the finish is blistered or flaking, let the piece air dry before cleaning it.

Water can cause veneer layers to separate. If this happens, weight or clamp the areas. Put a soft cloth under the weight or clamp to protect the finish.

To speed up drying, remove all drawers and shelves. You want to expose as many surfaces as possible to the air.

Finished and/or painted furniture often develops a white haze or bloom when damp. It's unsightly, but it can be repaired later. Don't worry about it now.

Upholstered furniture can be tricky to restore. Start by rinsing it off. If you can remove the covers from cushions and pillows, do so and hang them up to dry. Wrap the piece with towels or sheets—this will soak up water from the frame and other immovable parts—and let it dry.

## Artwork

Heirloom and antique pieces should be assessed as quickly as possible by a restoration expert. It's best not to attempt to dry or clean these yourself.

All other artwork should be taken out of their frames and allowed to air dry. Paintings on stretchers should remain on them.

## The Least You Need to Know

- It's important to dry out your house and your belongings as soon as possible to arrest mold and mildew growth.
- When in doubt about anything that's been water-damaged, it's best to throw it out.
- Always isolate any moldy areas or items you're working on.
- Proceed carefully when cleaning things like books, photographs, and other paper items, as they're very fragile when wet.

# Part 2

# House on Fire!

If you're reading this part of *The Complete Idiot's Guide to Common Household Disasters*, we hope you're doing it at the right time—either after you've had a fire and you need to know what to do next, or you want to know what you can do to prevent one from happening in the future.

A fire can engulf your home in a matter of minutes. More than 4,000 Americans die in fires every year, and almost seven times that number are injured in conflagrations.

If there's a fire raging somewhere in your home, even a small one, now's not the time to learn what to do about it. Get out and call the fire department. Now!

IS IT GETTING HOT IN HERE?

# Chapter 8

# Heat in the Kitchen

## In This Chapter

- Keeping your kitchen from going "bam!"
- Sprucing up your stovetop
- Practicing safe cooking
- The one piece of must-have kitchen equipment

It happens to just about everyone. You put something on the stovetop to cook. Then you get sidetracked. Maybe it's an important phone call. Perhaps the doorbell rings. Or a bruised knee needs soothing. You get caught up in something else and forget you put a pan on the stove.

Until a fire starts and the smoke alarm goes off.

## The Heat Is On

It doesn't matter what kind of fire you have going on. Get everyone out of the house. Next, call 911 and report it. You might not need the fire department, but it's a good idea to have firefighters on the way in case the fire gets out of control.

If it's a small fire, you might be able to extinguish it. Here's what to do:

- For a fire that's confined to a pot or pan, snuff it out by carefully sliding a lid over it—preferably a tight-fitting lid. A flat cookie sheet will work, too. Or grab a box of baking soda, tear it open, and dump the contents on the flames. Never use water to extinguish a cooking fire. It can cause spattering, which can spread the flames. And don't use flour. It's combustible. Then turn off the burner.
- A fire that has spread to the cooktop can also be extinguished with baking soda. Better yet, grab your fire extinguisher. (You have one, right? If you don't, it had better be one of your first purchases after this disaster is over.) Stand a few feet back to keep burning oil from spattering all over the place, then pull the pin, aim the nozzle, squeeze the handle, and sweep the base of the flames with the contents. Don't aim at the top of the flames. That's not where the fuel is.
- For oven fires, turn off the heat and leave the door closed. Don't try to extinguish an oven fire. These fires will burn themselves out most of the time. Opening the door will add oxygen to the mix and could cause the fire to spread.
- For microwave fires, turn off or unplug the unit. Again, keep the door closed. These fires also burn themselves out most of the time.

CAUTION

**A Fine Mess**

Don't try to carry a grease fire outside. You could spill the grease and further spread the fire. If you can't contain it on the stovetop, leave it and get out of the house.

After you've done what you can, leave the house and wait for the fire department to arrive.

If it isn't a small fire, or if you're too flustered to put your hands on a lid or cookie sheet, or you don't have a fire extinguisher, don't put yourself at risk. Get out of the house and let the fire department do its job.

After the fire is out, don't use the appliance it started on or in until you get the okay from a qualified repairperson. Don't use any other appliances that were involved in the fire or located near it until you know for sure that they're okay, too.

## Firing Things Up

When life gets busy, it's easy to extend multitasking to the kitchen, but there are lots of reasons why it's best to narrow your attention to food preparation when you're cooking. Kitchen fires lead the list.

There's no way around this simple fact: Food left to cook unattended—especially on a stovetop—is the number-one cause of kitchen fires. They happen for a couple of reasons:

- Water or moisture boils out of the pan. When this happens, heat buildup scorches the food that's left behind and causes a dry fire. These fires typically create lots of smoke but don't cause much structural damage. However, the heat from the fire can damage the surrounding area, and the smoke can deposit stinky, sooty residue. (For tips on cleaning it up, turn to Chapter 11.)
- Grease or oil gets hot enough to smoke, and the oil vapor in the smoke ignites. These are grease fires, and they can do a lot of damage, especially if the flames spread to cabinets or other nearby combustibles.

Dry fires and grease fires can happen on a stovetop or in an oven. Oven fires are usually less of a problem since these appliances are designed to handle high temperatures. Fires here are easily contained and often burn out on their own as they consume the oxygen in the oven.

**Around the House**

According to the U.S. Fire Administration, cooking is the leading cause of house fires in the United States. In single-family and duplex dwellings, more than 25 percent of all fires start in the kitchen. That figure swells to almost 50 percent in apartments. Human error, including not keeping an eye on food as it cooks, is almost always to blame for kitchen fires. Malfunctioning stoves or ovens are rarely the cause.

Not only is it incredibly easy to set food on fire, the chances of it happening are high, simply because of how often we use our kitchens. As an example, say you cook, on average, 10 meals a week. Multiply that by 52 weeks, and you've got 520 opportunities to set your kitchen ablaze. Kind of a scary thought, isn't it?

Unattended food isn't the only cause of kitchen fires. So are the following:

- Combustible items near a stovetop. These include oven mitts, paper towel dispensers, and wooden cooking utensils. Surprised that oven mitts are combustible? They're only designed to protect your hands from heat. They'll ignite at 400°F. Electrical coils can reach 800°F. Gas flames can burn at temperatures over 1,000°F.

- Grease residue on burners, vent hoods, filters, and so on—even cabinets.
- Metallic cookware used in microwaves. They can cause sparking, which can ignite a fire.
- Electrical appliances used near a cook top. Overloading electrical circuits by plugging in too many kitchen appliances can cause overheating and/or arcing, which can result in a fire. Cords that come too close to a heat source will themselves generate more heat and be at greater risk of overheating. Frayed or cracked cords are fire risks on their own. They can also catch fire if they get too close to a burner.

How we use our kitchens can also contribute to kitchen fires. Today's kitchens are usually more than food preparation areas. Over the years, they've turned into the center of activity for most families. Many kitchens sport home office areas, crafting areas, and more. They're fun to have and they're as convenient as all get out, but they also increase fire risks.

Kitchens are kind of like cars. We appreciate having them and they make life convenient, but we don't often give them much thought. As such, they don't get the respect they deserve. Both are safe when operated correctly. Both can be very unsafe when they're not.

**In the Nick of Time**

Older homes typically have only one 15- or 20-amp circuit to the kitchen, which isn't enough for modern appliances and this can easily become overloaded. Current electrical codes require two 20-amp circuits. Any appliance that generates heat uses a lot of electricity. If you have an older house, you may want to consider having a second circuit run to the kitchen to split the loads.

**Around the House**

It can cost anywhere from $5,000 to $15,000 to repair the damage caused by even a small kitchen fire. A big one can result in six-figure damages.

# Smokey the Bear Redux

If you're like most people, you've seen and heard messages on fire prevention and safety since you were a kid. Who doesn't remember Smokey the Bear? Chances are pretty good that you've retained a lot of it. But it's pretty easy to get lax about things, especially when life gets busy.

We won't give you any Smokey lectures here. You know you shouldn't play with matches. You know smoke detectors are an essential element in home decor. (You do, right? If you don't, get this wisdom, and fast. If your home doesn't have hard-wired detectors, buy and install battery-powered ones, and make sure you keep them in proper working order.)

But we will say this: The best way to deal with kitchen fires is to keep them from happening in the first place. You, and everyone else who uses the kitchen in your home, are the biggest players in this equation.

> **In the Nick of Time**
>
> If your local fire department offers home fire-hazard assessments, sign up for one. Professionals often spot things that others take for granted.

## Home Economics Redux

If you're a woman and a baby boomer, you probably received cooking lessons as part of your home economics education in junior high. If you're not or you didn't, you may not have learned the basics of food preparation.

Even if you did, your skills may have become a bit sloppy over the years. So, let's review the basics. This isn't everything you need to know, but it will go a long way toward keeping you and yours safe when you're practicing kitchen alchemy:

- Always match food and pan size. Don't use a pan that's too big or small for what you're cooking. A big pan can boil dry too quickly. Food can slop over the sides of a small pan and cause grease spatters.
- Use the minimum amount of heat and oil necessary to create the desired results. Sure, turning a burner too high will heat things up faster, but it also increases scorching and spattering risks.
- Don't heat oil to its smoking point. Not only will it make food taste bad, smoking is what happens right before oils ignite. If oil gets to this point, immediately remove it from the heat source and let it cool down.
- Always use cookware as intended by the manufacturer. If something isn't labeled as safe for stovetop use, don't put it on a burner. The same thing goes for anything you put in an oven or microwave. If in doubt, don't use it.

- Don't use anything other than a deep fryer to deep-fry food. If your family loves French fries, do the right thing and invest in one of these devices. Using anything else is simply too risky.
- If food has been washed or is damp, drain or pat dry before placing in cooking oil to avoid spattering.
- Use a spatter guard when cooking. This is a screenlike device that you place right over pots and pans. They come in lots of different sizes. Having two is a good idea.
- Never wear loose-fitting clothing when cooking. Long-sleeved garments, and especially sleeves with some fullness to them, can catch fire in a flash.
- Don't use towels when handling pots and pans. They can easily ignite if brushed against a heating element. Use potholders or hot pads instead. Even better are fireproof gloves, which you can buy at a hardware store. They aren't pretty, but they're much safer.
- Turn pot and pan handles inward when cooking. Depending on what the handles are made of, this could make them very hot if other burners are on, so be sure to keep hot pads on hand.

Finally, turn the burners off if you have to leave the kitchen for any reason.

## Taking Your Kitchen Up a Notch (with Apologies to Emeril)

All kitchens are fire hazards. But some present greater risks than others for a variety of reasons, ranging from their age to how well they're maintained to what else they're used for besides cooking.

**Around the House**

Homeowner insurance policies typically cover things like structural damage to a kitchen, including paint and wallpaper replacement, repairing or replacing damaged appliances, and cleaning up smoke and soot damage.

If you're in an older home, faulty and/or overloaded wiring can be a concern throughout your home. It's an even greater concern in kitchens, and especially near cooktops and ranges, as plug-in appliances typically congregate in these areas. All it takes is one spark from a frayed electrical a wire to kindle a fire. If that spark were to come from a wire near a stovetop … well, we probably don't need to tell you what happens next.

You'll find more details on electrical fires in Chapter 10. As far as appliances and cords go, keep them away from stovetops. If you have to use them near burners, keep their cords as short as possible. Take up the slack with a Velcro cord keeper, a twist-tie, or a rubber band. Don't let them dangle long and loose about your cooktop. Never overload outlets around your stovetop with these devices. Doing so can overload a circuit, overheat an outlet, and … you get the idea, right?

Other tune-up tips include …

- Clearing the clutter from cooking areas. For some reason, people tend to load up stovetops with things that do and don't relate to cooking. That cute little plaque your nephew made in wood shop? It's wood, and it will burn. Those adorable potholders you got as a wedding present? They'll burn, too. Find another place to hang the plaque. Stow the potholders in a drawer near the cooktop.
- Keeping cooking areas clean and free of grease residue. This includes stovetops, range hoods, backsplashes—basically anything that makes up the cooking area. Wipe up splatters as soon as they happen or as soon as it's safe to do so. Plain old vinegar and water works fine on new grease spots. For caked-on grease, scrub with trisodium phosphate (TSP) or very fine sandpaper. And don't forget your cabinets. Grease builds up on them, too.
- Minimize paper pileup. If kitchens are doing double duty as home offices or crafting spots, paper and other flammables can be a real problem. Keep all paper products away from appliances. Keep newspaper and junk-mail piles to a minimum. Better yet, throw them away as soon as you're done with them.

Finally, keep kids and pets away from cooking areas. Establish a safe zone, and teach your kids about it as soon as they're able to understand.

## Fire-Fighting Equipment

All kitchens should have a portable fire extinguisher near or in them. Period. The best choice is a multipurpose dry-chemical extinguisher. You can find one in just about any hardware or home store. Look for an extinguisher labeled ABC. This stands for the three types of fires they can put out:

- Class A: Ordinary combustibles (paper, cloth, and wood)
- Class B: Flammable liquids (oil, grease, gasoline, and kerosene)

- Class C: Electrical equipment (appliances, wiring, fuse boxes, and circuit breakers)

Read the instructions that come along with the extinguisher so you'll know how to operate it. Hang it in a conspicuous location, preferably in or near the kitchen and close to a door or similar exit. This way, you can grab it, use it, and get the heck out.

**In the Nick of Time**

Be sure to inspect and maintain your fire extinguisher according to manufacturer instructions. If you use the extinguisher, have it serviced or replace it right away. And keep an eye on the gauge. If the needle is out of the normal range, the internal pressure is either too high or too low and the device may not operate properly. Have it inspected by a qualified professional. Ask your local fire department for advice on finding one. See if the department offers free extinguisher checks. Many do.

A fire extinguisher is always your best bet for fighting a fire. Lids, cookie sheets, and baking soda are all good to have on hand, too, but none of them will put out a fire as well, and with less risk to you and your belongings, as an extinguisher can.

Finally, if you need to use your fire extinguisher, use it! Don't empty it half-way. You can't save any of the contents. So fire away. Make sure the fire is out.

## The Least You Need to Know

- Kitchen fires are the most common household fires in the United States.
- Most kitchen fires are caused by operator error, not by appliances on the fritz.
- Using cookware and appliances appropriately can significantly decrease kitchen fire risk.
- A fire extinguisher is the most valuable piece of kitchen equipment you can own. Buy one if you don't have one, learn how to use it, and keep it in working order at all times.

Chapter 9

# Heat in the Chimney

## In This Chapter

- A roaring fire?
- Anatomy of a chimney
- Building the perfect fire
- Sweeping things clean

A crackling warm fire in the fireplace. Is there anything more romantic on a cold winter evening?

If you have a fireplace or a woodstove, you probably can't wait until the weather gets cold enough to fire them up. There's nothing that beats the warmth of a good fire—that is, when it's burning where it's supposed to be.

If it's burning in your chimney instead of the fireplace or stove, and it's accompanied by a roaring sound, you don't just have a fire. You have a chimney fire.

# Fire in the Hole

Most chimney fires happen for one simple reason: improper usage and care of wood-burning appliances like fireplaces and woodstoves. (Faulty installation is another key reason, but it ranks a distant second to the first.) We'll talk about proper usage and maintenance in a minute. First, let's address the problem at hand.

As mentioned, a roaring sound—some people describe it as sounding like a freight train or a low-flying airplane—is typically the first indication of a chimney fire. If you hear this sound, and it's growing louder, you have every reason to believe there's a fire raging in your chimney.

CAUTION

**A Fine Mess**

Chimney fires are often dramatic events, with flames and cinders leaping high enough to come to the attention of neighbors and passersby. But they're not all like this. They can also burn quite slowly if they aren't being fed by much air or fuel. These sleeper fires are no less dangerous than the more visibly dramatic ones. They still reach high temperatures and can damage the chimney and nearby combustible parts of the house. The heat can be so intense that it can actually pick the mortar out from between bricks or stones.

Clouds of black smoke and sparks pouring out the top of your chimney are other indications of a chimney fire. If it's a big fire, flames can leap several feet above the top of the chimney.

If you see or hear any of this, here's what to do:

1. Call the fire department. The fire could be out before firefighters arrive, but it's a good idea to call them anyway.
2. Get everyone out of the house.
3. Close the damper or the air inlet controls to the fireplace or stove. This will limit air supply and reduce the fire's intensity.
4. Grab your fire extinguisher (you do have one, right?). Open the door to the fireplace or stove just enough so you can insert the extinguisher's nozzle. Shoot the contents of the entire canister inside and shut the door. If you don't have a fire extinguisher, baking soda or salt pellets work, too. But you'll have to use a lot of

either substance. What you don't want to use is water. It could make things worse by causing more steam and gas to enter the chimney, which could crack or warp it.

5. Go outside. If the water to your hose connections is still turned on, wet down the roof and the area around your house. This will lessen the chances of sparks igniting other combustibles like shrubs and trees. Keep the water away from the chimney—wetting down a hot chimney could cause it to crack or even collapse.

**In the Nick of Time**

A quick way to snuff out a chimney fire is to use a chimney-fire suppressor. Available under several brand names—Chimfex Fire Suppressor is one—these flare-type devices snuff out flames by filling the chimney with a mixture of gases that rise up the chimney and cut off the oxygen supply to the fire. If you use your fireplace regularly, it might be worth keeping several of them around.

Don't go inside your home until the fire department tells you it's safe to do so. When you do, don't be surprised if things don't look too good. A large chimney fire can dump a ton of smoke and soot inside. There might be water damage to deal with as well. For information on putting your house back in order, turn to Chapter 11.

Don't use your fireplace or woodstove until you've had a professional such as a fireplace or woodstove installer or a chimney sweep come out and inspect the chimney. Chimney fires can cause a lot of damage to the chimney structure, including cracks and holes in the chimney wall, the *flue*, the *flue pipe*, and the *flue liner*. If the damage isn't repaired, any subsequent fires could move beyond the flue and engulf adjoining areas.

**Tool Chest**

A **flue** is the void or passageway through which the products of combustion are removed from the fire to the outside. A **flue pipe** is a pipe used to connect a fire or appliance to a chimney. A **flue liner** is the material used to form the flue in the chimney. They can be made of fire clay, refractory quality concrete, or metal. Some older chimneys may not have liners.

If you're not that familiar with fireplaces or woodstoves, some of the terminology used to discuss them might be unfamiliar to you. So, let's start with a quick anatomy lesson. While the following terms primarily apply to fireplaces, woodstoves are pretty similar in design. If you have one, you can follow along, too.

Chimneys are the physical structures that allow fire by-products to escape outside. They're usually made of brick or stone. The following is inside a chimney:

- **Flue.** This is the actual tube that smoke travels up through.
- **Flue liner.** This is the material that the flue is made out of. It's usually constructed of fire clay, refractory quality concrete, or metal. Some older chimneys may not have liners. Older unlined masonry chimneys may be used for gas appliances, but they should not be used for wood-burning appliances. The flue gases are corrosive to mortar and can weaken the chimney. Unlined chimneys should be relined before using them with woodstoves or fireplaces.
- **Flue pipe.** This is the pipe that connects a fire or appliance to a chimney.
- **Smoke chamber.** The area where the flue starts. It sits right above the damper.
- **Damper assembly.** Located between the smoke chamber and the firebox, these are adjustable louvers that open and shut to control airflow.
- **Firebox.** Where the fire burns. Consists of firebrick, outer hearth, inner hearth, and sometimes an ash dump door.

**A Fine Mess**

Older unlined masonry chimneys can be used for gas appliances, but they should not be used for wood-burning appliances. Flue gasses are corrosive to mortar and can weaken the chimney. Unlined chimneys should be relined before using them with woodstoves or fireplaces.

Woodstoves have stovepipes instead of flue pipes. They also have more vents for controlling airflow and temperature.

Now that you know how a chimney is put together, let's take a closer look at how they work, and why they sometimes don't work as well as they should.

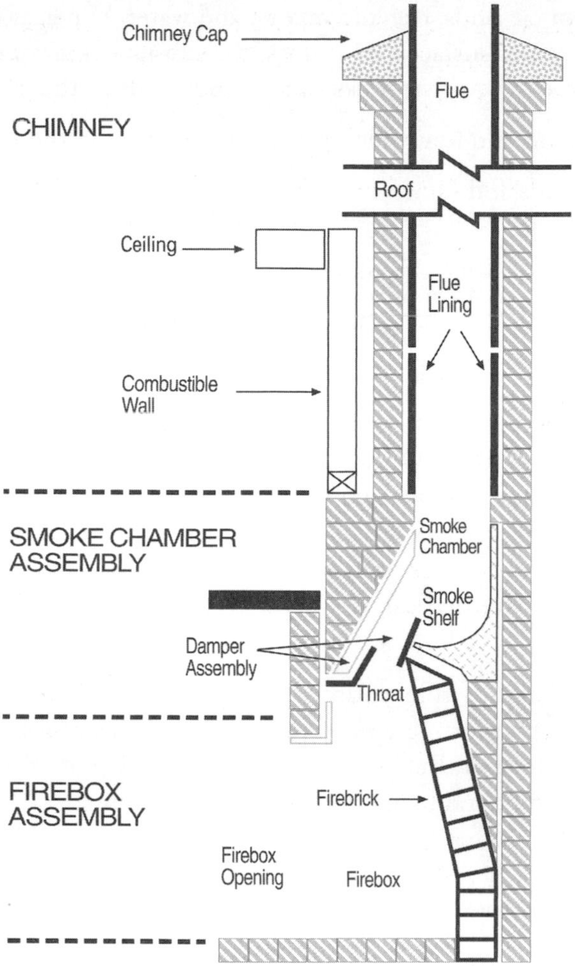


*Here's what the inside of a fireplace and chimney look like.*

# Dirty Business

As mentioned, dirty chimneys—or, more properly put, dirty flues—are prime breeding grounds for chimney fires. But it's not just the ashes and wood particles that travel through chimneys that make them dirty. *Creosote*, a natural by-product of burning wood, makes them dirty, too, and is at the heart of most chimney fires.

**Tool Chest**

**Creosote** is a flammable tarlike substance that's created when hot smoke flows up into the chimney.

Wood smoke consists of tar acids, organic vapors, and water. When it goes up into a chimney, it wafts over cooler surfaces. As it does, the substances it contains condense and forms a residue—creosote—that sticks to the inner walls of the chimney.

How much creosote forms and how quickly it forms depends on the following:

- How thick the smoke and fumes are
- How hot the fire burns
- The temperature of the stove pipe or flue

Cooler temperatures and slow-burning fires cause greater buildup.

Creosote is pretty unsightly stuff. It can be black or brown, crusty or tarlike, and drippy, or even shiny and hard. Look up inside your chimney, and you'll probably see more than one form of it. But appearance is secondary. What's most important to know is that all forms of creosote are highly flammable. Even small amounts of it can cause a fire. Let it build up over time, say over a winter or two, and there will be enough to fuel a long, hot fire that can destroy your chimney—and possibly your home.

Getting rid of creosote buildup in its entirety isn't possible. Moisture and cooler temps produce the gases that form creosote. All wood contains moisture and no fire can burn bright and hot forever. But you can keep creosote in check by using wood-burning appliances correctly, and by taking good care of them.

**A Fine Mess**

Creosote buildup in a chimney or stovepipe can be compared to cholesterol building up in arteries. Both substances reduce the diameter of the structure they flow through. As they build up, things don't function as well as they used to. Creosote, which has amazing insulating properties (even better than asbestos), impairs chimney function by putting down a layer of insulation on chimney walls. This hampers effective heat passage in and out of the chimney. When this happens, the temperature inside the chimney goes up fast. If it reaches 1,000°F, the creosote can ignite.

As mentioned, every fire produces creosote, and it builds up in every chimney. However, certain factors can make it worse. They are …

- **Poor air supply.** Fires need oxygen to burn well. On fireplaces, not opening the damper wide enough or closing glass doors restricts the amount of air that flows into the fire. When this happens, the heated smoke from the fire can't travel as quickly up the chimney as it should. The longer the smoke stays in the flue, the more creosote it forms. With woodstoves, stopping down the damper or air inlets too soon or too much or not using the stovepipe damper correctly can cause the same problems.

- **Green wood.** Green wood is higher in moisture than seasoned wood is. Burning it takes a lot of energy, which results in a cooler-than-normal fire that doesn't burn very efficiently.
- **Cool chimney temperatures.** Creosote-creating condensation forms faster in exterior chimneys that are exposed to the elements than in chimneys that run through the interior of a house. Packing woodstoves tightly for an all-day burn creates large, cool fires instead of small, hot ones. When fires burn cool, chimneys can't heat up like they should.
- **Burning things other than wood.** Plastic substances in things like boxes, wrapping paper, and trash can emit a corrosive acid that can worsen an existing creosote problem.

**A Fine Mess**

Some people believe that having a chimney fire from time to time is a good way to clear creosote from a chimney. Bad idea! Allowing a chimney to catch fire on a regular basis increases the chances of damaging your home. Even a small fire can make a chimney unsafe to use.

Woodstoves, fireplaces, and the chimneys they're attached to cause an estimated 100,000 residential fires every year and some 200 deaths. Makes you want to avoid one at your home, doesn't it? What's more, chimney fires are not only deadly, they're expensive. A good-sized chimney fire can warp a metal chimney and crack or break the tile liner on masonry chimneys.

These are major repairs, and they should be made before using the chimney again. Let even a small crack or hole in a flue go unfixed, and the next chimney fire could be much more serious. Sparks from a regular fire could float into the attic or framework near a chimney and cause a house fire.

**In the Nick of Time**

Wondering how much creosote is in the stove pipe on your wood-burning stove? Here's an easy way to find out: Give the pipe a sharp rap or two with your knuckles. A clean stove pipe will answer back with a ping. If you hear a dull thud, creosote buildup is hampering the pipe's ability to sing.

As already mentioned, there are two basic ways to keep chimney fires from happening: using fire-burning appliances correctly and keeping chimneys clean.

# Fire-Building 101

Lots of people build fires, but many people don't know how to build good fires. Doing it right is essential for keeping chimneys in good working order. To understand why, it helps to know how wood burns:

1. In the beginning stages of a fire, the heat of the flames removes water from the wood via evaporation and vaporization. This heat doesn't make the fireplace or room any warmer. It just dries out the wood.
2. As wood dries out, the temperature begins to rise. When it reaches 500°F, the materials in the wood begin to break down and form volatile gases. These gases contain roughly 50 to 60 percent of the wood's heat value.
3. Temperatures continue to rise. At approximately 1,100°F, gases will break into flames if enough oxygen is available.

Once combustion takes place, the remaining material burns at temperatures above 1,100°F. As it burns, it leaves ash behind as a by-product.

## Starting a Fire

Since wet wood contributes to creosote buildup, it's important to use dry, seasoned wood for your fires. You'll sometimes read that hard wood is better than soft, but moisture content is really more important. That said, hardwoods such as oak, ash, hickory, and juniper burn cleaner than softwoods like cedar, pine, and fir do.

Here's how to build a good fire:

1. Open the damper completely.
2. Put about a half-dozen crumpled sheets of paper or softwood kindling in the bottom of the firebox. If possible, use both. Stack the kindling in a pyramid or in a crossed pattern on top of the paper. Spread over the entire bottom for an evenly burning fire.

**Around the House**

Always get your firewood from a trusted source who can tell you when the wood was cut and how it was stored. If you cut it yourself, be sure to give it enough time to dry out before you use it. Store it in a protected area away from water and damp surfaces.

3. Place a few small pieces of wood on top of the paper or kindling. Use small, split logs instead of big, unsplit logs. Big logs hamper airflow and cause fires to burn slow and long, resulting in increased gas and tar levels. Stack the wood loosely, leaving enough room between logs to facilitate airflow.
4. Roll up a handful of sheets of paper, light it, and hold it near the flue opening. This will warm the flue and improve the draft.
5. Light the wood and paper in the firebox. After it ignites, adding more wood will increase the fire's heat. Add wood carefully at first—you don't want to smother the fire by adding too much.

*How not to build a fire in a woodstove.*

The woodstove fire in this photo is a perfect example of what not to do. Note the closely stacked large logs, loaded tightly in a dirty stove. You can bet the chimney on this stove is full of creosote.

## Keeping It Going

If you're using a fireplace with a metal curtain, close and secure it when the fire is going. If there are glass doors, leave them open while the fire is burning.

> **A Fine Mess**
>
> Never use flammable liquids such as gasoline, lighting fluid, or kerosene to start a fire. Doing so could result in a fire that's much larger than you intended it to be, and possibly an explosion.

You can close the flue partway at this point. Doing so will regulate how fast the fire burns. If the room starts to smoke up, open the flue as necessary to increase airflow.

If you're using a wood-burning stove, close the fire door. Use the draft regulator to maintain the desired heat. Be sure to check the manufacturer's instructions for how to operate this device. How you set the regulator will depend on the wood you're using, how much space you're heating, and how warm you want things to be.

## Putting It Out

When the time comes to call it a day with your fire, it's best to let it burn out on its own. To expedite things, you can use fire tongs to move any unburned pieces of wood away from the coals. If possible, stand them on end in the corners of the firebox.

> **A Fine Mess**
>
> If at all possible, never extinguish a fire quickly by pouring water on it. Cooling things down fast increases gas and water emission.

Leave the fire alone until it's completely burned out. This can take anywhere from 10 to 15 hours. By this time, there should be no heat coming from the ashes, and they should be completely gray.

Keep the damper open as long as there's wood smoldering in the firebox, and keep the screen pulled until you know that the fire is completely out.

## Cleaning It Up

When the fire is completely out, remove the ashes with a metal scoop and bucket. Metal is the preferred material in case any glowing embers remain. If you're not sure everything's completely out, you can add water to the bucket.

Finally, give the ashes a proper burial. If you have a compost heat, they can be added to the mix. If not, place them in a heavy plastic bag and add them to the trash.

# A Clean Chimney Is a Happy Chimney

Keeping chimneys clean is the other key step in preventing chimney fires. If you don't use your fireplace very often, or you just moved, you might not know whether your chimney is clean or not.

The following signs indicate a chimney in need of a cleaning:

- Burned wood odors coming from the fireplace when it's not being used.
- Fires that seem to burn poorly or that dump a bunch of smoke into the room.
- A black damper. Since it sits right above the firebox, the damper is often the easiest thing to see and reach. And it gets caked with creosote. Look or reach inside, and see what you can find. If you see black gunk or you can pull out chunks of the stuff, there's a good amount of creosote built up inside.

How often you need to clean your chimney depends a great deal on how much you use it. The kinds of fires you build and the type of wood you use also govern frequency. As a rule of thumb, it's a good idea to have chimneys cleaned at least once a year, usually before cold weather sets in. Some people prefer to do it in the spring, and some chimney sweeps offer special promotions at this time of year to keep business going. This is fine, too, but scheduling a fall cleaning will also clear out anything that might have fallen into the chimney during the summer.

**Around the House**

If you're using a fireplace or woodstove as a heat source, have it inspected more frequently than once a year. A good rule of thumb is after every two to three cords of wood.

Most people hire chimney sweeps. We recommend it as well. It's dirty work, and not something that's okay to do half-way. A certified, well-trained sweep will do a better job in a shorter amount of time than you can. Look for someone who is credentialed by the National Chimney Sweep Guild or the Chimney Safety Institute of America.

You can, however, clean your chimney yourself.

Here's what you'll need:

- Ladder for climbing onto the roof.
- Drop cloth or old sheet to cover fireplace opening, and additional drop cloths or sheets to cover any rugs or furniture in the area.

- Duct tape or another product for attaching the drop cloth or sheet to the fireplace opening.
- Vacuum cleaner with crevice attachment. If you plan on making chimney cleaning a regular habit, you might want to think about investing in a vacuum designed for exactly this.
- Chimney rod and brushes. You can buy these at some hardware and home stores, or from a chimney sweep supplier. Some fire departments keep brushes and rods for people to borrow to clean their chimneys.
- Stiff-bristled cleaning brush. Buy one with a long handle for easier access to the damper.
- Broom for sweeping up ash and other debris.
- Eye protection, gloves, and a dust mask. While you can get away with a cloth mask, a respirator mask is strongly recommended. You don't want to inhale creosote dust or soot.
- Old clothes. Wear things you won't mind getting dirty.
- Flashlight, for checking your work.

**In the Nick of Time**

If you're going to be serious about cleaning your own chimney, and do a good job of it, be sure to buy the right size of brush for the job. To determine this, you'll need your chimney's interior measurements, which are taken from the top of the chimney. To do it, climb on the roof. If you have a metal or prefab chimney, remove the chimney cap and measure across the diameter. If it's a masonry chimney, measure the length and width of the flue liner and compute the dimension from these measurements. Be sure to buy a brush that comfortably fills the chimney without being too tight. A too-large brush will be harder to maneuver, but it will work unless it's really huge.

There are a couple of different ways to clean a chimney. We'll give you the preferred method, which is from the top of the chimney down. If possible, do it when the chimney is still warm from a fire. Creosote is easier to remove from warm surfaces. But make sure the fire is completely out:

1. Tape or otherwise attach the drop cloth or sheet around the fireplace opening. This will keep ashes and other debris in the firebox and off your furniture and floors. Drape other drop cloths or sheets around the area as necessary.

2. Open the fireplace damper.
3. Don your protective apparel, grab your chimney rod, brushes, and flashlight, and climb onto the roof.
4. Remove the chimney cap. While it's off, clean it with the stiff-bristled brush. Check for damage.
5. Assemble the chimney brush and rods. Make sure all fittings are securely fastened. Just attach a few rods at first. You'll put more on later.
6. Lower the brush into the top of the chimney. Attach more rods as necessary for the brush to reach the bottom of the flue. You'll know you're there when you hit the damper assembly.
7. Work the brush up and down in a scrubbing motion. Check your work with the flashlight. Typically, you'll see the largest concentration of creosote in the upper one third of the chimney, but it's important to scrub the entire length.
8. When things look good from up above, climb down and go inside. Remove the cloth from the fireplace opening. Be sure there's a cloth on the hearth and the floor where you're working. Use the stiff-bristled brush to scrub the damper assembly and the sides of the firebox.

When you're done, sweep or vacuum up all ashes and other residue. Be sure to check behind the damper and around the smoke shelf for pieces of creosote. If you're cleaning a stovepipe, check all elbows or T connections. Clean your equipment with kerosene to remove creosote residue, and store it away for the next time.

Using creosote prevention products inside the firebox on a regular basis between cleanings will help keep creosote levels down. However, they won't remove existing creosote, so don't substitute them for regular cleaning.

## The Least You Need to Know

- Woodstoves, fireplaces, and the chimneys they attach to cause an estimated 100,000 residential fires every year.
- A sound like a freight train and flames leaping from the top of a chimney are classic indications of a chimney fire.
- Even a very thin layer of creosote inside a flue can reduce how well a fire burns by as much as 15 percent. Burning efficiency goes down as creosote increases.

- Creosote preventatives are not a substitute for regular chimney cleaning.
- Building fires correctly can help prevent chimney fires. So will annual inspections and cleaning by a professional chimney sweep.

# Chapter 10

# Burning the House Down

## In This Chapter

- Causes of residential fires
- One homeowner's story
- Wiring woes
- When lightning strikes

Lots of different things can cause a fire in your home: kids playing with matches, frayed wires on the cord of a lamp, even a spark from a boiler that wasn't put together properly after it was serviced.

Many house fires definitely are avoidable and preventable. For those that aren't, all you can do is know how to respond to them. We'll take a closer look at both types in this chapter.

# The Wide World of House Fires

We could write an entire book on house fires. As such, it's impossible to present an exhaustive discussion of them in the space we have here. We all know that smoking in bed is a no-no, and that kids plus matches is always a dangerous combination. No need to recap them.

**Around the House**

According to the Federal Emergency Management Agency (FEMA), residential structures account for only one quarter of all fires, but result in three quarters of fire fatalities and injuries as well as half of all dollar losses.

We covered several leading causes of household fires in the previous chapters. In the pages ahead is information on other ways household fires happen. You'll find advice on what to do to prevent them, if they are preventable, and how to respond to them if they do happen.

We also discuss some interesting things that can cause house fires. As an example, did you know that between 25 to 50 percent of all fires of unknown origin are believed to be caused by squirrels and other small animals chewing through electrical lines?

To set the stage for what's ahead, here's a quick rundown on the leading causes of residential structure fires, courtesy of the United States Fire Administration.

## Causes of Residential Structure Fires

| Cause | Percent |
|---|---|
| Cooking | 26.0 |
| Heating | 15.0 |
| Incendiary/Suspicious | 11.4 |
| Open Flame | 8.6 |
| Electrical Distribution | 8.3 |
| Appliances | 8.0 |
| Smoking | 6.4 |
| Exposure | 5.1 |
| Children playing | 3.4 |
| Natural | 2.8 |
| Other Heat | 2.7 |
| Other Equipment | 1.3 |

As you can see, mishaps related to cooking cause the highest percentage of fires in the United States. If you read Chapter 8, this should come as no surprise to you. Combine the percentages for heating, open flame, and other heat, and you'll find that home heating, in its various forms, is also right up there. Again, that's probably not much of a surprise if you read Chapter 9.

How about the rest? Incendiary or suspicious relates to arson fires, which we won't go into here. Natural and exposure refer to things like lightning fires and spontaneous combustion, which we'll discuss in this chapter.

There are also fires that fall into the undetermined category (not reflected in the previous list), which means no one knows for sure what causes them.

One more piece of information, and we'll move on. The next chart shows where house fires are most likely to break out. Just keep it in mind as you move through this chapter.

### Residential Structure Fires by Leading Areas of Origin

| Area of Origin | Fires (%) |
|---|---|
| Cooking Area, Kitchen | 30.6 |
| Bedroom with less than 5 people | 13.1 |
| Common Room, Living Room | 7.0 |
| Laundry Area, Wash House | 4.8 |

*Source: National Fire Incident Reporting System (NFIRS)*

Again, given the causes of residential fires, there probably aren't many surprises here. However, did you know that a number of bedroom fires start in closets? And it's not just little kids playing with matches or candles who start them.

## One Homeowner's Story

In the introduction to this chapter, we mentioned a fire caused by a spark from a boiler. This really happened; well, it's certainly happened more than once, but we personally know someone it happened to. The story illustrates some important points we want to make about household fires.

We present the story as told by the homeowner in its entirety first, and then recap it as we go through some of the points it makes:

> We had just finished a year-long renovation of the ground floor, taking it from an unfinished space to a laundry room, master bath and bedroom, hallways of closets, etc.
>
> The furnace was spurting out brown soot every now and then, but because there was so much dust going on, it was hard to tell if something was wrong. We finally called in a service man, who said everything was fine. A few weeks later, I called him in again, and was told the same thing. A few days later, the fire started.
>
> The smoke alarms went off at 7 A.M. Fortunately, my husband has been a volunteer firefighter, and he knew what to do. While I was grabbing my son and our pets, throwing on coats and shoes since it was snowing, he turned off the furnace and sealed all the vents and windows.
>
> We live in the country, and it took the fire department 45 minutes to reach the house while smoke poured out of the windows. We didn't have time to save both cats so we left one in the house.
>
> When the firemen finally arrived, they were able to save Elmer, the cat we left behind. It was amazing to see the firefighter come out of the building holding him, just like in the movies. I swear I heard dramatic music and started crying.
>
> The fire chief told us my husband saved the house by shutting off the fuel to the furnace. We had to rebuild the entire ground-floor interior, and insurance was terrific. They paid to have us live in a hotel for a month, cleaned our entire house, rebuilt and replaced all our missing items, and dry-cleaned every piece of clothing and fabric in the house. They paid for repainting the entire house as well.
>
> Our moral is to always replace batteries in the fire alarms and have an escape plan.

## Electrical Fires

Renovations—especially the do-it-yourself kind—are a leading cause of electrical fires. Sometimes it's the tools themselves that cause them, thanks to frayed cords or not using extension cords appropriately.

**In the Nick of Time**

If you're doing a remodeling that requires new wiring, get a permit before you start and have it approved by a qualified electrical contractor. If your municipality doesn't require these inspections (most do, however) or you can't find a qualified inspector, call your local fire department or building department for help.

However, most electrical fires are caused by problems with *fixed wiring*. Often, it's because the renovation adds an additional burden to existing electrical systems, and they can't handle it.

## Goings-On Behind the Walls

Because electrical wiring is usually hidden inside walls, it's easy to not give it much thought. This oversight can and does lead to problems. According to the National Fire Protection Association, nearly 40,000 house fires and 350 deaths in the United States every year are caused by faulty home wiring and other electrical equipment such as plugs, lighting, and extension cords.

It's especially a problem if you live in an older home, as the wiring in older homes wasn't designed to handle the higher demand that newer appliances place on it. Although it's true that today's appliances are more energy efficient than they were in the past, they're also bigger and we use more of them.

**Tool Chest**

**Fixed wiring** is the permanent wiring in the walls of a structure that connects things like wall sockets and light fixtures to a power source.

**A Fine Mess**

Electrical inspections typically aren't required when houses are sold, which means that worn-out wiring and "fixes" made by previous owners often aren't discovered until they cause problems.

Problems like the following could very well be lurking behind your walls and in your ceilings:

- Burned wire insulation in ceiling lights, typically caused by using bulbs with higher wattage than old fixtures can handle.
- Frayed insulation around lights. Using improperly sized bulbs causes this, too.

- Damaged insulation around fixed wiring. This happens over time from wires rubbing together. Nicks in the insulation or overloaded circuits are other culprits. Wires get hot, and the heat buildup causes insulation to crack or fray.

**Tool Chest**

**Arcing** takes place when an electrical current jumps through a tiny gap of air.

All of the above can cause a nasty little phenomenon called *arcing*, which is pretty much what the name implies: electrical current jumping between two things. Here, the current leaps through the air between the ends of broken wires or at loose receptacle connections. The energy from the current heats up the surrounding area, causing … you guessed it, a fire. If there's not much oxygen to feed it, it can smolder for hours before bursting into flames.

Devices called arc fault circuit interrupters (AFCIs), which are installed in circuit-breaker panels, detect arcs that are so subtle that they typically don't trip circuit breakers. They're not a substitute for good wiring, but they do offer a measure of protection for older or damaged wiring. If you're in an older home, consider having them installed. If your home was built after January 1, 2002, circuit interrupters were installed on all bedroom circuits, as per national electrical code requirements.

## Alternative Wiring Products

During the mid-1960s to the mid-1970s, many homebuilders substituted less-expensive aluminum wiring for copper wiring in branch circuits—the circuits that feed electricity from a house's main circuit panel to its rooms. While aluminum was believed to be a safe substitute, it didn't prove to be over time, as the wiring oxidized and loosened at connections, resulting in arcs and overheating.

Many home electrical systems have been upgraded to safer copper wiring, thanks to a public information campaign conducted by the Consumer Product Safety Commission. However, experts believe that thousands of homes from this era have yet to be repaired and are still at risk.

Aluminum wiring is permitted, and is commonly used, for main incoming lines and any dedicated 220-volt loads such as stoves or ovens. Houses that have aluminum branch wiring can be made safer by replacing outlets and switches with aluminum-rated outlets and switches—a cheaper solution than rewiring with copper wire.

## Signs of Problems

How do you know if your house's electrical wires are a potential fire risk? The following is a list of warning signs that you shouldn't ignore:

- Flickering lights
- Outlets that feel hot to the touch
- Circuit breakers that repeatedly trip

If any of this is going on in your home, disconnect all appliances that are plugged into the overworked circuits and call a licensed electrician right away.

## Other Causes of Electrical Fires

As previously mentioned, animals like squirrels and other rodents are a leading cause of fires with unknown origins. Typically, it's their lifelong need to chew that causes the problems, but their nests can also be fire hazards. You'll find lots more on these critters and others that you need to know about in Part Four.

Lightning strikes cause almost 20,000 fires every year. Most happen outside, but they can and do happen indoors, too, thanks to the natural attraction between the electrical currents in wiring and lightning bolts.

**In the Nick of Time**

If you live in a lightning-prone area, consider installing a lightning protection system. These devices consist of external ground rods and conductors that divert damaging electrical energy to the ground, away from your house. Surge protection devices installed at the main electrical switch or meter and on key electronics like computers, stereo systems, and big-screen televisions add another layer of protection.

# Combustion Gas Fires

Combustion appliances such as the following ones are also a leading cause of house fires:

- Oil-fired furnace, boiler, or water heater
- Gas-fired furnace, boiler, or water heater

- Fireplace (discussed in Chapter 9)
- Other fuel-burning device

**In the Nick of Time**

Carbon monoxide poisoning, which can be lethal, is the most common problem associated with combustion spillage. Smoke alarms will not detect carbon monoxide, but carbon monoxide alarms will. If you have a home with an older furnace, it's a good idea to install one near the bedrooms in your home.

All of these devices produce flammable gases as a by-product of the fuel they burn. If everything works as it should, these gases should vent to the outdoors through a chimney or pipe vent. However, they can escape into your home. This is called *combustion spillage*, and it can create a lot of problems, ranging from carbon monoxide poisoning to fires.

Older furnaces can develop cracks that allow gas to seep out. The lines themselves can also become cracked. Seals and fittings can loosen, also causing gas seepage. The best way to prevent these problems is to have your furnace inspected before cold weather sets in.

**Tool Chest**

**Combustion spillage** is the unwanted flow of combustion gases into an indoor area.

Help your furnace do its job properly by keeping the area where it's located free of clutter and debris, and be sure to keep all venting systems, chimneys, and so on in good working order.

## An Ounce of Prevention

We were going to spare you another lecture on the value of smoke alarms and escape plans … but we can't. It goes without saying that you should have both. It also goes without saying that homeowners are amazingly lax on both fronts. According to FEMA, 53 percent of the residential fires that occurred in 2000 happened in homes that didn't have smoke alarms.

**In the Nick of Time**

Be sure to check local codes and regulations if you need to install smoke detectors in your home. Depending on where you live, you might have to use a specific type of detector.

Both smoke alarms and escape plans can and do save lives. Don't wait until after a fire disaster to find this out for yourself. If your home doesn't already have smoke detectors, buy them and install them. Put one in each bedroom and on every level of your home.

Most people know that smoke detectors need to be tested every so often, and that their batteries should be changed twice a year, in the spring and fall. But what you may not know is that they also require some looking after beyond this. Dust, grease, and other materials, if allowed to accumulate, can clog the detectors' grillwork and impair their operation. Remove this buildup on a regular basis with the upholstery attachment on your vacuum cleaner.

**A Fine Mess**

Never disconnect a smoke detector. If steam from cooking or showers are setting one or more off on a regular basis, move it to a better location.

Escape plans tend to fall into the "I'll get around to it … someday" category. Don't wait until someday comes. Put a plan together and make sure everyone in your family knows what it is. Figure out at least two possible exits from each part of the house. Sketch it out on a piece of paper. Rehearse it a couple of times when you first formulate it, and at least annually after that. Yes, you may feel silly doing so. But it's a proven approach to saving lives.

If your house has more than one story, buy a collapsible escape ladder and store it in an accessible spot—preferably a closet that everyone in the family can easily reach. Make sure everyone knows where it is and how to use it. Better yet, buy ladders for each upstairs bedroom and store them under the beds.

# Savvy Saves

Knowing a little bit about how things work in your home can pay off big time when it comes to many kinds of disasters. It's especially important with water- and fire-related disasters.

Right now, before you forget, find the main shutoff valves to any gas lines coming into your house. Also find the shutoff valves on any appliances or heating systems that use it. If need be, label them so you know what they are. Give each a quarter or half turn to make sure they're working properly.

Do the same thing with your electrical system. Find the main shutoff and label it, if it isn't already.

## Fire or Not Fire?

We've pretty much gone through everything we wanted to glean from our homeowner's story. Now let's look at some other causes of residential fires. Each of the following scenarios illustrates situations that can happen in just about any home. All were taken from real-life stories. One or both of us have experienced more than one of them as well.

### Light at the Top

There's a cavernous storage closet on the lower level of your home. It has just one wimpy light fixture—an exposed bulb in a basic light holder. Pretty much everything gets stored here when not in use. Over the years, what used to be manageable stacks of clothing and other household items have grown tall, and a couple of them are inching near the light bulb. Cause for concern? Yes, especially if clothing is allowed to pile up near the fixture. An estimated 12 percent of all house fires begin in a closet. An incandescent light burns at between 212 and 572°F. Wool can ignite at 442°F, cotton at 482°F. Even a 40-watt bulb can generate enough surface heat to ignite fabric or plastic.

Clothing should always be kept away from closet light fixtures. If the fixture in your closet is mounted too close to shelves or rods, remove them. If it's a bare-bulb fixture, often found in older homes, replace it with a glass-globe fixture.

### Room with a View

You have a large closet in your master bedroom. So large, in fact, that your thoughtful architect decided to install big skylights to let more light in. During the summer, nearby trees shade the area, keeping your closet nice and cool. When the leaves leave the trees, however, things really cook in your closet.

Cause for concern? Possibly. Remember, fires need three things: an ignition source, fuel, and oxygen. Here, the ignition source is the heat from the sun's rays. It could build up high enough to cause spontaneous combustion. However, sun-scorched clothing is the more likely problem. If you're concerned, check into installing UV film on the skylights.

## Let the Light In

You were shopping at your favorite thrift store and found a lamp you couldn't live without. When you got it home, you discovered that its cord was frayed, so you replaced it. You can't read what the lamp says about maximum wattage, so you figure it's okay to stick a 100-watt bulb in the socket. You also fitted it with a new, larger shade. It makes the lamp a little tipsy, but boy, does it look good.

Cause for concern? Possibly. Exceeding a fixture's recommended wattage can cause overheating. Fitting a lamp with a too-large shade compounds the problem. If the lamp were to fall over and come to rest on something flammable, the overheated socket could cause a fire.

## Nice and Toasty

You love sleeping under an electric blanket. Your dog, a Great Dane, loves sleeping on top of it. When it's really cold out, you crank the blanket up almost as high as it can go, and you and Rover hunker down for the night.

Cause for concern? Yes, and especially so if you also tuck that blanket in. Both practices can cause excessive heat buildup that can start a fire.

## Rays and Rainbows

Out thrifting again (you just can't stay away), you find a beautiful old cut-glass vase. It probably isn't Waterford, but you don't care. It's big and heavy and you know it will look great on the new side table in your living room.

You bring the vase home, fill it with water and flowers, and place it on the table, which is located dead center under the picture windows in your living room. Your kids love the rainbows the sun creates when shining through the cuts in the glass, and delight when they fall on the upholstered sofa that sits near the table.

Cause for concern? Definitely! Water inside a bottle focuses the sun's rays to a very specific point—a point concentrated enough to cause a fire.

## How Dry I Am

Aunt Bea and family decide to stay with you for the summer. Instead of your usual four or five loads of wash a week, you're running about 20. Young cousin Betty Sue, however, is shouldering the lion's share of the work. It seems like she spends more time in the laundry room than outdoors, which is a sad state of affairs for someone who's just 11 years old, but she seems to enjoy her work. She also seems pretty competent at it, so you aren't hovering over her.

**Around the House**

Dryer fires are amazingly common. According to the Consumer Product Safety Commission, they spark almost 16,000 fires annually, resulting in more than $84 million in property damages, about a dozen deaths, and more than 300 injuries.

**A Fine Mess**

Dryers that run noisy, that take too long to dry, and that make clothes feel really hot are fire risks. Don't keep running yours if you spot any of these warning signs.

The last few loads of wash that Betty Sue has delivered to you are covered with dryer lint. You make a mental note to ask her about it, but it falls off your to-do list.

Cause for concern? You betcha. What little Betty Sue might not know is that she needs to clean out the dryer's lint trap before and after every load.

Lint buildup and improper venting are both concerns. Improperly maintained vents and screens impede the flow of hot, moist, linty air to the outdoors. Let it go for long enough, and the hot air can cause a fire.

Always clear lint filters before and after you run a dryer, and wipe away any lint that accumulates around the drum. Don't run your dryer when you're not home, and keep the vent pipes unobstructed. Check the outdoor vent flap regularly to make sure it's clear and working properly. They collect dirt and debris easily.

## Hubby's New Hobby

Dear husband comes home loaded with gear for his newfound hobby: making furniture. You smile and nod; maybe he won't discard this one after a couple of weeks like all the others. As it turns out, he likes making furniture and is creating all sorts of things in your garage. He's not the neatest craftsman, however, and you notice a growing pile of oily-looking cloths near his work area. He's also dumping funny-smelling rags in your wash basket on a regular basis.

Cause for concern? Yes, on both counts. Many of the products used in furniture building are flammable. Leave them sit in a pile in a hot garage, and they can ignite. Put oil-soaked rags in your dryer, and the hot air can ignite them.

Always let rags and cloths used with flammable liquids dry out before you wash them. When they're not in use, store them in metal containers with tight lids. Label the containers so everyone knows what's in them.

Other flammables to be careful with include …

- Barbecue charcoal. Damp coal can ignite. Always store it in a cool, dry place—preferably an open area where self-ignition, should it occur, presents less of a problem. A metal pail or garbage can with a tight lid is ideal.
- Stacks of newspaper. Yes, recycling is admirable and good for our planet. However, stacks of newspapers are fire hazards. Stack up enough newspapers, and they can generate enough heat to ignite. Store your stacks in a cool, dry place at least 3 feet from heat-generating sources. And don't let them stack up too high.

**In the Nick of Time**

Small storage fires are easily smothered by throwing a blanket or rug over them. Better yet, keep a multipurpose fire extinguisher near storage areas.

## Hot Rock

Dear teenage son has caught the thrifting fever. He comes home from a foray thrilled to death over an amazing find: an electric guitar from the '60s and a larger-than-life amp to match. He hauls his booty downstairs to the cave he calls a bedroom, and you're soon treated to his eager rendition of some Jimi Hendrix tune. As you search for your earplugs, you reflect on the fact that you haven't entered your son's bedroom in months, and that you probably need to, as most of what goes into it rarely comes out of it.

Cause for concern? Probably. If a bedroom is crammed with stuff, chances are that lots of it is flammable. A guitar amp, like all electrical appliances, throws off heat. If placed too close to flammable materials, the heat could cause a fire. Given the amp's age, bad wiring and burned-out insulation are also possibilities.

## Waffling Over an Iron

Now your dear teenage daughter is getting into the thrifting act. She comes home one day with a very neat old waffle iron, which she proudly presents to you. You've wanted one for a long time, and you're thrilled. This one even looks like it's in great shape.

You decide to make waffles for breakfast the following Sunday. As you plug in the waffle iron, it smells kind of funky but it seems to work just fine. You figure the funky smell is from disuse, and you figure it will dissipate as you use the iron, so you go ahead and pour in the batter.

Cause for concern? Definitely. Never use any appliance that smells funny when you plug it in, or that gives off a shock, no matter how slight, until you can have it checked out by a repairperson. The funky smell could be from deteriorated insulation around internal wires, which could cause a fire.

Remember, all it takes is one tiny spark.

## The Least You Need to Know

- Never assume that a fire can't happen to you. Being vigilant about all the things that can cause a fire is the best way to prevent them.
- Seemingly innocent things like incorrectly sized light bulbs and tucking in an electric blanket can cause house fires.
- Devices like lightning-protection systems can help protect your home from fires you can't prevent.
- Never put oil-soaked rags through the wash without drying them out first. Doing so is a great way to start a laundry-room fire.
- Both smoke alarms and escape plans can and do save lives. Don't wait until after a fire disaster to find this out for yourself.

Chapter 11

# After the Fire

## In This Chapter

- First response
- Searching for valuables
- Sponging things off
- Airing things out

Fires rank near the top of the list of life's stressors. A large fire can rock your world and turn your life around. Even a small fire that doesn't cause much damage can leave you feeling shaky and wondering, "What if?" What if it broke out when you weren't home? What if you hadn't found it in time?

There are always lots of things that need to be done after a disaster. Recovering from a fire is no exception. But fires often affect people on a more emotional level than other disasters do. If this is the case, dealing with the emotions raised by the experience needs to be on your to-do list, too.

Like any disaster, it can be difficult to know where to begin and who you should call in the aftermath of a fire. This chapter tells you what you need to know.

## Actions in the Aftermath

At some point after the fire is out, you'll either be allowed back into your home or told to stay out. If it's the latter, it's because the fire department or fire inspector has determined your home isn't safe for you to enter. If this is the case, about the only thing you can do is call your insurance department. They'll tell you what you'll need to do to get the loss recovery process underway.

If you're allowed back into your home, you'll probably be allowed to do one of two things, based on the extent of the damage:

- Locate valuables and other important personal property. This is a typical scenario in homes that have suffered structural damage but aren't a total loss. You'll be told where you can and can't go, and damaged areas might be taped or even boarded off. You'll probably also be advised to keep your visit short.
- Start the cleanup process. There might be some structural concerns, but not at a level where officials believe they'll present a significant risk. Smoke and soot levels might be high and there might be water damage, all of which should be addressed as quickly as possible.

Cleaning the aftermath of a fire is probably the last thing you want to do, but it's also about the first thing you should do. Here's why: Smoke deposits an acidic film on everything it touches. If left on surfaces too long, it can damage them.

**In the Nick of Time**

Ask anyone who has experienced a damaging fire, and they'll tell you it's a disturbing experience on many different levels. Having to swing into action so quickly after a fire is out is one of the toughest things about them, but it's essential for preserving and protecting your belongings. It's also essential for your financial recovery from your insurance company. If you don't take the appropriate steps to protect your property from further loss, your insurer can deny reimbursement based on neglect.

Smoke also has a nasty, permeating odor. Some items, such as wood and fabric, retain that odor extremely well because they're so porous. The longer they're exposed to smoke odor, the harder it is to get rid of it.

Before you touch a thing, however, call your insurance company. They'll tell you what they will want you to do about such things as documenting the damage and getting your home put back into order. They'll also be able to answer any questions you have regarding what your policy covers.

**Around the House**

Fire coverage is a major part of homeowner policies. Typically, policies will pay for cleaning up smoke and soot damage throughout the house, repairing structural damage, repairing or replacing damaged appliances, and paying living expenses until structural damage is repaired and the house is safe to live in. If faulty wiring or appliance installation is determined to be the cause of a fire and you're covered by a new or existing home warranty, talk to your builder or check with the policy issuer.

If you need a place to stay and food to eat, contact a local disaster relief service or a local branch of a national disaster relief service, such as the Salvation Army or the American Red Cross.

## In the Cinders

If you are allowed back into your house, be prepared for what awaits you. Roofs and floors may be buckled, sagging, or bearing other signs of damage. Paint and wallpaper might be blistered and burnt.

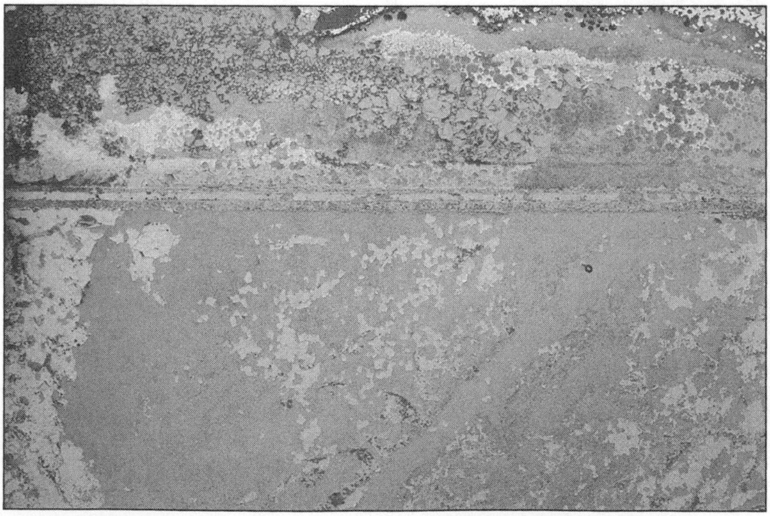

*This is what paint on a wall can look like after a house fire.*

**A Fine Mess**

We've said it before, but it bears repeating. Do not enter a fire-damaged house until the fire department or a structural expert has evaluated the damage and gives the go-ahead. In addition to structural damage, there could also be a risk of smoldering cinders rekindling.

If the fire was limited to one room and damage is minimal, you can probably handle cleanup duty on your own. If it's more than you think you can do (or want to do) on your own, leave everything as you found it, and call a company that specializes in fire cleanup. You'll find them in the yellow pages under Fire and Water Damage Restoration or Carpet and Upholstery Cleaners.

These people are specially trained in techniques for getting rid of the smell and soot that fires deposit, and they have special equipment and chemicals for smoke and soot cleanup that typically aren't available to consumers.

If you're allowed in only long enough to search for personal items and valuables, try to find the following:

- Identification such as driver's licenses, birth certificates, and so on.
- Important documents such as wills and insurance information.
- All necessary prescription drugs and/or medical equipment.
- Eyeglasses, contact lenses, hearing aids, prosthetic devices, and so on.
- Valuables such as jewelry, cash, credit cards, checkbooks, and so on.

When you're done, make sure your home is secured against vandalism and/or trespassers. Broken windows, doors, and other holes should be boarded up. You might want to hire a security service to keep an eye on things if it's going to be a while before you're allowed back in.

## Clearing the Smoke

Burning things leave different types of residue and odors, which makes fire reclamation and restoration difficult. Techniques that remove smoke and smell from some substances don't work on others, and vice versa. Knowing what does and doesn't work and what to use on various surfaces and materials is often beyond the skill set of most homeowners, which is why insurance companies usually recommend hiring experts.

But let's say you had a small fire that only affected a single room—for our example, we'll use your kitchen. There's no structural damage—the fire was out before the fire trucks arrived—just a lot of soot everywhere and an awful smell from the fire. What's more, you didn't file an insurance claim because the damage is pretty much limited to the smoke and soot, and you figure the cleanup costs are going to be less than your deductible. So, you either have to hire and pay for the help out of your own pocket, or do it yourself.

Here's what you'll need if you choose the latter option:

- Wet/dry vac. Preferably a unit that can handle wet and dry substances.
- Dry-cleaning sponges. These are special sponges that do a great job of cleaning soot from just about anything. You can find them in art-supply (they're also great for keeping artwork clear of dust and whatnot while it's being created), cleaning, and paint supply stores. Expect to pay around $4 to $5 each.
- Tri-sodium phosphate, or TSP. This is a caustic chemical commonly used as an all-purpose cleaning agent. It's a powerful degreaser and cleaner and makes short work of things like grease and soot. You can use TSP to clean clothing, walls, floors, and some furniture. Pine cleaners will work, too, and are typically less caustic. As such, using them will take a little longer.
- Bucket for mixing the TSP or other cleaner. Get at least a gallon-size one.
- Sponges, rags, mop, and so on for cleaning hard surfaces.
- Rubber gloves, both for wearing while mixing cleaner and during cleanup. Oils from your fingers can mix with soot and smoke to further damage everything you touch.
- Vacuum cleaner with edge attachment. You'll use this for getting into hard-to-reach nooks and crannies.

> **In the Nick of Time**
>
> The smell of smoke can overwhelm you, especially if you're working in a small area. Using a room deodorizer can help you breathe a bit easier while you're working. Or buy some dried eucalyptus branches, stick them in a pot or vase, and keep them with you as you work.

One of the first things you want to do is get fresh air circulating through your house. This will lessen the smoke smell, but it won't get rid of all of it.

If it's dry outside, open all windows and doors to grab as much breeze as possible. If things are soggy from the water used to hose down the fire, you might want to run some fans or a dehumidifier as well. Be sure to check the status of the electrical wiring and outlets in the damaged room before you plug in anything. And, keep central air or heat turned off until after the room is cleaned. This will help keep soot from circulating through your house.

Next, figure out your game plan. It's usually best to work from the top down, as fire debris tends to float downward, which means you'll probably want to tackle hard surfaces like the ceiling and walls first.

> **In the Nick of Time**
>
> It's notoriously difficult to get smoke smells out of fabric and textiles. Having these items professionally cleaned might be your best bet.

Before you do, use your wet/dry vac to remove all dry soot and any chemical residue from fire extinguishers that is underfoot. You don't want to track this stuff through your house. If you're vacuuming carpets or rugs, hold the nozzle of the vac slightly off the surface to avoid working the soot further into the fabric. Cover soft surfaces with plastic after you're done to protect them from accumulating soot that's still circulating in the air and from dirt that might be tracked in by inspectors or workers.

Next, remove loose soot from hard surfaces with the dry-cleaning sponges. Unlike regular sponges, these are used dry (hence the name). Wipe the ceiling first, then do the walls. Start each stroke at the top and work down. As you work along, the sponge will collect soot. You can use a knife to skim it off the sponge and expose a new cleaning surface.

The extra-soft surface of dry-cleaning sponges work well on many surfaces, but not all. For example, they aren't good on oil-based paint, acrylic paint, or vinyl wallpaper, and they also aren't very effective for removing the soot from grease fires. You'll need to use a regular sponge and TSP or a similar cleaner on these surfaces.

Work quickly, but be thorough. The more soot you're able to remove, the faster the smoke smell will dissipate.

Use your sponge and cleanser to wipe down all the surfaces in your cupboards, pantry, and other storage areas. Throw away any open food packages as you go. The smoke makes it unfit to eat. Dishes, glassware, and cooking utensils can be washed as you normally would.

If there are soft surfaces such as curtains, carpet, or rugs in your kitchen, you might want to consider hiring a professional fire restorer. Incorrect cleaning methods here can hurt more than help, as the oils in soot easily damage these materials. Vacuum up as much soot as you can from a distance of about an inch or two from the surface you're cleaning. Then cover it up and let someone else tackle it.

> **A Fine Mess**
>
> Don't use upright vacuum cleaners or vacuum cleaner attachments with brushes on carpets, upholstered furniture, and curtains. Doing so can force soot deeper into fibers.

# Getting Rid of the Smoke Smell

The smell of a fire can be tougher to remove than the soot and ash it deposits. Cleaning things thoroughly will take care of some or most of the smell, but you may never be able to entirely get rid of it without some professional help.

Professional fire restorers (some dry cleaners, too) use special equipment like thermal foggers and ozone generators to eliminate odors. Thermal foggers release chemicals into the air that attack bad odors and replace them with more pleasant fragrances. Ozone generators produce an oxidizing agent that literally breaks up the smoke molecules. However, these devices can also damage fabrics and make them age more rapidly. If you're concerned about any of your items, you might want to think twice about this approach.

Repeated cleanings will gradually reduce smoke odors. So will pumping large amounts of fresh air in and through your home on a regular basis. Giving curtains and rugs a sun bath can also help. If possible, put them on green grass away from direct sun and let them air out for as long as you can. The combination of air, sunlight, and grass can work wonders.

> **A Fine Mess**
>
> Household deodorizing products will only mask smoke smells, not remove them. What's more, the ingredients in these products can interact with the smoke odor and make things smell even worse. Steer clear of them.

Other odor-clearing approaches include…

- Placing big boxes of baking soda around your home. Change them out every three months or so.
- Putting bowls of vinegar in strategic spots around your home.

- Making an aromatherapy air freshener by combining 30 to 40 drops of your favorite essential oil (odor-clearing essential oils like lemon grass, citronella, geranium, or orange are all good choices) with $1^1/_2$ ounces of distilled water and $1^1/_2$ ounces of vodka or grain alcohol in a 4-ounce spray bottle. Use as necessary; keep the mist away from food and food-prep areas.

- Running a powered air cleaner or air ionizer. These devices are good for removing smoke and soot smells after a fire and for sanitizing air and surfaces in general.

When you're all done, have all the heating and cooling ductwork professionally cleaned. This will remove the majority of soot, ash, and smoke residue. Lay in a good supply of filters, and change them at least once a month for the following year. Before you fire up your air conditioner or furnace, tape cheesecloth over the intake and outlet air registers. This will help trap loose soot, which can remain airborne for a long time.

## The Least You Need to Know

- Recovering from a fire can be a physical and emotional drain.
- Cleaning up after a fire isn't just about making things look good again. You also have to get rid of smoke smells.
- The longer soot and ash sits on surfaces, the tougher it is to get rid of them. Tackle cleaning projects as soon as it's safe to enter your home.
- Be sure to have all the heating, ventilating, and air-conditioning units professionally cleaned, and change the filters regularly. Particulates can remain in the air for months.

# Part 3

# Rock Solid? Maybe Not!

The exterior of a house—from the foundation all the way to the roof—is designed to protect the well-being of its inhabitants and make them feel comfortable and safe.

Unfortunately, lots of things can happen—and do—that disrupt this protection. Cracks develop in foundations and slabs. Birds peck holes on siding. The mortar between bricks crumbles away. Bugs and rot destroy wood. All of it can make you feel like you're living with one of the Three Little Pigs.

Want to know how to keep the big bad wolf at bay? If so, this part is for you.

# Chapter 12

# My Foundation Has a Crack in It

## In This Chapter

- Cosmetic cracks versus structural cracks
- Signs of shifts
- Foundations and water
- Crack patches

Just the word foundation connotes something that's rock solid and meant to stay in place forever. And that's what foundations are all about. That said, foundations can and do crack. Some cracks aren't much to worry about. Others are. In this chapter, you'll learn which are which and what you can do to keep your foundation in rock-solid condition.

## Foundation Faults

Cracks in foundations are amazingly common. In fact, you can pretty much count on them happening. For the most part, they're nonstructural

**A Fine Mess**

The soil that sits under a building's foundation is technically part of the foundation. For this reason, foundations are only as good as the soil they're built on. Some soils are worthy elements in a foundation system. Others can cause big problems.

and cosmetic in nature. As such, foundation cracks are rarely disasters. However, they can indicate factors such as construction defects, shifting ground, or moisture problems in the ground under and around the foundation, all of which can cause structural problems.

Foundation cracks can also lead to other household disasters, including wet basements, basement floods, and pest infestations. For more on dealing with these problems, turn to Chapters 5, 17, 18, and 19.

# Small Crack, Big Problem?

As mentioned, discovering a foundation crack or two is rarely cause for panic. There's really not much you need to do about them on an immediate basis as long as water or pests aren't streaming in. However, if you suddenly see some strange condition changes in your house, there's every good reason to be concerned about foundation cracks.

Here are some of the "strange" things that are cause for alarm:

- Door sills and frames that have suddenly come apart
- Doors and windows that suddenly don't open or close properly
- Big cracks in interior walls near door or window corners (or both)
- Diagonal cracks that suddenly appear in brick fireplace walls or on exterior brick or stone veneers
- Nails that have suddenly popped out of the wall
- Cracking or waving in floor finishes, or feeling like you're walking uphill or downhill when you walk across rooms
- Caulking pulling away from exterior surfaces, or caulked joints on exterior surfaces separating

These are all indications of possible structural damage due to differential foundation settlement, meaning that one part of the foundation has moved more than the rest, and they all warrant calling out a structural expert for further diagnosis.

# Why Cracks Happen

As mentioned, lots of things can cause foundation cracks. However, there are two main culprits: soil problems and construction defects. While both can and do happen, soil tends to be a problem more often than not, especially in newer construction.

## Settling Things Down

All houses settle into their sites to a certain extent after they're built. If things go well, you'll see few if any signs of it, as your house will nestle into place gradually and evenly. But this isn't always the case. Sometimes settlement is more abrupt and/or uneven.

Cracks that are wider at the bottom than the top indicate soil settling.

The direction of a crack can give you an indication of what's causing it. Settling cracks generally move away from the corner of the foundation as it goes down. A crack due to expansive soils is directed toward the corner as it goes down. All cracks will normally appear at the weakest point in the wall, which is generally where a window is cut into it.

**A Fine Mess**

Call an architect or engineer if you spot a foundation crack that is greater than ⅛-inch wide or you can see all the way through it. These cracks indicate significant foundation settlement or the presence of expansive soils.

## Soils of Clay

If there's clay soil in your area, your house's foundation might be at a higher risk for developing problems due to changes in the soil's moisture level. Clay soils act like sponges. They absorb water during wet weather—typically winter and spring—and shrink when it's dry—typically during summer months.

Foundations are designed to handle some movement. As the soil shrinks and swells, the foundation and the house will move up and down. The movement is subtle, not something you'd notice. What you might notice is damage

**Around the House**

Wondering about the soil conditions around your house? Go to www.usda.gov, where you'll find handy soil maps for most of the country, courtesy of the U.S. Department of Agriculture.

that seems to appear and disappear on a regular basis. This indicates that your house is returning to the same position on both its upward and downward swings.

Extremes of either condition, however, can literally push a foundation to the breaking point.

Cracks that are wider at the top than at the bottom indicate expansive soils.

## Keeping Foundations Happy

There's not much you can do about construction defects beyond remediating them. And there's not much you can do about the composition of the soil under and around your house. But you can help your foundation stay in good shape simply by keeping moisture levels in the soil around it on an even keel—not too wet, not too dry.

For tips on preventing too much water from entering the ground around your home, turn to Chapter 5. If you're in a situation where you need to temporarily add moisture—say, you're in an area that's experiencing a drought—you can do so by watering your foundation, just like you water your yard.

There are fancy, in-ground foundation-watering systems that you can buy. These systems can be worth the money if you live in an area where soil and weather conditions warrant them. If you have to cope with occasional drought conditions, you don't have to go to the expense of installing permanent solutions. Watering with plain old soaker hoses works almost as well and is much less expensive.

Simply position a soaker hose about 3 to 5 feet away from the foundation. Run the hose daily over a period of several weeks. How long you keep the water running depends on how hot, dry, and sunny it is. You want to run it long enough to give the subsoil a good soaking, down to a depth of about 3 to 4 feet.

CAUTION

**A Fine Mess**

When watering your yard, don't make the mistake that many people do and just water parts of it. Keeping your front yard lush and letting other areas dry out will cause foundation expansion in the wet areas and contraction in the dry areas.

Be careful when adding moisture to the ground. Do it too quickly or add too much, and you can cause the opposite problem—soil expansion, which can also cause a crack.

Once the soil is sufficiently saturated, keep watering it as needed to maintain moisture levels. Obviously, you'll water more when it's hot and dry than when it's cool and damp.

# Patching Cracks

Foundation cracks that allow water to seep into your basement should be fixed. This can be done from the inside or the outside. Working from the inside is typically easiest, so we'll start there.

Polyurethane caulk can work well on small cracks. For the best results, make sure the concrete is dry before applying it, and force the material into the crack as far as you can. If there's any loose material in the crack, remove it before you apply the caulk.

Larger cracks take a little more work, and more materials. Here's what you'll need:

- Wire brush.
- Masonry chisel and heavy hammer.
- Quick-dry hydraulic cement. This is a special waterproof cement that will even set up underwater. It expands as it dries.
- Bucket for mixing cement.
- Safety goggles.
- Spray bottle of water.

Here's how to do it:

1. Put on your goggles.
2. Chisel out a groove with the masonry chisel and hammer. You want to make the inside of the crack larger than the outside. If you're familiar with furniture construction, you're basically making a dove-tail groove. This shape is best as it will lock the cement in place as it dries.
3. Clean out the crack with the wire brush.
4. Mix the cement. Be sure to follow the package directions.
5. Spray the patch area with water. Doing so will keep the moisture in the patch so it can set properly.
6. Fill the crack almost full. About ½ inch from the surface is good. Let this layer dry.
7. When the first layer is dry, completely fill the crack with a second layer. Smooth it so it matches the surface of the surrounding area.

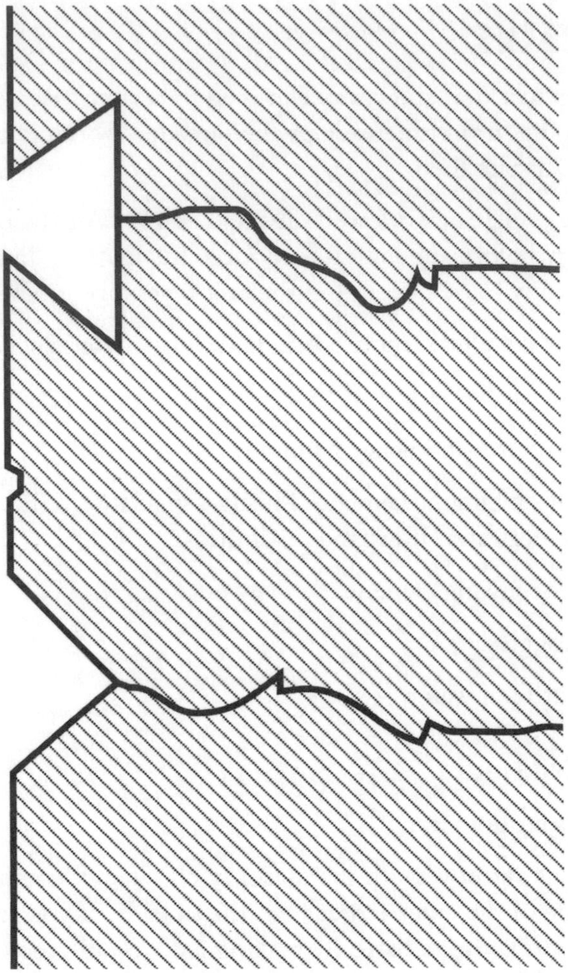

*Foundation crack repair.*

The dove-tail shape on the top works best for foundation crack repairs. The bottom shape, which is wider on the outside than on the inside, won't hold the patch material as well.

Cracks can also be repaired from the outside. Since these repairs prevent water from entering the foundation in the first place, they can be more effective and are typically longer lasting. However, they often require excavating the area around the crack. The repair process is pretty much the same as doing it from the inside—you'll clean the crack, then fill it with cement. When the cement is dry, apply a coat of waterproof coating over the repaired area. Choose a product designed to be used below grade. Then refill the excavated area.

After the cracks have been patched, you can apply a waterproof sealer to your basement walls. Doing so will prevent additional moisture from seeping through porous surfaces. There are a variety of different products available for this. Make sure the walls are dry and clean for the best results, and follow the label directions when applying.

## The Least You Need to Know

- Most foundation cracks are cosmetic and don't cause problems. Some, however, can indicate structural issues that need immediate attention.
- Soil problems and construction defects are the main culprits behind foundation cracks.
- Clay soils, which act like sponges, increase the risk of foundation problems due to fluctuations in moisture levels.
- Watering a foundation is the best way to keep cracks from happening due to insufficient moisture in the soil. Once the soil is sufficiently saturated, it's important to keep watering it to maintain consistent moisture levels.

Chapter 13

# My House Has a Hole In It

## In This Chapter

- Exterior problems
- Mortar moisture
- Keeping wood happy
- Solving stucco problems

We expect the materials on the outside of the structures we live in to help keep us warm in the winter, cool in the summer, and keep water out year-round. For these reasons, exterior materials must be able to stand up to anything that Mother Nature can and does throw at it.

For the most part, these exterior materials are up to the task. But things can happen to even the most durable of them. Some of the problems are of a more cosmetic nature. Others are more serious and can wreak havoc inside your home.

## Old Friend Water

Problems with exterior materials often mean that rain or snow can penetrate the building envelope. This manifests in—you guessed it—interior water problems. They can also provide entry for pests. For more on handling these problems, turn to Chapters 6, 16, 17, 18, 19, and 21.

**Around the House**

Defective materials and/or shoddy installation can cause cracks, gaps, holes, and other breaks in exterior materials. Exterior problems can also stem from other material failures and even deeper problems like shifting foundations. As such, these problems can be difficult to diagnose and remedy. Solving them might mean hiring a qualified professional to do a thorough investigation and suggest possible solutions.

Any of the following can cause exterior surface problems:

- Physical damage, such as debris flying into the house during a storm
- Old or bad paint on wood siding
- Waterproofing or protective coating failure
- Flawed roof construction and/or materials
- Flawed or incorrectly installed flashing at the base of walls or over windows and/or doors
- Problems with wall sheathing or sheathing membranes installed behind the finishing
- General wear and tear, such as cracks, dents, or buckles, on metal or vinyl siding
- Crumbling mortar, cracked or loose bricks, and/or bricks that are losing their exterior layer
- Cracks or loose areas in a stucco finish
- Improper fastening and/or support of all exterior finishes
- Animal damage, such as woodpeckers drilling into wood siding

If you're seeing water damage inside your home, chances are good that one or more of the above are to blame.

In most cases, there aren't any immediate fixes for exterior finish problems beyond finding the source of the problem. However, some of the long-term fixes are things homeowners can do, including …

- Sealing cracks with caulking.
- Repairing splits and holes in wood with waterproof glue.
- Fixing dents or cracks in vinyl or metal siding.
- Removing and reapplying wood siding (within reason).
- Repairing mortar around bricks (known as repointing), within reason.
- Sealing small stucco cracks.

You'll need an expert for any extensive brick, siding, or stucco repair or replacement.

For repairing interior damage from water problems, turn to Chapter 6.

**Tool Chest**

Pointing involves applying a small amount of mortar in the opening around bricks. In new brickwork, it's done to add extra protection from the elements. In old brickwork, repointing is done to repair eroded or damaged mortar.

# Finding the Break

Because exterior finish problems typically manifest in water penetration, and because water has a funny habit of traveling long distances in various directions, it can be difficult to find the exact spot where the water is coming in. Holes and cracks are obvious entry points, but the obvious isn't always the answer when it comes to exteriors. Or water.

**A Fine Mess**

Exterior materials can look just fine even when they're not. Sometimes leaks happen due to breaks in the waterproof sheath beneath the finish. The material over the sheath might not have any problems at all.

For this reason, you might need to call in an expert to help diagnose the problem. Most general contractors can do this for you. Those who specialize in the exterior product covering your house (vinyl siding, brick, stucco, and so on) will be your best bet.

Knowing more about how exteriors are constructed and the things that can damage them will help you keep your home's exterior in good shape. Let's take a look at some of the more common finishes, the problems that erupt with them, and what you can do to mitigate them, as well as what's underneath those exteriors.

## The Inside Scoop on Exterior Construction

It may seem odd, but most people don't even know how the exteriors of homes are built. What you see on the very outside is just part of the process.

From the inside out, here's what a typical wall looks like:

- Walls are constructed with 2 × 4 or 2 × 6 pieces of wood (wall studs).
- Insulation is placed between the studs.
- Wood sheathing is nailed over the studs and the insulation.
- Building paper or Tyvek, a vapor barrier, is applied to the sheathing to help keep moisture out.

The next layer varies a bit depending on the exterior finish. Wood, metal, or vinyl exteriors are installed directly on top of the building paper or Tyvek.

Brick and stone veneers are attached with short metal brackets called ties. This creates a slight break between the layers for moisture control. For stucco homes, a wire framework is first attached to the sheathing or to wooden slats nailed to the sheathing. The stucco is applied in three layers over the armature.

## How the Brick Crumbles

Brick is amazingly durable and an excellent insulator, which is why it's so widely used and has been for centuries.

Older brick homes usually feature solid brick construction. Most modern brick homes, however, are made with brick veneers. These surfaces give the appearance of solid brick at a lower cost.

**Around the House**

Brick-veneer siding is applied to a wood frame over building paper. It can cover an entire wall, or serve as an accent to other exterior surfaces. You can tell the difference between a brick veneer and structural brick by the brick pattern. Structural brick normally requires two layers of bricks tied together every few rows. The ties are bricks placed on edge so you can see a row of the short ends of the brick.

Both solid brick and brick veneer is applied with mortar, which is cement, sand, and lime mixed together with water. Both substances are solid yet porous, with mortar being more so. In wet climates, and especially climates that experience extreme temperature swings, water-repellant coatings are sometimes applied to brick buildings to preserve their finish.

Both types of brickwork can deteriorate for a number of reasons. Sometimes it's just one thing that causes the problem; other times it's a number of things that come together to create havoc.

## Spalling

*Spalling* happens when moisture inside the brick expands and contracts due to temperature changes. It causes brick to lose its topmost layer. It is more of a problem in climates with temperature extremes, and especially in areas where there are repeated freeze-thaw cycles.

**Tool Chest**

**Spalling** describes brick that is shedding its topmost layer.

Spalling can also indicate mortar that is too dense or too high in cement content. Mortar should never be denser than the brick it holds in place, but it definitely can be. When it is, it's stiffer than the brick that it surrounds, and it won't allow the bricks to expand as much as they need to when they get wet. Because of this, stress builds up inside the brick because the mortar doesn't let the moisture escape to the surface of the brick where it can evaporate. Instead, the surface cracks off due to the pressure.

Properly installed and maintained brick is less likely to develop spalling. That said, about the only way to fix spalling when it happens is to replace the affected bricks with salvage or replica pieces. Depending on the extent of the damage, it might be possible to remove individual bricks, clean them, and put them back into place with the undamaged side facing out.

For more extensive damage, painting the brick or applying a breathable, water-repellent coating might slow down additional deterioration.

## Cracks

Cracks in brickwork are pretty common and can happen either along mortar joints or in the bricks themselves. Typically, they're caused by things like structural movement, construction defects, temperature and moisture extremes, mortar problems and/or erosion, and tree roots growing too close to foundations. If you see cracks in mortar, these factors are most likely to blame.

Cracks in bricks, however, can indicate more serious problems, such as unstable soil, uneven weight distribution, and foundation problems.

Brick veneer sidings typically will develop cracks along mortar joints. Very rarely do the bricks in these surfaces crack.

**Around the House**

As discussed in previous chapters, bricks sometimes develop a "bloom" on their surface, known in the business as "efflorescence." It's caused by soluble salts moving to the surface of the brick, and it can indicate moisture problems inside the brick, but it can also be caused by high relative humidity levels. Efflorescence should be checked out to make sure it isn't a sign of a more serious problem. If it's weather-related, you can clean it off by scrubbing it with a damp brush. If bricks are dirty, add a little trisodium phosphate (TSP) to the water to dissolve the grime. Rinse thoroughly; TSP can stain if residue remains behind. For more on using TSP, turn to Chapter 7.

# Fixing Brick

Superficial cracks in brick aren't much of a concern, and can be left as is. Cracks that are a little wider than this also aren't cause for concern. If they bother you, you can touch them up with grout tinted to match the color of the brick.

If you have brick that's cracked all the way through, it should be replaced. This is best left to a bricklayer, especially if the damage is extensive.

**Tool Chest**

Weep holes are regularly spaced small holes in the vertical mortar between the first course of bricks in a wall. The holes allow the space between the brick and frame walls to breathe and allow any water that accumulates behind the brick to escape.

## Water Problems

As mentioned, waterproofing can be applied to brick surfaces to slow down spalling. Keeping *weep holes* clear in brick veneer will also help eliminate some water problems. Unfortunately, this is easier said than done, as weep holes are often clogged with mortar that's dropped by the bricklayers during the building process. If this is the case, it's possible to have special vents installed to improve ventilation. These vents are the size of a brick and are held in place with caulking.

## Mitigating Mortar Problems

Even the best mortar will break down over time. The lime in it leaches out, cracks develop, and water seeps in. When this happens, mortar starts to crumble.

As mentioned, you can replace crumbling mortar by repointing it. You'll need the following:

- A chisel or similarly pointed tool.
- Safety goggles.
- Mortar. You want dry, ready-mixed mortar. Buy a bag marked water-resistant type N.
- Something to mix the mortar in. A plastic bucket (plan on throwing it away when you're done) is fine.
- A small trowel.
- A spray bottle full of water.

Here's what you'll do:

1. Don your goggles and use the chisel to chip out the old mortar.
2. Mix the mortar according to the package directions.
3. Dampen the area you're going to work on slightly with the spray bottle. Doing this will help keep the moisture in the mortar you're applying from migrating to the surrounding areas, which could result in mortar failure due to insufficient moisture.
4. Pick up a good amount of the mortar on the trowel and pack it into place.
5. Firmly press or pack the mortar into place with the flat edge of the trowel. Try to match how the mortar is finished in other areas. Slide the trowel along the wall to remove excess mortar.
6. Clean any additional excess from the wall.
7. Keep the repaired area damp for three to four days while the mortar cures.

## Special Problems with Brick Veneer

Brick veneer houses are legendary for developing water intrusion problems. Homes that are built in the open with little or no protection from trees or nearby structures are particularly at risk, but they all can suffer from it.

Here's why: Brick veneers are installed over building paper or Tyvek. There needs to be a minimum ¾-inch space between the veneer and the wall behind it, and this space has to remain free and clear to allow the water that gets behind it to evaporate and/or drain. Weep holes must also be placed at the base of the wall for water elimination.

Most contractors leave enough space between the veneer and the wall, but they might not clean away excess mortar that collects behind the veneer when it's built. This material can wick water right into the wall behind the veneer. Excess mortar can also obstruct weep holes.

Severe storms can quickly drive water into the space between the veneer and the wall. If there are blockages in this space, the water can't evaporate like it should. Instead, it will seep into the building paper or Tyvek, which, while being an effective moisture barrier, is not waterproof. When it does, it can sit there for many days—definitely long enough to cause interior damage and mold growth.

Once water problems develop behind brick veneer, about the only thing you can do is remove and replace the veneer.

# Wood Siding

Wood siding, which includes clapboard, shingles, and shakes as well as plywood and hardwood sheets, can last up to 30 years if well maintained. This means keeping it sealed, stained, or painted to protect it from weathering, decay, and insect damage.

**In the Nick of Time**

The best way to keep wood siding in good shape is to inspect it regularly. Look for cracks, holes and warps, paint that is cracked or blistered, missing shingles or shakes, and insect and bird damage.

Many wood siding repairs are pretty easy to do, and they should be done as soon as you spot problems. Before you do any repairs, however, it's a good idea to figure out what caused the problem and correct it to prevent problems from continuing. Typical culprits include the following:

- Leaky or clogged gutters
- Damaged gutters and/or downspouts

- Downspout problems
- Damage along the edges of eaves and roofs
- Tree or shrub branches
- Termites or other wood-loving pests

Depending on the type of siding that's on your house, it might be easier to repair it than replace it, as finding a perfect match might be difficult. However, if damage is extensive, plan on replacing the material.

If you suspect damage from insects and/or birds, turn to Chapters 15 and 21 for more help.

As mentioned, minor damage to wood siding, such as splits and small holes, is easy to repair. Some splits can simply be glued back together with waterproof glue. Drive a nail or two into the board to hold it in place while the glue dries. Paint over the glue, if necessary, when it's dry.

Replacing entire boards, shingles, or shakes can be a little tougher, especially if you can't find products to match. One approach is to remove what you need from an inconspicuous area on your house, and replace what you removed with new product.

**In the Nick of Time**

Some hardboard siding products, such as Masonite, have hard surfaces, but if water penetrates the surface, the material will quickly deteriorate (this problem has also made them the subject of class-action lawsuits). The edges of these products are most susceptible to water penetration. Painting the edges every fall—particularly edges that are low enough that snow can drift over them—will help protect them.

# Stucco

Stucco is plaster with a cement base. Although it's pretty durable, it can develop cracks and holes, especially if it's not applied well or if it's not good quality to begin with. Some cracks on new construction can be expected as the house settles into place. Significant cracks are something to be concerned about, as they can indicate poor application or problems with the base that the stucco was applied over.

Both plaster and cement are porous materials, which means that stucco is, too. Most of the time, water isn't that much of an issue, but it can be if there are holes and/or cracks in the stucco. Both should be repaired as soon as you see them.

Hairline and small cracks can simply be painted over with acrylic paint. If necessary, fill them in first with latex caulking compound, and then paint them.

Larger cracks are also fairly easy to fix. You'll need the following materials:

- Chisel
- Trowel
- Stucco patching compound
- Concrete bonding agent
- Paint, if you need to cover your work
- Spray bottle full of water

Here's what you'll do:

1. Open up the crack slightly by chiseling around the edges. Brush away any loose stucco.
2. Apply concrete bonding agent to the edges. This will help keep the patch material in place.
3. Mix the patching compound according to the package directions.
4. Apply to the crack. Try to match the texture to the existing stucco.
5. Let the area cure for three to four days. Keep it damp during this period by spraying it with water.

Hole repairs are pretty similar. However, since stucco is applied in layers, you'll have to do your repairs in layers, too. You might also need a small piece of wire mesh if the existing armature is damaged.

1. Remove any loose stucco. Use a chisel if necessary. Brush away any dust or dirt.
2. If you need to repair the armature, staple or nail the mesh patch into place.
3. Wet the area with water from a spray bottle.
4. Partially fill the hole with stucco patch. Let it set up for several days.

5. Apply the next layer. Again, don't fill the hole all the way. Let this one sit for several days, too.
6. Apply the final layer. Keep the surface damp for three to four days.

If cracks reappear or appear to be widening, have the stucco inspected by an expert.

Synthetic stucco, also called EIFS (exterior insulation and finish systems) has been the subject of class action lawsuits. EIFS are multi-layered exterior wall systems consisting of a finish coat, a base coat, and insulation board, all of which are secured to plywood or another substrate.

EIFS is available in various external textures designed to look like traditional stucco. If not installed properly, it can cause water problems behind the wall. Ensure that there are no openings in the seals around windows and doors. If there is any doubt, contact a professional.

# Vinyl and Metal Siding

Vinyl or metal siding is often applied over existing finishes, such as masonry or wood, to freshen the appearance of older houses, to improve their insulating abilities, and to better protect them from the elements. Both products are extremely durable and stand up well to weather. However, they can crack, crease, or puncture. Heavy winds can also rip siding right off a house.

Keep siding in good shape by inspecting it regularly. Keeping trees and shrubs trimmed back will also help minimize damage.

Slight surface damage, such as cracks, creases, and other small blemishes, can be repaired on vinyl siding with color-matching caulking. Dents and dings in metal siding can be filled with auto body filler and painted.

Anything more than this typically calls for removing and replacing the entire section, which is best left to the experts.

## The Least You Need to Know

- Problems with exterior materials typically manifest as interior water problems.
- Both bricks and mortar can develop cracks. Anything more than superficial cracks in each should be investigated and repaired.

- Sealing or painting wood siding will go a long way toward keeping it in good condition. For the best protection, plan on reapplying every three to four years.
- Slight blemishes in vinyl or metal siding can be repaired with caulk or auto body filler.

Chapter 14

# My House Is Rotting Away

## In This Chapter

- Rotten luck
- Types of rot
- What rot needs to grow
- Getting rid of rot

Is there a step on your wood deck that seems a little soft and springy when you walk on it? Maybe you came home one day and found that a door fell off its hinges. Maybe you've noticed some paint cracking on the exterior trim on your house, and the wood around it doesn't look so good. Or your kids found something that looks like a big mushroom growing on a beam in your basement.

These are just a couple of things that can happen when wood goes rotten. Consider them warning signs, and don't ignore them. If you do, you might have to deal with an even bigger problem, like your bathroom floor caving in when you're filling the bathtub.

It happened to Tom Hanks in a movie called *The Money Pit*, and it can happen to you, too.

## Rot Repair

What you're immediately going to do about rotten wood depends a great deal on what's rotting. If you're dealing with a structural collapse (and we definitely feel for you if this is the case), you'll need to take immediate action to prevent further damage and/or injury.

> **A Fine Mess**
>
> Wood rot can be and often is a hidden menace. Boards that look solid can be completely rotten inside. If they are, windows and doors can literally fall out of walls. Deck railings can crumble off of porches, and floors can cave in. What's more, a good case of wood rot can cause these things—and more—to happen in a matter of years, not decades.

First, cordon off these areas so others don't enter or come near them. This might mean blocking off outdoor steps and rerouting people to a different entrance. If the damage is extensive and it's indoors, take whatever steps necessary to protect your family, including, if necessary, moving everyone out until the damage can be assessed and fixed.

Next, call a pest-control company that specializes in evaluating and remediating wood-rot damage. They should send out someone who can determine the extent of the problem and help you figure out what to do about it. For assessing the extent of the structural damage caused by wood rot, call a licensed professional engineer.

There are two things you have to do about wood that has rotted: Fix it, and stop it from happening again. Fixing it is a two-step process. First, you have to remove the rotten wood. Then you have to replace it. Depending on where the wood has rotted and the extent of the damage, cosmetic fixes might be possible, which you can do yourself if you have the tools and the inclination. If this is the case, and you want to get to work right away, turn to the end of the chapter for repair tips.

> **A Fine Mess**
>
> Most insurance policies exclude losses caused by rots. They also exclude coverage for losses caused by collapse unless the collapse was caused by hidden decay.

If the damage is extensive, you'll probably have to hire a contractor to do the repairs for you. But there are things you can do right away to keep the rot from getting worse and to prevent it from happening in other parts of your house.

# Something's Rotten

Wood rots for one simple reason: It gets wet. It can happen to wood anywhere in your house—in structural timber, door trim, eaves, exterior trim—you name it. Wood rot is also common on boats and plants and can even be found in musical instruments.

All wood has the potential for rotting, as it contains a certain amount of moisture. If moisture content is below 20 percent, rot typically isn't a concern. Anything over this provides a potential breeding ground for *fungi*, which is what causes wood rot.

Moisture is just one thing that fungi need to survive. They also need the following:

- Favorable temperatures. Anything in the 40°F to 100°F range will do.
- Oxygen.
- A food source. The fungi that attack wood prefer carbohydrates in the form of cellulose and lignin.

Wood is made up of cellulose and lignin, and the other factors are pretty hard to control, so fungi abatement efforts generally focus on the one variable—moisture—that we can do something about.

> **A Fine Mess**
>
> Virtually every homeowner has to deal with wood damage at some time or another. It's so common, in fact, that the materials for replacing and repairing damaged wood makes up an estimated 10 percent of all wood products annually produced in the United States.

> **Tool Chest**
>
> **Fungi** are plantlike organisms. They can't synthesize food on their own, however, so they have to absorb nutrients from other sources, such as wood. Mushrooms are a well-known fungi.

## Dry vs. Wet Rot

People used to distinguish between different kinds of wood rot as being dry or wet. This was misleading, as it made it seem like dry wood could develop rot. This simply isn't possible. All rotten wood is wet wood, or has been wet at one time.

We'll repeat it one more time: Dry wood cannot decay.

**Tool Chest**

**Brown rot** causes infected wood to turn dark brown, hence the name.

Still, you'll hear people call certain types of rot "dry rot." What they're really referring to is *brown rot*, which is one of three types of wood rots. This rot cracks wood against the grain, causing it to split and crumble. In advanced stages of brown rot, after the rot has taken all the nutrients out of the wood, it can also become dry and powdery.

The other types of wood rot are …

- White rots. As the name suggests, these rots cause affected wood to take on a white appearance, which can range from grayish-white to yellowish. In their advanced stages, white rots make wood look stringy and feel spongy or springy.
- Soft rots. These are rare inside of homes, but they have been known to attack wood shingles in wet climates.

Some rots can grow inside wood for a long time and cause extensive damage before they are detected. Others develop crusts called "fruiting bodies" on the surface of the wood.

## Rot vs. Mold

As discussed in previous chapters, mold (and mildew) are also fungi that spring up around moisture. While they indicate moisture problems and can cause discoloration, they themselves don't cause wood decay. They can, however, increase wood's absorption ability, which can make it more prone to fungal growth.

Another type of fungi called "sap stain fungi" looks like surface mold. However, it, too, doesn't weaken wood structures; it only discolors them. Sap stain fungi stops growing when wood dries out. Its presence typically indicates wood that was wet at one time but no longer is.

*Both brown and white rot have virtually destroyed this old wall.*

## Why Wood Goes to Rot

Since there's always some moisture in the air, even in pretty arid areas, wood is always susceptible to rot. But there are situations and conditions that will make it rot faster than others. The biggest is direct contact with wet soil, cement, concrete, or masonry. If it happens for more than a brief period, wood will rot. It's that simple.

Other things that cause wood rot include:

- Condensation, which can build up in areas like wall voids in cool areas and poorly ventilated crawl spaces.
- Plumbing leaks. Rots are very common in bathrooms and kitchens where these occur.
- Rainwater and/or groundwater seepage from gutters and downspouts.
- Construction or design defects. Things like improperly installed flashings or shingles can cause water to pool on roofs. Wood that comes into contact with these areas can wick up the water. As it does, it becomes a breeding ground for fungi. Improperly sealed crevices, cracks, and corners in railings, decks, and staircases are also prime water-collection and fungi-breeding areas.
- Poor ventilation in attics with insufficient venting. Bathroom exhaust fans often empty into attics. Without proper ventilation, moisture buildup can cause mold and mildew growth and rot.

> **A Fine Mess**
>
> Poria incrassate, a water-conducting fungus, can transport water for several feet through rootlike structures called "rhizomorphs." It's typically a suspect when rot is found in wood that's nowhere near a water source.

Some forms of wood rot develop *rhizomorphs*, which are strands of material that can transport water. These rots can feed fungi located quite a ways away from water sources, and can even permeate dry materials to do so.

Wood rot is often associated with older homes, but it can attack any structure built of wood. Modern homes, in fact, can develop severe rot problems as they're often built so tightly that interior moisture can't escape to the outside.

# Rooting Out Rot

The best time to prevent rot is when homes are built. Some wood used in home-building, such as Western red cedar and redwood, contains substances that make them naturally fungi resistant. But these fungi-resistant woods are in short supply, and are too expensive to be used widely.

> **In the Nick of Time**
>
> If you're doing any repairs to wood on your home, building a deck, even building wood flower planters, always use pressure-treated lumber or lumber substitutes. Yes, they're more expensive, but they'll save you money in the long run.

Alternatives to these woods include …

- Pressure-treated lumber, which is impregnated with chemicals that protect it from insect and fungal damage. There are different types, rated for various placements: above ground, ground contact, and wood foundation.
- Wood-polymer lumber, which bonds wood with fungi-resistant plastic.
- Extruded plastic lumber made from recycled plastic containers.

Building on well-drained sites with proper grading will also help prevent wood rot.

In existing homes, periodic inspections can go a long way toward fighting off many problems, including wood rot. If you're picking up a musty smell in your basement or it's been raining more than usual, it's definitely a good idea to take a good look around.

Before you go, arm yourself with a pointed tool, such as a screwdriver, ice pick, or awl. You'll need it for probing suspect wood.

Inspect the following areas. Use the tool to dig into any suspicious areas. If it enters easily, you've got rot.

- Exterior trim. Pay close attention to horizontal or nearly horizontal areas that don't drain well, such as window sills. Cracked, peeled, or blistering paint are signs of moisture damage. Be sure to check underneath exterior doors, too, as water often pools here.
- Behind porches or patios. Wood here often sits close to the ground, concrete, or masonry. Rot can also develop in the wood behind concrete steps.
- Interior crawl spaces. Pay particular attention to joints, which typically retain water longer than other areas.
- The areas around plumbing fixtures, especially in the cabinets under kitchen and bathroom sinks.

If you have a fireplace, also check the flashing on the roof around the chimney, and the areas around the chimney (especially subfloors) where it runs through your home. While you're up there, check flashings around vents, skylights, around the roof—anywhere water can pool and cause problems.

## How Dry Am I?

If you don't find rot, but you still think there might be a problem, get your hands on a wood moisture meter. These handy devices are available at many hardware and home improvement stores and at stores that carry woodworking supplies. They're not cheap—the low end is around $100 or so—but they're worth the price if they detect a moisture problem before fungi sets in.

**Around the House**

If you have a friend who builds wood furniture or does other woodcrafts, ask about borrowing a wood moisture meter. Serious woodworkers almost always have one, as wood that is too wet or dry can wreak havoc with their projects.

**In the Nick of Time**

Some cities, especially those located in areas where things tend to be a bit damp, have inspection programs to assist homeowners in identifying wood rot. If you live in one of these areas, see if your municipality offers this service.

Most moisture meters use electric impedance to test moisture levels. These devices have two little pins on one side. You stick the pins into the wood, then press a button or flip a switch. This sends a quick jolt of electricity through the wood. Internal circuitry measures how quickly the electricity makes the rounds from one pin to the other. Wet wood conducts electricity faster than dry wood does.

Other models are pinless and use electromagnetic radio waves to test wood density. The denser the wood, the wetter it is.

## Drying Things Out

Any rotten wood you find during your inspection must be replaced and repaired to prevent further damage. However, it's also important to locate the source of the moisture and stop it from affecting the wood. If you don't, any repairs you make will be temporary at best. As long as there's water available, rot fungi will continue growing.

As previously noted, there can be some distance between a leak and the rot that grows from it, which can make it difficult to find the actual source of the problem. Don't be surprised if something that looks like a small rot problem turns out to be a lot more once you start looking around.

Breaking all contacts between wood and soil, concrete, or masonry is essential. Doing so will dry out decayed wood and stop further decay. You might also have to take steps to improve the ventilation, such as adding vents in crawl spaces, attics, basements, and any other areas where moisture builds up. It might also be necessary to run a dehumidifier in these areas to keep moisture levels down when relative humidity is high.

## Repairing Wood Rot

It's important to determine the extent of the damage before you begin to repair and replace the wood. As before, you can do this with a sharp-ended tool like a screwdriver or awl.

Remove as much rotten wood as possible (and economically feasible) before beginning repairs. In structural wood—columns, beams, girders, and the like—it's important to cut back to sound wood; if possible, the cut should be made at least 1 foot beyond the last evidence of rot. You don't have to be as aggressive on things like window trim, but you still should remove as much rotten wood as you can.

**A Fine Mess**

It's essential to find out how badly the rot has traveled around as eliminating it from one area will not stop it from traveling to other parts of your home. It must be destroyed in its entirety.

If you're replacing structural wood, keep the new lumber away from the old if at all possible, and be sure to use pressure-treated wood. For repairs in hard-to-maintain areas or in wood that's constantly exposed to the elements, you'll want to treat existing wood, too.

**Around the House**

It's really not that necessary to determine what kind of rot you have. Rot is rot. That said, white rot damages the structural integrity of wood more slowly. Wood infected with white rot is often still useable in the early stages of decay. Not so with brown rot. Even a small amount of it can have a significant effect on wood's strength.

*Borates* are the chemical of choice for treating and stopping rots, and have been used for this purpose for many years. They are water-based, low in toxicity, environmentally friendly, and they last a long time. Since they are water-based, they actually use the water in wood as a carrier. When wood is dry, borates stay in place. When wood gets wet, the borates move through the wood. As they do, they both kill fungi and protect the wood from future infections.

**Tool Chest**

**Borates** are chemicals derived from boron, a naturally occurring mineral.

Borate products are sold under a number of brand names, including Bora-Care, Guardian, Jecta, Tim-bor, Shell-Guard, and IMPEL Rods. All of them both protect and treat wood and wood-foam composite materials against fungi and wood-destroying insects (more about these in Chapter 15). Some are solutions that you spray or brush on. Tim-bor is available as a dust that you inject into cracks and hard-to-reach spaces. IMPEL Rods, as the name suggests, are rod-shaped devices that slip into holes drilled in wood.

Choose the product that best suits your needs, and follow the label directions for mixing and application.

## Fixing Minor Rot Damage

As mentioned, extensive structural repairs should be done by someone with experience in making these repairs. It's a good idea to have all structural repairs inspected by a pest-control company to make sure that all rot was removed.

The following approach can be used to fix minor rot problems that you might find in things like door and window trim, old porch posts, and so on. It's fairly easy as long as you have the necessary tools and supplies, which are as follows:

- Basic carpentry tools, including screwdriver and wood drill
- Moisture meter
- Heat gun or hair dryer (for drying out wet wood)
- Putty knife
- Sanding tools
- Borate wood preservative
- Epoxy resin, such as LiquidWood

Here's how to do it:

1. Remove all decayed wood. A flat screwdriver, wood chisel, or similar tool works well for this. If there's a lot of rotted wood, digging it out with a claw hammer will be faster. Remember to extend your removal a bit beyond obvious decay areas.
2. Check the moisture content in the newly exposed wood. If it isn't below 18 percent, the wood must be dried out before you continue. Exposing it to the air will help a lot, but you can hasten the process with a heat gun or hair dryer.
3. When the wood is sound and dry, brush or spray on a liquid borate. Or drill several small holes and inject a borate into the wood. As mentioned, the borate will seek and destroy any remaining rot and minimize future damage.
4. Apply an epoxy resin. This product will soak into damaged wood fibers and harden them. Most of these products consist of a primer and filler. They can be

a little tricky to work with, so be sure to follow the product directions for mixing and application. Use a putty knife to shape and mold the epoxy to fit the repair.

5. Let the repair harden. This takes longer in cool weather than in hot. You'll know the process is complete when the epoxy doesn't feel tacky. When it's completely dry, shape and blend the patch, if necessary, with medium or coarse sandpaper.
6. Apply freshly mixed epoxy, if necessary, to any areas that need additional fill or shaping. Let harden and treat as before.
7. Sand the repair area smooth with fine sandpaper, then apply an acrylic primer and two coats of acrylic paint.

This is just one approach for repairing wood rot. In areas where damage is more extensive, you might have to replace parts or all of the damaged wood.

## The Least You Need to Know

- Dry rot is a misleading term for something that is anything but dry.
- Wood that comes in contact with or is imbedded in wet brickwork or masonry is a prime fungi breeding ground.
- Wood-rot damage can range from minor to severe. It's always wise to consult with professionals if rot has damaged structural wood.
- Borates, which are naturally occurring minerals, are an effective treatment for wood rot and will protect against future rotting.

Chapter 15

# Something's Eating My House

## In This Chapter

- Diagnosing danger signs
- Telling termite from ant
- Choosing a termite-control service
- Doing it yourself

Sometime in early spring, typically around March or so, but it could be as late as May, you might find a bunch of insects in your home that look like winged ants. Or you come across some shed insect wings on a windowsill or along the edges of floors.

The bugs could be a variety of different ants in their winged reproductive stage. They're a nuisance, but they're pretty harmless. However, there's also a chance that the insects you're seeing are termites or carpenter ants.

If they're from the latter group, you've got evidence of a potential wood-destroying insect problem. And that's not good.

# Immediate Fix

Both termites and carpenter ants have a swarming stage, typically in the spring, during which time they commonly come into homes. It could be a few, or they could fill your rooms. It's not a good thing to find either insect in your house, as it's virtually always an indication that you've got a bigger problem on your hands. But there's also no need to go into a blind panic when you see one. The reason? For starters, termites aren't fast workers. As such, your house isn't in immediate danger. It won't collapse overnight.

**Around the House**

Termites cause an estimated $2.5 billion worth of damage to homes and businesses every year. What's more, experts believe that one in five homes has a wood-destroying insect problem. Given the right conditions, termites can start attacking a house anywhere between 10 to 20 years after construction. Some start their attack as soon as a house is built. However, it can take three to eight years before a termite colony causes appreciable damage.

Carpenter ants, while also a nuisance, typically don't cause the same kind of damage that termites do, so there's no need to panic when you see them either. And finding them in your home doesn't necessarily mean that they've taken up residence. They could be coming in from an outside nest.

Either way, you don't have to rush into finding a pest-control company or buying products to treat your house yourself. While you shouldn't wait forever to do either, it's a good idea to take the time to do your research and make an informed decision. If it takes you a couple of weeks to do so, it won't make much of a difference, if any, on what happens to your home.

That said, you'll definitely want to do something relatively soon, because termites, if left alone, can cause thousands of dollars of damage to your home and your belongings. As mentioned, carpenter ants aren't as destructive, but a large, well-established colony living somewhere inside your home can also cause structural damage over time.

# Insect I.D.

Determining the kind of insect you're dealing with is an immediate action you can take, and it's an advisable one as there are different approaches for attacking termite and carpenter ant infestations.

Here's how to tell insect from insect:

| | Termite | Ant |
|---|---|---|
| Wing | Paddle-shaped, equal size, twice the length of body | Pointed, only slightly longer than body, forewings longer than hind wings |
| Antennae | Straight, fairly short | Bent |
| Body Parts | Two components: head and ribbed abdomen | Three components: head, thorax (midsection) and abdomen |

It's important to know that many termite and carpenter ant infestations aren't visible. Both insects often keep the evidence of their destructive ways behind closed doors—in this case, in walls or other concealed areas. For this reason, locating termite or carpenter ant infestations often requires calling in a professional.

Because termites are the bigger problem between the two insects, we discuss them first.

# The Trouble with Termites

Termites are wood-eating insects. Although they like to eat things like trees and shrubs, they're also extremely fond of residential structures, as well as anything made of wood, including a wood product that's inside a structure they've already infested. Unfortunately for homeowners, their passion for cellulose—the fiber in wood—comes with a huge price tag. Every year, termites cause billions of dollars in damage to wood structures.

There are three main types of termites in the United States: subterranean, drywood, and dampwood.

## Subterranean Termites

As the name suggests, these termites live in the ground, where they build large nests and long tubes, called mud or shelter tubes, through which they travel. They're the most common type in the United States, making up about 90 percent of all termite populations.

Subterranean termites need a good deal of moisture, which is why they like to nest in or near the ground. The mud or shelter tubes that they build helps them stay connected to their moisture source. Foundations and structural wood are where you'll find the majority of subterranean termite damage. Because they like moisture, they're also common in rotten wood.

A type of termite called the Formosan subterranean termite is a fairly new species in the United States, but is rapidly becoming a real problem due to its aggressive foraging behavior and living habits. These "super termites" have much larger colonies than other subterranean termites and will attack more than 50 species of plants. As such, they can cause widespread property damage that is costly to treat and repair.

**Around the House**

Formosan termites are believed to have entered the United States through port cities on the Gulf of Mexico and southeast Atlantic coast by ships returning from the Pacific Ocean after World War II. The first record of Formosan termites dates to 1957 in Charleston, South Carolina.

Formosan termites typically live in the ground, but aboveground colonies are common where there's enough moisture to sustain them. Currently, Formosan termites are found in Texas, Louisiana, Mississippi, Georgia, Florida, Hawaii, North and South Carolina, and Tennessee.

Subterranean termites typically favor warmish temperatures and the humidity that typically comes along with them. As such, they're more widespread in parts of the United States where these conditions are common, but they're not unknown in other parts of the country where temperatures are cooler and humidity is low.

Give these termites the right conditions, such as allowing structural wood to come into direct contact with soil, or allowing moisture to puddle or accumulate along foundation walls, and you're opening up your house to a termite infestation even if you live in a low-risk area.

These termites typically enter homes through foundations, which is one reason it's essential to repair cracks in basements and concrete slabs when they appear. For more information on this, turn to Chapter 12.

## Drywood Termites

These termites attack and live in sound, dry wood located above soil level. They don't need soil contact or any other source of moisture, as they get what they need from the wood they eat, and they also manufacture some on their own. They're secretive and live deep inside the wood they infest, building small, widely dispersed colonies that can take years to mature. They typically enter homes through attic vents, windowsills and frames, and shingle roofs.

**In the Nick of Time**

Drywood termites create small holes, about the size of a BB shot, called kickout or kick holes through which they push small, hexagonal-shaped fecal pellets from their nests. Finding these pellets, which vary in color depending on the type of wood being eaten and typically accumulate on surfaces near the holes or in spider webs below them, is a sure sign of an infestation.

Drywood termites can be difficult to detect as they only show themselves when they swarm or when their nests are disturbed, typically during repair or remodeling work. Their nests, or galleries, have smooth walls, pockets or chambers connects by tunnels that cut across the grain, and few or no surface deposits.

Homes in southern California, southern Arizona, and southern Florida are particularly susceptible to drywood termites, which can infest buildings soon after they're constructed. That said, it can take a very long time for these termites to do much structural damage. If they attack furniture, hardwood floors or wood trim, damage can become apparent in a couple of years or so.

## Dampwood Termites

These termites are typically found in fallen or buried logs in forests. They need lots of moisture to survive and are uncommon structural pests, but they will attack forest cabins and beach houses, building their colonies in damp or decaying wood. Once their nests are established, some will attack dry wood as well. Removing the damp or decayed wood and treating nearby soil are effective controls for these pests.

**A Fine Mess**

Traditional homeowner's policies classify termite infestations as home-maintenance issues and exclude damage from termites and other subterranean pests. However, if hidden insect damage caused your home to collapse, costs to repair the collapsed area would be covered. The actual damage caused by the insects wouldn't be.

As an example, say termites ate away a support beam. It collapses, causing damage to walls, floors, and roof trusses in that part of your home. Costs related to damage caused by the collapse would be covered. Repairing or replacing the support beam wouldn't be.

# Preventing Termite Infestations

The best way to prevent termite problems is before construction even starts. For all termites, using building methods and materials—pressure-treated wood or wood treated with borates—to minimize the chances for termite infestations is a good practice. Typical approaches where subterranean termites are a problem include treating the soil with termiticidal chemicals where the home is to be built.

Drywood termites will not attack painted wood; however, there is currently no effective treatment or method to keep them from entering through or under wood shingles.

Another proven method for keeping termites at bay is making life miserable for them.

**Around the House**

Depending on where you live, a soil pretreatment might have been required when your house was built. These treatments are typically covered by a multiyear warranty period, but problems can still happen, especially if structural changes are made to the home. Anything requiring breaking or cutting into a concrete slab or digging into the soil around the foundation of a structure can disrupt and even destroy the treated barrier. If you know your home was pretreated and you're thinking about remodeling or adding on to it, be sure to contact the pest-control company that did the original work. They'll keep your warranty intact by re-treating the soil.

## Eliminating Wood-Ground Connections

Structural wood that touches the ground is prime real estate for subterranean termites, as it gives them quick access to the three things they need to thrive: food, moisture, and shelter. Take the wood away from the ground, and you thwart their access to each.

Make sure that wood products—siding, latticework, door and window frames, and so on—end at least 6 inches above ground level. If they don't, do what's necessary to create this clearance. It might require regrading the soil around your house or pulling soil and mulch back from the foundation of your home.

Other wood-abatement efforts that are effective for preventing both types of termite infestations include:

- Storing firewood, lumber, or other wood debris away from the foundation of your house. Keep it out of your crawl space, too. Not only does wood stored in these locations provide a free meal for hungry little chompers, it also gives them an easy way to get into your home.
- Remove all dead wood, stumps, tree roots, and so on from your property.
- Use mulch sparingly, if at all. This goes for organic mulches like sawdust and wood chips as well as crushed stone and pea gravel. Termites don't find much nutritional value in mulch, but they do appreciate its moisture-retaining and temperature-insulating qualities. If you're going to use mulch in your flower or shrub beds, apply about 2 to 3 inches thick at the most. Never let it come up to wood siding or the framing of doors or windows.

## Keeping Things Dry

As mentioned, subterranean termites are attracted to moisture. Preventing water from pooling around your home's foundation by keeping gutters, downspouts, and splash blocks in good working order is a key termite-abatement step.

Other moisture-abatement efforts for termite-control include …

- Repairing all leaking faucets (especially outside faucets), water pipes, and air-conditioning units.
- Adjusting sprinklers and irrigation systems to keep the spray away from the foundation.

- Grading the ground next to the foundation so the surface water drains away from the house.
- Keeping the moisture in crawl spaces in check by removing leaves, dirt, and debris from soffit vents. If necessary, install additional vents.

### Keeping Things Screened and Sealed

Installing screens on attic and foundation vents will help prevent drywood termites from entering through them. Also seal cracks and holes in window- and doorframes with wood putty.

## Taking on Termites

Termite-control services are expensive; exterminator bills can run into thousands of dollars. There are much cheaper do-it-yourself products on the market for termite eradication, but taking matters into your own hands when dealing with this pesky insect typically isn't a good idea.

> **Around the House**
>
> Most lenders require termite-free certification before they close the deal. Many won't accept self-treatment as part of this certification, as there's no way to guarantee the effectiveness of the application or the products used.

Not only are termite infestations difficult to treat, doing it yourself can cause problems should you decide to sell your home.

Other reasons for not doing it yourself:

- Termite infestations can be hard to find. While they can be located by probing wood with a knife, screwdriver, or ice pick, this doesn't mean you'll be able to find all the infested areas or that you'll be able to determine the extent of the damage.
- Depending on the extent of the problem and the type of termite, effective treatment may require special equipment such as sub-slab injectors, hammer drills, large-capacity holding tanks, hoses and pumps, and rodding devices.
- The most effective baits and insecticides are available only through pest-control professionals, or can be purchased only by a state-certified commercial applicator.
- Some treatments, such as fumigation, are simply beyond the skills of the average homeowner.

While you might save some money on the front end by doing it yourself, just about anyone who has dealt with a termite problem will tell you to hire a pro. Since we agree with this advice, we won't go into do-it-yourself termite-control methods here.

# Going with the Pros

Because termite control is typically an ongoing process, it's important to find the right pest-control company for this service. It's a good idea to call at least three of them, as costs and terms can vary significantly between companies. Ask friends and neighbors whom they've used. If they're happy, chances are good that you'll be, too. If necessary, check their references with the Better Business Bureau or the local chamber of commerce.

Once you have the names of a few companies, call and ask about their services. A good company will give you a general overview of the services it offers, but will want to schedule an inspection of your home before providing specific details and pricing.

Other indications of a quality pest-control company:

- Licensed by the Department of Agriculture or the agency that regulates termite control in your state
- Membership in a state pest-control association and/or the National Pest Management Association
- A permanent address and phone number that you can verify in the phone book
- Membership in a local chamber of commerce
- Few or no Better Business Bureau complaints

If you like what you hear, book inspections with these companies. You may have to pay for the inspection. Some companies offer it for free.

**Around the House**

Stay away from any pest-control company that says it will treat your home with a "secret chemical formula." All termiticides must be registered for use with the FDA. And don't use any company that tries to pressure you into signing a contract right away by offering a special deal that you have to agree to right away.

A good inspector will carefully examine both the interior and exterior surfaces of your home's foundation, paying particular attention to areas where wood is sitting on or near soil. Other areas that should be inspected include …

- All wood construction in the basement and crawl spaces if you have them.
- Frames and sills around basement doors and windows.
- Cracks in cement or bricks; hollows in cement-block construction.
- Exterior frames on basement doors and windows.
- Scrap wood near the structure, tree stumps, fence posts, etc.

When the inspection is over, the inspector should provide a written report that covers the following:

- Locations of all active and/or inactive infestations.
- Recommended treatment, where it'll be done, and the number of treatments necessary to control the infestation. Locations should be marked on a diagram of your home.
- Suggestions for remediating other problems, such as wood-to-soil contact areas and areas with drainage or moisture problems.
- Estimated control cost. These estimates can differ by as much as $1,000 or more between companies, so don't be surprised if you see big differences in your numbers. The company's treatment plan and the guarantees offered are more important than the total dollar figure. Choose the company that will give you the most thorough treatment and the best guarantee for the most reasonable price.

## All About Warranties

Reputable termite-control specialists will warranty their work for one year—if they can. If for some reason they feel they can't treat a home in accordance with industry standards, no warranty will be offered. Reasons for not offering a warranty include infestations located in areas that are difficult or impossible to treat, such as inaccessible crawl spaces. Wells, cisterns, and drainage systems located near infestations can also impede treatment.

If a warranty is offered, it should cover retreatment if termites return during the warranty period. Most warranties will not cover damage repair; some companies will offer this coverage on damage caused by subsequent infestations.

Most companies offer extended warranties. You don't have to purchase this protection, but it's generally a good idea to do so.

**Around the House**

It's a good idea to keep termite-control warranties in place by purchasing an extended service agreement or warranty for at least two to three years after the initial treatment. Doing so won't guarantee that termites won't return, but you'll be covered if any reinfestations should occur during this period.

# Treatment Options

Pest-control companies use a variety of approaches for termite control. They vary depending on the type of termite that's causing problems and the extent and degree of infestation. Since there are more choices now than ever before, it's important to understand what they plan to use before you sign a contract.

## Soil Barriers

This approach creates a perimeter barrier by placing a termiticide into the soil under and around a structure. Protection lasts for as long as the chemicals in the termiticide remain effective. Older products repelled rather than killed termites. Newer chemicals are nonrepellent and kill termites as they enter treatment areas.

Soil barriers have been the standard for treating subterranean termites for many years, and are still widely used. However, they have their drawbacks. Breaks in the barrier can develop if the soil isn't thoroughly saturated with the termiticide. Termiticides also lose their effectiveness over time.

These days, since some of the longer-lasting termite pesticides are no longer approved for use, soil barriers are often paired with other control methods.

## Colony Elimination

This newer approach for controlling subterranean termites uses poisonous bait to kill workers. Bait stations and/or stakes are placed in the ground around the outside of the house. If there are active mud tubes indoors, bait might be placed over them as well. Foraging termites eat the bait and share it with others, causing a gradual decline in numbers.

**Around the House**

Experts estimate that about half of all termite-treatment programs today rely on colony elimination, either alone or paired with liquid termiticides.

Bait systems are good for structures that can't be adequately treated with soil barriers. They're also recommended for structures where soil treatments have failed or where there are concerns about pesticide use.

Baiting is an ongoing process. It requires more than one visit by a termite-control specialist for installation and monitoring. Control can take anywhere from a few weeks to more than a year.

## Wood Treatment

This approach calls for applying termiticides directly to and inside wood. It's typically used in conjunction with other treatments.

Borate and silica gel dusts are often used for this treatment. Foams and gels are other options. Both are directed into active termite galleries to kill foraging workers. Treatments can also be combined with baiting systems or liquid soil treatment.

## Approaches for Drywood Termites

What's done for drywood termites greatly depends on the extent of the infestation and damage. If it's limited, simply removing and replacing damaged wood can be effective. Replacement wood should be pressure- or borate-treated.

**Around the House**

Termite control can be costly. When it comes to drywood termites, those costs might not justify chemical treatment if the damage is limited, slight, or cosmetic. Remember, these colonies develop slowly and it can take years for any damage to appear. However, if you decide not to treat an infestation, you'll need to keep an eye on things to determine if and when treatment is needed.

For widespread drywood termite infestations or infestations in areas where removing and replacing infested wood isn't possible, fumigating is a time-honored control tactic. It calls for draping tarps over the entire structure and filling it with fumigant gas. It also requires leaving the house for up to five days, and removing everything that could be contaminated—plants, animals, food, you name it. When treatment is complete, the tarps are removed and the building is aired out.

Heat can also be used to kill drywood termites, and is just slightly less effective than fumigating. Like fumigating, this approach requires tenting the infested structure with nylon tarps. All non–heat-resistant items are removed from the house. Water is left running inside to protect plastic pipes. A large propane-heating unit is then connected to the tent. It blows hot air in and around the structure. Depending on how hot things get, treatment lasts from about half an hour to an hour.

Other controls for drywood termites include spot treating with liquid and dust insecticides or treatments that use heat, freezing, microwaves, or electricity. The effectiveness of these approaches varies and often depends on accessibility to the infestations. Some methods, such as microwaves and electricity, can also damage the areas being treated.

# Repairing the Damage

If caught early enough, termite damage might not require repairs. If you're concerned, have a structural engineer inspect things and make recommendations for any needed repairs.

If repairs are necessary, you might be able to do them yourself, depending on the extent of the damage. Repairs that are within the realm of a do-it-yourselfer include …

- Framing. You'll need to replace it from the bottom up, just like it was built.
- Replacing doorsills, window frames, and so on.
- Installing reinforcement (sistering) rafters and joists.
- Plugging termite holes in wood. This is a particular problem in log homes in which a variety of insects can and do penetrate wood. Special epoxies are available that will both plug the holes and restore strength to damaged wood.

When replacing or repairing termite-infested wood, keep in mind that repairs must extend at least 2 to 3 inches beyond the damaged area. Why? Termites tell other termites where food is available by secreting chemicals called *pheromones*. After repairs are made, other termites can smell where the old infestation was if you don't remove all signs of it.

**Tool Chest**

**Pheromones** are chemicals produced by organisms that signal their presence to other members of the same species.

If damage is more extensive or involves replacing structural components of the house, plan on hiring a contractor to do the work. For more on this, turn to Chapter 22.

## Other Wood Lovers: Carpenter Ants

Like termites, carpenter ants damage structural wood. However, unlike termites, they don't eat it as they lack the ability to digest cellulose. Instead, they tunnel into it while building or expanding nests for their colonies.

Carpenter ants establish a main nest with several satellite colonies. The main nest, or parent colony, contains an egg-laying queen, her brood, and thousands of worker ants. These nests are usually outdoors, often in rotting stumps, trees, or decaying landscape timbers, but they can be established indoors in wet, decaying wood. They have to stay moist—if they don't, the brood will die.

Satellite colonies have workers and older larvae and pupae that can stand drier conditions. Most indoor carpenter ant nests are satellite nests. They're often located in hollow doors, wall voids behind dishwashers, attics, insulation, and hollow decorative beams.

**Tool Chest**

**Frass** is the debris carpenter ants expel from cracks and crevices or from slitlike openings they make in the wood. It contains fecal matter, wood dust, and other debris from the nest.

### Diagnosing Carpenter Ants

The most obvious sign of a carpenter ant problem is the ants themselves, which are large reddish-brown or black critters with a circlet of hairs at the end of their abdomen. However, like other ants, these ants come inside to forage for food. Finding them indoors does not always mean they're living there. Good indications of indoor nests are piles or bits of *frass*, which is the debris carpenter ants expel when they're excavating.

## Preventing Carpenter Ant Infestations

Like subterranean termites, carpenter ants are attracted to wet wood. As such, controlling moisture in and around your house is key to preventing infestations. So, too, is keeping ants out where they belong. The following will help you do both:

- Fix any water problems, inside and out.
- Keep all structural wood or siding from coming into contact with soil.
- Caulk all cracks and openings through which carpenter ants can enter.
- Keep trees and shrubs near your home trimmed back.
- Discourage nest building near your house by placing gravel or stone mulch around the foundation.
- Store all ant-friendly foodstuffs, such as ripe fruit, in ant-proof containers.
- Store firewood off the ground and away from your house.
- Inspect the outside of your home for damaged wood. Replace as necessary and fix whatever caused the damage.

## Controlling Carpenter Ants

Finding and destroying nests is a proven approach for controlling carpenter ants. This can take some time as the nests can be located indoors and out and can be hard to find, so you might want to hire a pest-control specialist to do it. However, you can do it yourself by observing ant activity after dark, which is when they're most active.

For the best results, mix up some ant bait by combining equal proportions of honey and water. Place the mixture in small containers. Bottle caps work well for this. Place the caps along foundation walls or anywhere else you suspect activity. When ants appear, try to follow their trail. It could lead inside or outside, depending on where the nests are located.

Probing interior wood for hidden colonies is another way to find nests. Again, this can take some time, so you might want to hire a pest-control specialist to do it. If you do it yourself, tap along suspect areas—anywhere wood is

CAUTION

**A Fine Mess**

Don't try to control carpenter ants indoors by spraying areas where you see them. This doesn't get to the root of the problem, as it won't affect activity in the nest.

moist, soft, or rotting—with a blunt object. A screwdriver works well for this, and can also come in handy should you find a suspect area.

Listen for a hollow sound as you tap along. This indicates damaged wood. If a nest is nearby, carpenter ants often will respond by making a "rustling" sound similar to cellophane crinkling. If you want, you can confirm the location of a gallery by plunging the tip of the screwdriver into the wood.

If you can reach the nests with a vacuum, removing the nesting material and the ants can be an effective control. Be sure to caulk up entry cracks to keep other ants from coming in. Indoor nests in wall voids and other hidden spaces can be treated with boric acid or silica dioxide (also called diatomaceous earth) powder. Apply it by drilling small holes—about ⅛ inch—right into the ant galleries. Then puff the powder through them.

> **A Fine Mess**
>
> Spraying the outside of your house is not an effective control for carpenter ants. The ants will just avoid the treated areas and return when the insecticide wears off.

Killing inside nests and taking steps to keep ants outside might be all you'll need to do to control them. If problems continue, finding and treating outdoor nests might be necessary.

Baiting is another approach for carpenter ant control, and an option that many professionals rely on. If you decide to bait, choose a slow-acting formulation that the ants will carry back to the nest. These ants can be finicky eaters; if yours are, try attracting them to a nontoxic food first. A honey-water mixture works well. When they start to feed, replace the mixture with the toxic bait. You might have to try a couple before you find one that they like.

Baits are available from home and garden centers, or if you are lucky enough to have a retail pest-control outlet, ask them for the right bait for the right ant.

## Repairing Carpenter Ant Damage

Like termites, if you catch carpenter ants in time, it may not be necessary to repair any damage they caused. Long-term infestations, however, can cause serious structural damage and should be assessed by a structural engineer.

## The Least You Need to Know

- It's estimated that one in five homes has a wood-destroying insect problem.
- Establishing a termite-free zone by keeping wood from touching soil around your home is one of the best ways to keep termites from gaining access to your home.
- Baiting systems eliminate termite colonies. Barrier systems prevent termites from entering homes.
- Carpenter ants also destroy wood indoors. Baiting is an effective approach for eliminating them.

# Part 4

# Uninvited Guests

No matter where we live—city, country, or somewhere in between we share our surroundings with wild things—animals, bugs, plants, you name it. If you're an urban dweller, you might not see much beyond pigeons, ants, and squirrels, but other animals are definitely out there.

As their own habitats become more scarce, many species have adapted very well to living near humans. Being able to observe them close up can be a delight, but sometimes they get a little (or a lot) closer than we'd like. When they do, they can cause problems. Sometimes big problems.

Wild things are best experienced in their natural habitat, which doesn't include your home. If they're inside with you, it's time to let them know they're not welcome there.

Chapter 16

# There's a Mouse (or a Rat) in My House

## In This Chapter

- Getting rid of the "eek" factor
- Determining the size of the problem
- Control measures
- Picking your poison

The pitter-patter of tiny feet can be a welcome sound. But not if there's a rodent attached to them. If you're reading this chapter, chances are you've seen the flash of a small furry body or found evidence of its presence. Most likely, you're dealing with a house mouse, which is the most common warm-blooded household intruder. But it could be a rat. Or even a different kind of furry intruder.

What you're going to do to combat them varies a bit depending on what type of critter you have. You learn how to do it in the pages ahead.

# Getting Past "Eek!"

If you've seen one small, scampering critter, there's a good chance that the little guy (or gal) has skittered out of sight by now. If so, your immediate problem—removing a mouse or rat from your line of sight—no longer exists.

> **In the Nick of Time**
>
> Thinking about scooping up your little intruder for a humane release outside? You might want to consider another approach. A released mouse can return to your home within minutes, using pheromones in its urine to find its way.

However, know that one mouse is usually only evidence of the problem. You can rest assured that there's probably more than one. In fact, there could be many.

Depending on where you live, rats can also be a problem. Their habits, breeding patterns, the problems they cause, and the steps for controlling and eradicating them are similar to what is done for mice, but there are some differences between the two.

For simplicity's sake, from here on out we'll refer to both mice and rats generically as "rodents." However, more often than not, you'll be dealing with a mouse, as they're the most common intruders, and the one you're most likely to encounter.

Other small animals can also invade your home. Raccoons, for example, can enter homes through windows, chimneys, and roof vents. Squirrels can also gain entry in a variety of ways. Some of what you learn in this chapter, especially when it comes to critter-proofing your home, applies to these animals as well. However, what you'll do to rid your home of them is often quite different. For more detailed information on dealing with these animals, turn to Chapter 17.

# Meet the Enemy

Mice and rats are often referred to as *commensal* rodents in recognition of their close association with humans. Because of their affinity for the luxuries available in human dwellings, they are particularly troublesome pests. People spend a lot of money getting rid of them. And getting rid of them. And getting rid of them.

> **Tool Chest**
>
> **Commensal** animals are those that live on, in, or in close association with other animals, but are not parasitic on them.

Once rodents take up residence in your house, it can be difficult to control them. But it's not impossible. Diligent use of traps or rodenticides will kill them.

## The House Mouse

Known formally as *Mus musculus*, the house mouse is the most common rodent pest in the United States.

A female mouse can have between 5 and 10 litters every year, with five or six babies in each litter. Young mice are capable of reproducing when they're six weeks old, and mice typically live to between 9 and 12 months old.

Do the math, and you'll quickly see how one pair of mice turns into many more. In fact, one pair of mice can produce more than 15,000 offspring in a year. Definitely a scary number.

## The Rat on Rats

In the United States, the roof rat (*Rattus rattus*) and the Norway rat (*Rattus norvegicus*, also called the brown rat or sewer rat) are the two most common rat pests.

As their name suggests, roof rats claim roofs as their home turf. They're excellent climbers, and often gain entrance to houses by scurrying along overhanging tree limbs to a roof. They can also climb up almost every type of siding material, including smoother ones like stucco. These animals also like to live high up, and typically take up residence in attics or cabinets. They enter homes through bathroom vents, gable vents, spaces around soffits, exhaust pipe holes, spaces between fascia boards and roofs—just about any vulnerable spot. They can even chew holes through roofs.

Norway rats, which are ground nesters and often dig burrows in gardens and along foundations, can enter homes through cracks and holes in crawl spaces, slabs, a foundation block, you name it. Once inside, they lay low, preferring to nest in kitchens and bathrooms.

In the United States, Norway rats are more common in the North, roof rats in the South. Of the two, roof rats are less common and less aggressive. Like mice, rats are prolific breeders, with short gestation periods and large litters. They can live as long as three years.

Other common names for Norway rats are dump rats, river rats, sewer rats, and city rats.

# Why They Come Inside

In general, rodents aren't all that picky about their surroundings, which means they can survive and thrive in many different conditions. That said, they love living the high life when they can. This means being indoors in houses, barns, and similar structures where they have shelter from the elements and predators, and where food is easily available.

**Around the House**

Mice, once inside a home, often live out their entire life cycles without ever setting foot outside. Some rats will forage for food outside, come inside at night in search of more food, and return to outside burrows.

Water isn't much of an issue for mice, as they can live without it for up to several weeks. Rats, on the other hand, need water to survive, and will come inside to drink from toilets and sinks.

Rodents can come into your home at any time, but fall is prime-time infestation season. As the weather turns cooler and their summer breeding season ends, Mother Nature tells them to eat more food, hoard what they can't eat, and find shelter from the harsh weather ahead.

If they're in the neighborhood, and there's a way they can come into your house to do these things, they will.

# Why They're a Problem

One of the biggest reasons why rodents are such a nuisance is because they'll eat practically anything. They prefer grains and grain-based foods, but virtually nothing is off the menu for these critters. As such, they rob people and animals of their food, both by eating it and contaminating what they leave behind.

As rodents nibble and gnaw their way around wherever they've taken up residence, they damage structures and property. Finally, they transmit diseases. Two that are most commonly associated with both mice and rat contamination are salmonellosis and leptospirosis, which are bacterial infections.

Most people call salmonellosis salmonella, which is actually the bacteria that causes it. Salmonella causes diarrhea, fever, and abdominal cramps 12 to 72 hours after infection, usually lasts four to seven days, and rarely requires treatment.

Leptospirosis, also known as Weil's disease in its more advanced stages, is of greater concern. Contracted through food or water contaminated with rat or mice urine, it is a bacterial infection that affects both humans and animals. In humans, it can cause high fever, chills, severe headaches, muscle aches, and vomiting, and can also cause jaundice, abdominal pain, and diarrhea. Or it can cause no symptoms at all. If left untreated, it can lead to meningitis, kidney damage, liver failure, and respiratory distress.

Rats are also known for carrying such nasty human diseases as bubonic plague and typhus. Rat-bite fever, which is caused by a bite from an infected rat, is also a concern, but is rare in the United States.

Certain species of rats and mice have also been identified as carriers of Hantaviruses. Many aren't a concern for humans, but some can cause Hantavirus pulmonary syndrome, or HPS. HPS is rare—as of 2004, less than 400 cases had been reported in the United States—but it's deadly, and it's been grabbing headlines over the past several years because of it. Of those 400 cases, 40 percent resulted in death.

Hantaviruses are transmitted by infected rodents through urine, droppings, or saliva. Humans can contract the disease by …

- Breathing in tiny droplets of the virus released into the air through cleaning or otherwise stirring up substances containing it.
- Eating rodent-contaminated food.
- Touching something that's contaminated, and then touching a mucous membrane—eye, mouth, nose.

Rodent bites, although rare, are another means of contracting the virus.

Several rodent species, particularly the deer mouse, have been linked to Hantavirus, but it's not associated with common house mice, Norway rats, or roof rats. Not yet, anyway. That said, the risk presented by Hantavirus speaks to playing it safe no matter what kind of rodent you come in contact with, especially since the different species can be difficult to tell apart.

## Recognizing Rodent Infestations

Not sure you're sharing your home with a rodent? One or more of the following are surefire signs:

- Droppings, typically left behind in kitchen cabinets, pantries, cupboards, drawers, bins, and anywhere else they think they might find food, or where they scurry to avoid predators. Rodents are prolific poopers, so it's pretty easy to spot if you have an infestation. It's also not uncommon to see droppings along walls, on top of wall studs or beams, near nests, and in boxes, bags, old furniture, and other objects.

**In the Nick of Time**

You can often identify the kind of rodent you're dealing with by the size and shape of their droppings. Mice, being the smaller of the two types, leave behind the smallest droppings, measuring on average $\frac{1}{8}$ to $\frac{1}{4}$ inch. They're about the size of a grain of rice, thin or rod-shaped with pointed ends. Roof rats are larger than house mice but smaller than Norway rats. Their droppings average about $\frac{1}{4}$ inch and are spindle-shaped with pointed ends.

Droppings left by Norway rats are the largest, measuring between $\frac{1}{4}$ to $\frac{1}{2}$ inch in length. They're moon- or crescent-shaped and are typically shiny black in color, but this can vary, depending on what they eat.

- Squeaks and other noises. Rodents aren't what you'd call quiet. If they're in your house, you'll hear squeaks, rustling, and scampering sounds as they move about and nest. Noises are often more apparent at night as you're going to bed and they're waking up.
- Urine pools or trails. Rodents are notorious for having weak bladders, and they'll dribble all over the place. House mice sometimes make things called "urinating pillars," which are small mounds consisting of grease, dirt, and yes, urine. Sometimes you'll see tiny drops of urine leading to a mound.
- Nibble marks on food boxes, food, or containers. These telltale signs are often accompanied by nearby droppings.
- Nests. Rodents build nests from soft, fuzzy, or warm materials, such as fabric, furniture stuffing, quilt batting, shredded paper, grass, and twigs, and will typically stuff them into sheltered, out-of-the-way places like boxes, cabinets and closets, walls, even the subspace between ceilings and floors. Other possible mouse nest sites include dressers, behind and inside appliances, and machinery, even computer cases—basically, anywhere it's cozy and warm.

**In the Nick of Time**

Mouse droppings can be easily confused with bat droppings. If in doubt, try to crush a dropping. Bat droppings easily crush into tiny dry fragments, mouse droppings will not.

- Grease marks. Mice can wedge through openings as small as a quarter of an inch in size. As they do, they often leave greasy smears—caused by oil and dirt in their coats—behind. The marks left by mice are fainter than those left by rats. If you find large greasy smears, you should suspect a rat infestation instead.
- Gnaw marks. Gnawing is a defining characteristic of all rodents. They do it to keep their incisor teeth, which grow continually, in check. Wood is a favorite, but they'll pretty much chew on whatever suits them. This includes electrical wire, which, as noted in Chapter 10, makes them a leading cause of structural fires. On wood, newer gnaws are light colored. They turn darker with age. Sometimes you won't see gnaw marks, but you'll see what looks like fine wood chips or coarse sawdust, especially along baseboards, door and window frames, and cabinets.
- Holes in food packaging. Rodents will nibble into anything they can smell, including boxes and bags of pasta, rice, beans, and grain products. Dog food bags are also prime-time rodent magnets, and especially so for rats, who like the meaty smell as much as canines do. Another popular nibble, although not a food product: soap.
- An "off" aroma, or smell. House mice have a distinctive musky odor. It's hard to describe, but once you smell it, you'll never forget it.
- Tracks. Look for footprints or tail marks in dusty spots. The type of track and tail marks can tell you what kind of rodent you're battling. Mice have the smallest feet, measuring $\frac{3}{8}$ inch or less. Rat tracks average between $\frac{3}{4}$ to 1 inch. Rats also drag their tails, which leaves a mark between their feet tracks. If tracks are hard to spot, shining a flashlight across a suspicious area can help illuminate them.
- Pet excitement. If Rover or Miss Kitty is acting a bit nuts (more nuts than usual?), especially around a possible mouse hiding area, chances are good a critter has been there or is still there.

**In the Nick of Time**

To track where rodents are traveling, you can create your own dust by sprinkling baby powder, cornstarch, or flour along suspicious areas. This is also an effective approach for monitoring rodent abatement efforts.

Rodents are nocturnal, so you probably won't see many of them unless you've got a big infestation going on. That said, mice tend to be more active than rats during daylight hours.

*This homeowner sprinkled cornstarch at various spots along a baseboard where her family had noticed what they thought were mice droppings. However, large footprints and tail marks indicate a rat problem instead.*

## Getting Rid of Rodents

As mentioned, it can be difficult to get rid of rodents, but not impossible. Pest-control experts suggest a three-pronged approach:

- Sanitation
- Rodent-proofing
- Population reduction

The first two steps are also effective methods for preventing rodents from setting up residence in structures that haven't had problems before. It's typically not necessary to call in an expert to accomplish either step, although you might need some help installing barriers or screens, especially in hard-to-reach places.

Reducing rodent populations can be a little trickier. If you're not comfortable handling traps or putting out poison, or you feel you're dealing with problems beyond what you can handle, call a rodent-control expert. You'll find them in the yellow pages under pest-control services.

# Sanitizing Your Home

Sanitation means keeping food away from rodents and making your home and its surroundings less rodent-friendly.

## Food Sanitation

Food-sanitation measures include the following:

- Storing bulk foods in rodent-proof containers or rooms. Metal canisters and glass containers with lids that seal tightly are as rodent-proof as you can get. In a pinch, very thick plastic is also an option. If you enjoy feeding birds, keep feed in rodent-proof containers, too.
- Keeping stored foods off the floor and away from walls. This is a step more suited to places where large quantities of foodstuffs are stored, but one to keep in mind if you have a pantry or closet where you keep food.
- Wiping or vacuuming up spilled food, from either cooking or storage, as soon as you see it. Flour and sugar easily migrate from their containers, especially if you store them in their original packaging. Rodents love both. Corn meal and other grain products are also prime rodent targets.
- Picking up animal food after your pets eat. Many owners "free-feed" their pets, allowing their animals free access to food 24/7. Switching to a controlled feeding program—you put food down, your pet eats what it wants during a specific period of time, after which you pick it up—may take some adjusting to for animals and owners, but it will also keep the food away from rodents.

**A Fine Mess**

All three control measures—sanitation, rodent-proofing, and reducing populations—are essential for a successful rodent-control program. Don't skip one of these steps!

**Around the House**

Food, water, and shelter provided for pets often contribute to rodent population problems. Pet food and bird food are two of the most common rodent attractors. The smells of both are extremely attractive. Once rodents get a taste, they'll try to feed there as often as they can—daily, if possible.

## Outdoor Sanitation

Making your home less hospitable for furry creatures involves outdoor and indoor measures. Outdoor sanitation includes …

- Clearing away brush and grass growing near or next to your home's foundation. Rodents use both to build nests, and as hiding spots when they're not in your house.
- Relocating bird feeders. If you have bird feeders near your home, move them to another spot farther away. If this isn't possible, use squirrel-proof feeders and clean up all spilled seed every night.
- Finding new places to stack wood, lumber, and other building materials if necessary. All should be located at least 100 feet away from your home.
- Hauling away trash or anything else that rodents can nest in, including old tires, fallen trees, abandoned cars, and old lawnmowers.
- Keeping trash and recyclables in rodent-proof containers with tight-fitting lids. Old-fashioned metal garbage pails are ideal.
- Keeping grass closely mowed. Also, cutting any limbs on trees that overhang your house will give roof rats less access to your roof.

## Indoor Sanitation

Inside sanitation measures include the following:

- Checking every nook and cranny of your house for debris that rodents could nest in or use to build nests. Leaving any kind of debris around for any length of time invites infestations and reinfestations.
- Eliminating water sources. This includes repairing water leaks and insulating cold water pipes to prevent condensation. If you store water, keep it in sealed, rodent-proof containers.
- Disposing of trash regularly. Put it in rodent-proof containers, and take it out often. Clean the containers inside and out with soap and water on a regular basis, too.

- Clutter-proofing all rooms. Keep all clothing off the floor. Don't store clothing and other soft goods under beds.
- Keeping exterior doors and windows closed. If they're screened and there are holes in the screens, get them fixed.

## Rodent Repellents

While they won't solve a rodent problem, rodent repellents are another way to make your home less rodent-friendly. These products use certain chemicals or scents of natural predators, such as fox and bobcat, to deter intruders. They typically come in liquid and granular formulations and have been shown to be moderately effective in reducing the number of rodents entering treated areas.

Repellents are usually broadcast or sprayed around the perimeter of the house. They can last up to three months depending on weather conditions. Water can dilute them and make them less effective.

Indoor repellents are also available, and many people like to include them as part of an overall pest-control program. One type uses a removable and reusable rope as its delivery system.

There are also all-natural repellents. These often contain essential oils like peppermint or spearmint that rodents hate the smell of. If you really don't want to use chemicals, they're worth a try. However, there's no scientific data to support their effectiveness, so be ready to try something more powerful if you don't get the results you're seeking.

> **CAUTION**
>
> **A Fine Mess**
>
> Don't use repellents where rodenticides or traps are in place. These products will contaminate them, and negate your baiting and trapping efforts. Not all states register rodent repellent for use. Check the regulations where you live before buying them.

Some people swear by dryer sheets as a rodent repellent. Mice supposedly can't stand the smell of them, and won't go near them. However, this is anecdotal information at best. Talk to a rodent-control expert after he or she has treated a building where a dryer sheet has been stuffed in every crack, and you'll be told it isn't an effective control measure.

Ultrasonic devices are another repellent with dubious results. While it's true that rodents can't stand the sound they emit, these devices are directional and can't be heard behind objects. What's more, distances affect their effectiveness. They might chase away the rodents, but all the critters do is take up residence somewhere else, typically in the same building.

Dogs and cats are also ineffective repellents. Yes, they can seek and destroy rodents, but both species are used to living close to other animals, and they're not particularly bugged by rodents. In fact, many pest-control experts agree that homes with pets are more likely to have rodent problems than those that don't, as mice and rats are attracted to pet food, and the pets don't do a thing to the little critters when they see them.

## Rodent-Proofing

This control measure will help prevent future rodent visitors from gaining entry to your home.

First, seal any rodent holes that you've already found, using one of the following materials:

- Steel wool, which is good for stuffing into small cracks and holes.
- Lath metal. Good for covering larger areas, and can be placed over steel wool for extra security.
- Caulk or expanding foam. Can be used to fill holes and reinforce repairs using other materials. Expanding foam alone can be highly effective.
- Cement.
- Hardware cloth.
- Copper-mesh cloth. Sold under the brand name Stuf-fit, it's resistant to rust (unlike steel wool), and easily molds into openings and gaps with a screwdriver or similar tool.

Next, do another sweep of your home and seek out holes that are any larger than a pencil inside your house. Look everywhere, and be sure to concentrate on the following areas:

- Kitchen cabinets
- Closets
- Around doors
- Under sinks

Look inside, under, and behind anywhere a rodent could potentially gain access. Seal any holes or cracks you find with one of the previous materials.

Outside your house, check for cracks, gaps, and holes around doors and windows; around electrical, plumbing, and gas fixtures; and between the foundation of your home and the ground. If you're living in a trailer, repair holes, cracks, or gaps in the skirting.

If your investigations uncover rodent burrows near or under foundations or trailer skirting, consider installing a pest barrier around the entire foundation. To do this, you'll need flexible material, such as wire mesh or hardware cloth. If using wire mesh, choose 6-millimeter mesh. If using hardware cloth, 16 to 19 gauge works best. Either product should be 14 inches wide.

Bend the material lengthwise into a right angle, with both sides approximately the same width. Use fasteners appropriate to the building, and secure one side to the side of the building. Bury the other side at least 2 inches below ground level, extending away from the wall.

# Reducing Their Numbers

Once you've made your home less hospitable to your furry guests, it's time to eliminate the ones that have already taken up residence.

There are several effective approaches for doing so, including trapping, poisoning, electrifying, and fumigating.

## Trapping

Trapping can be very effective if you're only dealing with a few rodents. Many people prefer this approach to chemicals, especially when there are young children and pets about. Another strong advantage to using traps is odor control. Rodents die in the traps, rather than behind walls or in other inaccessible places.

Traps range from the classic spring-loaded wooden snap traps that you probably remember from kiddie cartoons to deluxe live traps capable of capturing multiple critters.

If you decide to use traps, be sure to check them every day and dispose of trapped animals promptly. You'll find detailed disposal advice at the end of this chapter.

## The Skinny on Snap Traps

Wooden snap traps are widely available, cheap, and relatively easy to use. There are several different types; ones with an expanded trigger catch are more effective than older designs, and they don't have to be baited, which makes them worth seeking out.

If you're going to use snap traps, be sure to select the right kind of trap. There are different sizes for mice and rats, with the ones for rats being much bigger. Try to catch rats in mousetraps, and you'll probably end up with perfectly set traps, minus their bait.

> **In the Nick of Time**
>
> Rats often shy away from unfamiliar objects and will stay away from baited traps. Putting unset traps in areas where you think they hang out, and letting them sit unbaited for a week or two makes for confident rats and better trapping success.

> **A Fine Mess**
>
> Spring-loaded traps—especially the giant-sized rat traps—can be painful or even dangerous if they close on fingers. Handle them carefully, and place them where children and pets can't reach them.

Snap traps all work in much the same way, so the advice here goes for all of them, but be sure to read any instructions that come along with the trap before setting it:

- Always set traps in groups of two or three. This will ensure that the rodent hits the business end of one of them. Not doing so can cause false traps as the animal will set off the mechanism and not get hurt. Smart rodents get "trap shy," and learn how to grab the bait without setting off the trap. Also, position the traps so they form a "T" with the wall, with the bait end nearest the wall.
- If you're using bait, place a small amount on the trap's bait pan. Peanut butter is one possible choice, but you can use just about anything, as rodents will eat just about anything. Even chocolate.

If you're dealing with both mice and rats, you'll need to set snap traps that are appropriately sized for both. Or you can buy a trap designed to catch both.

If you're concerned about children or pets getting into your snap traps, look for tamper-resistant bait stations. Traps fit right into these handy devices, which keep fingers and nontargeted animals away from the traps and protect rodent bait from moisture and other possible contaminants.

### Bringing Them Back Alive

Some people prefer live traps as some of them can catch multiple rodents without being reset, which means you don't have to deal with the critters as often. Since they keep the animals alive, they're also viewed as more humane. However, experts don't recommend using them if Hantavirus is a concern, as they can scare rodents and cause them to urinate, which increases the risk of Hantavirus exposure.

Live traps can be found in hardware, home, farm-supply, and feed stores. They range from single-animal traps to large devices that can handle a dozen or so rodents at a time.

Like snap traps, live traps should be placed up against walls, behind objects, and in secluded areas where droppings, gnawing, and damage are evident. Orient them with the entrance hole parallel to the wall. Follow the manufacturer instructions for setting and baiting.

When releasing rodents from live traps, don't just put them out the front door. Find an open field far enough away from your home so they won't be tempted to come back in.

### Tips for Glue Traps

Glue traps or glue boards, as they're known in the pest-control industry, are the easiest traps to use as you don't have to set them. All you have to do is bait and put in place. As rodents run over the boards, they get tangled in the glue and eventually suffocate.

Glue traps are available for mice and rats. However, age and cold temperatures can diminish their effectiveness. They're also not recommended in Hantavirus areas, for the same reason discussed previously (the rodent can still urinate on them).

## Poison Control

Poisoning is another effective rodent-control measure. There are many different products to choose from. Most *rodenticides* are anticoagulants, and cause death by internal bleeding. Warfarin was used for many years, and is still found in some products. However, many rodents are now resistant to it, so you'll also see products containing newer rodenticides, such as

**Tool Chest**

**Rodenticide** is the formal name for rodent poison.

brodifacoum, cholorphacinone, pindone, and diphacinone. Bromethalin, one newer rodenticide, works a little differently than other substances by attacking the central nervous system. Another newer rodenticide contains cholecalciferol, or vitamin $D_3$. It causes heart failure by creating abnormally high levels of calcium in the blood. Rodenticides come in two basic formulations: single dose or multiple dose.

Most are formulated as food-based baits and contain seeds or grain to attract their quarry. As such, pets—especially dogs—are also drawn to them, so it's important to place these products in areas where pets (and, of course, children) can't get at them. Putting rodenticides in bait stations (preferably tamper-resistant) is another way to keep children and pets away.

It's important to choose the right product for your needs. Some rodenticides, especially ones that contain bromethalin, are safer to use around pets than others. Some do a better job of attracting rats than mice, and vice versa. Rodenticides also come in various forms, including blocks, pellets, and seeds. Some rodents will find blocks attractive, others are attracted to seeds. It's a good idea to use some of each.

## Zap 'Em

Rodent zappers, which use electricity to shock animals to death, are another time-tested rodent abatement approach. You can find these devices pretty much anywhere you'd find traps and other abatement products. They're easy to use and don't take much power as they use inexpensive batteries.

Zappers should be installed in areas where you know rodents are feeding, nesting, or gnawing. Baiting is the same as for traps. When animals enter the device to feed, they ground out the circuit. The device then delivers a fatal jolt of electricity. Many people like rodent zappers as they're painless and humane. However, they can be messy and a bit tough to clean.

## Fumigating

If you're dealing with a severe rodent infestation, fumigation may be your only hope. This approach, typically used to control rats instead of mice, is extremely effective. However, fumigants are poison gases. As such, they are highly toxic, and should only be used if absolutely necessary. This is a job for licensed pest-control operators only, as fumigants are restricted-use products and can only be used by operators who have a fumigation license.

# Disposing of Your Guests

It's important to be vigilant about getting rid of dead rodent bodies. Not only will they begin to smell before too long, but it's also a good idea to keep them away from pets and children.

Always keep dead animals an arm's length away. Use rubber, latex, or vinyl gloves to handle them, or pick them up with tongs or a similar long-handled device. Place them in a plastic bag—two bags are even better—close the bags tightly, and put them in a secure trash container for removal.

If Hantavirus is a concern, first spray the dead rodent with disinfectant or a 1:10 chlorine bleach solution. Be sure to thoroughly soak the body to ensure deactivation of the virus. Wait 10 minutes, then either take the animal out of the trap or place the trap and the animal in a plastic bag. Place them in a second plastic bag and seal it. Dispose of them by burning or placing in a covered trash container that is regularly emptied.

For cleaning infested areas, you'll need …

- Rubber gloves.
- A dust mask.
- Commercial disinfectant or ½ cup of household bleach mixed in 1 gallon of water.
- Rags or sponges for wiping up. Plan on discarding them when you're through.
- A damp mop. Use one with a removable head that you can throw away.
- Plastic garbage bags for disposing of debris.

> CAUTION
>
> **A Fine Mess**
>
> Never vacuum or sweep a rodent-infested area. Remember, mice and rats can carry diseases, and some diseases are spread by coming into contact with urine and droppings. Breathing dust in infested areas can expose you to Hantaviruses.

Here's what you'll do:

- Put on the dust mask and gloves.
- Wet down the area with the disinfectant or bleach mixture.

- Wipe up nesting materials, droppings, and whatever else is there with rags or sponges. If there are any dead rodents, spray them with the disinfectant or bleach mixture before handling. Put everything in the garbage bag when you're done.
- Mop the area with the disinfectant or bleach mixture. Allow to dry.
- Remove the mop head and throw it in the garbage bag with the rest of your cleaning materials. Wrap another bag around this bag and throw it out.
- Wash your gloves with soap or disinfectant before taking them off. After you take them off, wash your hands thoroughly.

## The Least You Need to Know

- Mice are the most common warm-blooded household intruders.
- Like all pest problems, the best way to avoid rodent infestations is to make it difficult for critters to enter your home.
- A successful rodent-control program consists of three control measures—sanitation, rodent-proofing, and reducing rodent populations.
- Understanding rodent feeding and nesting patterns will help you know where to place traps and baits.

Chapter 17

# Other Furry (and Not) Intruders

## In This Chapter

- Living with wildlife
- Obeying the laws
- Serving your eviction notice
- Keeping them out

While mice and rats are the most common mammalian household intruders, they're by no means the only critters that can gain entrance to your home. Other unwanted animal guests, including squirrels, opossums, raccoons, and skunks, are also common household visitors. Snakes and other reptiles can be, too. Some are solo travelers and just drop in for a spell. Others take up residence with their families.

If you've seen one of these critters, or you've found signs that lead you to believe that you're dealing with something other than a rodent infestation, this chapter is for you.

# Animal in the Room

Finding yourself in the same room with a wild animal can create a state of panic. Interestingly, you might be more excited about it than the animal is. Many wild animals simply aren't as wild as they used to be. Raccoons, for example, are such a fixture in so many neighborhoods that they rarely show fear around people. Skunks often belly up to a food bowl right alongside the family cat. Other wild animals exhibit a decidedly cool demeanor around humans and pets as well.

**A Fine Mess**

While they can seem somewhat scary, most wild animals are harmless. However, this doesn't mean you should relax your guard around any animal that has entered your home. There's a chance the animal could be ill, and some wild animals can carry diseases that you're better off not being exposed to. Always approach them with caution. If you see a nocturnal animal—a raccoon, opossum, or skunk—during the daytime, definitely approach with care. There's a strong chance of these night-time-loving animals being sick or injured.

## Overriding the Panic Button

Your first goal when dealing with a wild critter is to keep your cool. This will help you accomplish your most important mission, which is to get the animal to leave, preferably under its own steam. This is your goal, regardless of whether the animal is a casual intruder or has taken up residence.

**Around the House**

Keeping calm around animals is definitely the way to go. Skunks, for example, will only spray when they feel threatened. If your little black-and-white intruder starts to stomp its front feet or raise its tail, beware and back off.

### Say Buh-Bye!

Wild animals can wreak havoc while inside your house, so you definitely want to get them out as quickly as possible. The best way to do this is to make it easy for them to depart.

If the animal is in a room with outdoor access, open all exterior doors and/or windows. Block off the room, and wait a few hours for the animal to leave.

If the room doesn't have outdoor access, block off an area that includes a room that does. You might have to use a blanket or sheet to do this.

An intruder snake may slither off on its own. If it doesn't, try one of the following:

- Pick it up. Wear heavy leather gloves. Keep the snake calm by supporting its entire body. Hold the snake behind its head to keep it from biting you.
- Scoop it up using a shovel or scoop.
- Snare the snake with a hook or hoe.
- Put out a glue board designed for rats. This approach can be a little tricky, as it can be tough to get the snake off the board. A little cooking oil can ease the transition from stuck to slither.

Once you've corralled the snake, drop it into a garbage can or a strong paper or cloth bag with no holes. Take the snake outside and release it.

## No, No, I Won't Go

If the animal won't leave your house, trapping it might be your only solution. You'll need to use a live trap—something that most people don't keep around—and you'll have to dispose of the animals when you trap them, which is something that lots of people don't like to think about. For these reasons, you might want to have an expert—an animal-control officer, a wildlife-control expert, or a wildlife rehabilitator—do it.

**In the Nick of Time**

Some wildlife-control and animal-protection organizations rent live traps. If you don't want to buy one, but you do want to trap the animal yourself, it might be worth calling around to see if any in your area rent them.

If you decide to trap the animal yourself, buy an appropriately sized live trap. You'll find them at sporting goods stores, lawn and garden stores, farm-supply stores, and similar retailers. Follow the directions for setup and baiting. Place the trap in the room with the animal and leave it alone. Check the trap in a couple of hours. If the animal isn't inside, leave it alone for another couple of hours or so. After the animal is caught, cover the cage with a blanket to keep it from becoming frenzied.

For squirrels, capturing in a blanket is an option to trapping. Hold the blanket in front of you so that your entire body is obscured. When you get close enough, toss the blanket over the animal. Roll it up quickly, making sure you don't squish the critter. Take the animal outside and set it free.

*Live traps like this one can be used indoors and out to catch nuisance animals. This trap is large enough to catch a raccoon, and was placed outdoors where raccoon activity and damage was spotted. For best results, multiple traps should be set in different locations.*

## Next Steps

If you're dealing with a casual intruder—that is, a solitary wildlife animal that mistakenly entered your house—your immediate cause for concern is over once the animal leaves your home. You might have to do some cleaning or repair any damage caused by the animal.

**Tool Chest**

**Nuisance animals** are wildlife that cause property damage.

However, if one animal has made its way into your home, there's a good chance that more will follow. Things aren't easy and simple when it comes to wildlife intruders. They're not called *nuisance animals* for nothing.

Many different kinds of wild animals can, and do, make their way indoors. As mentioned, critters like squirrels, raccoons, skunks, and opossums are the most common intruders, but just about any animal can barge in if it's motivated enough.

## Why They Come In

Just like rats and mice, it's easier for wild animals to live indoors than outside. That said, some wild animals are accidental visitors. They fall through vents, come in through pet doors looking for food, you name it. They're not in your home to stay.

Others enter homes in search of food and a hospitable environment for nesting. Once they get a taste of the easy life, there's little incentive for them to move on as long as they can access food, water, and safe shelter.

Many wild animals will only stay long enough to raise their babies. When the young 'uns are old enough to survive in the wild, they leave.

# Why They're a Problem

Although it's folly to assume that every wild animal that comes indoors is disease-ridden, there's always the chance that it could be. Raccoons and skunks, for example, can carry several diseases, including rabies. If you see one during the day, which is when they're typically not very active, it might be sick. Or it simply could be injured. But it's best not to get close enough to find out.

Squirrels are rodents, and can carry the same diseases that rats do.

All wild animals can damage home interiors. As noted in Chapter 10, squirrels are a leading cause of house fires, which start when they chew through electric lines. Raccoons and squirrels can destroy roofs when attempting to reach their nests. Raccoons foraging for food indoors can cause extensive damage in kitchens, and it's not limited to food. Their little claws and tiny teeth can wreak havoc on drawers and cabinets, too.

# Removing the Nuisance

The approaches for dealing with nuisance wildlife are pretty similar to what you do for mice and rats—you sanitize, you animal-proof, and you control. But there's a difference between control measures for rodents and control measures for wildlife.

General sanitizing and animal-proofing measures were covered in detail in Chapter 16, so we won't repeat them here. However, you will find additional suggestions, when appropriate, related to the species in question.

## Can't Touch Me!

Extermination is an accepted control measure for rodents and insects. However, it often isn't for nuisance wildlife.

Some nuisance animals are protected species. This means there are federal, state, and/or local government laws and regulations that govern how they're treated. These laws and regulations differ depending on where you live, but most allow taking (capturing, relocating, or killing) small nuisance mammals such as squirrels, raccoons, opossums, and so on.

**In the Nick of Time**

For a state-by-state listing of threatened and endangered animal species (plants, too), go to www. endangeredspecie. com/map.htm.

In some areas, live trapping might be the only approved taking method. In others, trapping and releasing animals is against the law, as it's felt that doing so makes the animals someone else's problem.

If you don't know the status of the animal in question, call your state's Department of Natural Resources. Ask to speak with a conservation officer. This individual will know the statutes, and can advise you on what to do.

Because many different types of wildlife can take up residence inside domestic structures, we can't address them all in the space we have here. Instead, we'll sketch out basic procedures for dealing with the most common wildlife intruders. What works for these animals will usually work for others.

## Why Can't We Be Friends?

If your animal intruders aren't doing any harm, simply waiting for them to leave might be the easiest thing to do. You might have to put up with some noise as they skitter and fidget around in your walls or crawl space. However, given the short gestation and infancy periods for most wild animals, you won't have to wait too long.

Waiting things out isn't always practical, however, and some people simply don't want to let animals live inside their homes any longer than they have to. If you're one of them, you'll have to get more aggressive about getting the animals to leave. How you do it will vary a bit depending on where they are.

## Animals in the Chimney

Chimneys are a favorite roosting spot for raccoons. (Birds and bats like them, too. For more information on what to do with winged things in chimneys, turn to Chapter 21.) Squirrels often fall into chimneys. They can't climb out, but they typically don't nest in them.

If you hear chittering, barks, growls, soft grunts, and other noises in your chimney, chances are good a raccoon has taken up residence. Rustling and chittering indicate a squirrel. You can encourage either animal to leave by …

- Making lots of noise. Bang on the damper or the wall near the fireplace, or turn on a loud radio.
- Placing a dish of ammonia in the fireplace. Ammonia can't be used in all states, so be sure to check your state or local statutes before putting it out. Also, some wildlife experts say ammonia and other noxious smells, such as bleach or mothballs, aren't effective. It's worth a try, though.
- Giving it a way to escape. Make an escape ladder from a thick rope or a big piece of cloth, such as an old blanket or sheet. Tie some knots in it, roughly a foot or so apart. If necessary, tie two or more ropes or cloths together so it will reach the bottom of your chimney. Tie a weighted object—a hammer works well for this—at the end to keep it in place. Go up on your roof and drop the escape ladder down the chimney. Secure the rope or cloth at the top of the chimney. Leave the area alone. The animal should climb out in a day or so. When it does, remove the rope.

You'll want to do something to prevent reentry once the animal leaves. Installing a one-way door over the flue is one good approach. You can buy these, but they're also easy to make. Turn to Chapter 21 for one possible construction. This will let the animal leave, but it won't be able to get back in. For permanent reentry fixes, go to the end of this chapter.

If these approaches don't work, you might have to let the animal leave through your house. This requires opening the damper and the fireplace door, which some wildlife experts don't recommend doing as other things, such as nests and feces, can come down with the animal. If you take this approach, place a shallow box in the fireplace to catch any materials that might accompany the animal. Follow the tips above for removing an animal from a room before you open things up.

## A Family Affair

The approaches detailed previously are appropriate for adult animals. If you're dealing with a family of raccoons or squirrels, which can also nest in chimneys, you'll have to encourage the entire group to leave.

If there are animals in your chimney during spring or summer, there's a good chance that babies are around, too. Waiting until the babies are old enough to move around and survive on their own is the safest and most humane approach. When the babies are very small, you run the risk of the mother abandoning the nest. If she does, the babies will die.

Making their environment less inviting by placing ammonia in the fireplace is often recommended. This supposedly encourages the mother to move her babies to another location if one is near. As noted, it might not be that effective. In these situations, and especially since chimney nests can be hard to reach, it's typically easiest to ask a wildlife expert to remove the nest and its inhabitants.

Again, installing a temporary door on the chimney is a good way to keep the critters from coming back in. Once they leave, seal off all openings so they can't return. You'll find tips on how to do this at the end of this chapter.

Be sure to wait until you're sure the animals have left before you install permanent closures. If any are trapped inside, they'll starve to death and you'll have a bigger problem—the smell from their decomposing bodies. The best way to ensure their permanent departure is to construct a temporary door as detailed above. Or you can cover the chimney flue with a couple of layers of newspaper. Check the flue every day. If it stays in place, it's a pretty good bet that your critters have left the premises.

CAUTION

**A Fine Mess**

Never start a fire if there are animals in your chimney. Doing so can kill them before they get out.

## Animals in Crawl Spaces and Attics

Raccoons and squirrels often occupy crawl spaces and attics. Squirrels, in fact, are such common attic dwellers that many people don't do anything about them. This isn't necessarily a good idea, however. While they may not cause a lot of damage, what damage they do cause will accumulate over time. What's more, their nesting area will develop an odor that will attract more squirrels. They'll keep coming back as long as the nest is intact.

The approaches for ridding animals from these areas are the same as for chimneys. Trapping can work well, as there's typically enough space in these areas for setting them up.

If you don't trap, use any of the other approaches detailed earlier. Before you do, locate the spots where the animals came in.

For squirrels, inspect the following:

- Soffits, soffit vents, and trim around soffits
- Utility chases and conduits
- Rooftop vent fans
- All household trim, especially along corners, where signs of wear typically appear first

If you can't get close enough for a good visual inspection, use binoculars. Signs of entry include chew marks and rub marks (caused by oil and dirt in the animal's coat) around holes.

For raccoons, inspect the following:

- Vent covers. Look for bends in the covers—a classic sign of raccoon entry.
- Chimney caps. Same as vent covers. Raccoons will pry up edges or take them completely off.
- Building corners and downspouts for scratch marks.

When you find entry spots, seal them up using any of the methods detailed at the end of this chapter. Leave one hole open. If you only find one hole, leave it open. You want to give the animals a way out. Put a temporary door over this spot so they can't come back in.

How will you know if they're really gone? For starters, you shouldn't hear scampering sounds. If you're not sure you're really alone, sprinkle some flour around the open exit hole. Check for tracks over the next several days. If you don't see any, you can be pretty sure that everyone's gone. Once you are, seal this hole, too.

## Animals Under the Porch

Lots of different critters can take up residence under your porch. While it's never a good idea to let them do so, it's often easiest to let them leave on their own, especially if there are babies involved. Skunks are the obvious exception, thanks to the obnoxious stink they release when provoked.

Trapping works well for evicting skunks. So does a one-way door, but only if there aren't babies. If your skunk has taken up residence during May or June, it may very well be a female tending to her litter. If so, either wait for the family to leave or try some mild harassment techniques, such as ammonia or loud noise. Since skunks are nomadic and switch dens fairly regularly, this can be an effective approach. Packing the hole with soft organic material—rags or newspaper—can also be an effective deterrent, but a mother skunk will simply remove the material to get to her babies.

To be on the safe side, don't seal any openings until you can determine that they're gone for good. The flour test is one way to do this. So is packing the hole. If the packing stays in place, you can be pretty sure that the skunk is gone.

Skunks can also get trapped in window wells. If there's one in yours, give it a way to get out and it should depart on its own. A long board works well, but you'll have to be careful about getting it into the well. If you startle the skunk, it will probably spray. One approach is to tie a rope to the end of the board, and lower it in from a safe vantage point high above the animal. Or tie it to a long pole and fish it in from a distance. When the board is in place, keep everyone away until the evening, which is when the skunk will probably climb out.

## Keeping Them Away

The best way to keep wild animals out of your house is to make it impossible for them to enter. The next best way is to quit being so nice to them. Yes, this sounds harsh, but it really isn't. Wild animals are meant to live in the wild. Give them their space and treat them appropriately, and they'll be less likely to want to invade your space.

For squirrels:

- Don't feed them! Attracting squirrels to your house with corncob feeders might be lots of fun for the kiddies, but it's also like flinging your doors wide open to the furry critters.
- Don't feed the birds, either. If you must, use squirrel baffles to keep them off feeders. Locate feeders as far away from your house as you can.
- Keep tree limbs trimmed back. Squirrels jump from them onto roofs.
- Repair all damaged or missing trim on your house. These are prime squirrel-entry areas.

For raccoons:

- Keep all outdoor trash in secure trashcans. Best are metal trashcans with tops that you can strap down, but heavy plastic cans will work, too.
- If you have fruit trees, pick the fruit as it ripens. Keep it picked off the ground, too.
- If you have outdoor fish ponds, cover them with nylon netting in the evening, which is when raccoons are most likely to forage for one of their favorite foods.

For skunks:

- Block entrances to all possible denning sites.
- Install covers on window wells.

For all wildlife:

- Install chimney caps.
- Make sure all screens are intact, including the ones on rooftop ventilation fans. If necessary, replace flimsy aluminum screens with ¼- to ½-inch hardware cloth. Cut the cloth to size and fasten securely.
- Install covers on all external air vents.
- Seal all openings and holes in your house. Use ¼- to ½-inch mesh hardware cloth or sheet metal flashing, and fasten it securely. Extend the patch at least 6 inches around the hole in all directions.
- Keep doors and windows closed.
- Use a repellent. Two possible choices are Ro-Pel and Get-Away. Ro-Pel makes everything it touches taste bitter. Get-Away contains oil of mustard and capsaicin, which act as odor and taste repellents.
- Place ammonia stations around your yard. As mentioned, the jury is out on the effectiveness of this approach, but it doesn't hurt to try it. Ammonia will burn grass; keep it off turf by placing soaked rags in bowls or dishes.
- Secure pet doors at night. Also, don't feed or keep pet food outdoors.

## The Least You Need to Know

- Most wild animals enter homes by accident or only take up residence long enough to have their babies.
- Unlike rats and mice, extermination sometimes isn't possible when dealing with wild animals.
- Trapping is one effective approach for removing wildlife from residences. However, releasing the animal can be problematic.
- Never try to smoke animals out of fireplaces. Doing so can cause a bigger problem—getting rid of the stench from decomposing bodies.

Chapter 18

# Ants, Cockroaches, and Other Creepy Crawlies

## In This Chapter

- Identifying insect intruders
- Nuisance bugs versus pest bugs
- Understanding IPM
- Bugs in the pantry

Is something chomping on your wool sweaters? Have you found bugs in your flour bin? Are hoards of insects climbing out of your antique furniture?

Entomolgists—insect experts—have identified some 1 million species of insects, and they believe that this is only the tip of the iceberg. So it stands to reason that you're going to share your home with a certain number of creepy crawlies. But you definitely can control how many you have to live with.

# Under Siege!

The best approach to insect infestations, of course, is to keep them from happening in the first place. But if you're under siege, it's too late for prevention. That can—and should—come later. Right now, your goal is to get the pests out of your house.

> **Around the House**
>
> Be sure to dispose of any bugs that you swat or squish. Even tiny dead bug bodies can entice other bugs to come inside for an impromptu feast.

Quick fixes include stomping, squashing, swatting, or otherwise getting rid of the intruder(s) in your immediate vicinity. While it's never a good idea to use pesticides to excess, a few shots from a can of quick-kill spray insecticide is the fastest way to knock down a pesty bug or two.

> **Around the House**
>
> Insect problems are typically more noticeable in the fall, as that's when insects look for hiding places to protect them from cold winters. Houses contain food, water, and shelter—all the things insects need for survival.

# Living the Bug-Free Life

There is no such thing as a bug-free home. As such, you shouldn't feel bad when you find them in yours. It doesn't mean you're a bad person. Nor is it necessarily a reflection on your housekeeping skills, although cleaning and vacuuming regularly goes a long way toward keeping bugs in check.

It does mean you're providing ideal conditions for infestations, whether you know it or not. And it means that insects are finding it easy to get into your home and take advantage of your hospitality.

# Taking Control Over Bugs

Humankind has battled against bugs since the earliest times. In the 1960s, some of the various approaches we've taken were formalized into a strategy called *Integrated Pest Management* (*IPM*).

IPM began as "integrated control," in the early 1960s as a response to concerns over excessive pesticide use. At the time, the use of heavy-duty chemicals, such as DDT, to kill insects and nuisance plants was acceptable, and these products were in wide use. While these substances were effective, experts feared they would cause more problems than they solved down the road.

There were already signs that pesticides were becoming less effective. Strains of pesticide-resistant insects were developing. In some cases, pesticide treatment backfired as it killed both the intended bugs and their natural predators. Instead of eliminating infestations, it created them. The theory behind integrated control was that cutting back on pesticide applications would allow chemical and biological controls to work in harmony.

**Tool Chest**

IPM relies primarily on nonchemical means, such as controlling climate, food sources, and building entry points, to prevent and manage pest infestation.

By the end of the decade, IPM was further developed and formalized into a holistic approach toward pest management. The goal was not to completely eliminate pest insects, but to use a variety of methods to keep their levels in check. This philosophy continues to this day.

IPM consists of the following control measures, ranked in order of their preferred use:

1. **Sanitation.** Includes keeping things clean inside and out, removing food and water sources, storing foods properly, and keeping indoor temperatures and humidity at appropriate (meaning insect-unfriendly) levels.
2. **Controlling entry points.** Includes sealing exterior gaps and cracks around windows, doors, eaves, roofs, siding, and other points of access; keeping window and door screens in good repair; and screening and otherwise blocking other potential insect entryways.
3. **Passive controls,** such as fly paper strips, bug traps, electric zappers, and so on.
4. **Natural controls,** such as other insect predators.
5. **Chemical controls.** Used as the last resort.

IPM is an ongoing process, and it's not necessarily easy. Ensuring that pests don't find hospitable environments requires ongoing housekeeping and maintenance. However, this approach will minimize the use of strong chemicals to control pest numbers. It also saves money, is friendlier to the environment, and poses fewer risks to children and animals. Since it primarily relies on passive controls, it's even effective when you're not around.

We've included IPM suggestions for each insect species in this chapter. Finally, a quick disclaimer. This is a long chapter by necessity, as there are so many bugs to battle in the world around us. However, even with the extra length, we couldn't cover them all here. Instead, we've included information on some of the offenders you're most likely to encounter. We also focus more on IPM measures than on physical descriptions.

This chapter deals with bugs that, for the most part, travel by foot. For winged pests—bees, flies, and the like—turn to Chapter 19.

## Name and Number Please!

Effective IPM begins with knowing the kind of bug (or bugs) you're dealing with. Here's why: Simply finding a crawly critter in your house isn't necessarily a problem. Some insects are casual intruders; they come in with the morning paper, perhaps, or nestled into the grain on a piece of firewood, and don't mean to take up residence in your home. You don't have to worry about these guys. Just shoo them on out.

That said, others definitely mean to come in and stay a while. In some cases, a long while.

How can you tell which from which? There is a variety of methods available for identifying insect intruders, including the following:

- **Field guides.** Available online and at the library, these guides can give you a general idea of the kind of insect you've found and whether or not it's a problem. Most field guides are pretty general. Unless the guide was written specifically for your region, it might not identify the exact bug you're dealing with, but it should get you close enough.
- **County extension offices.** These helpful agencies usually have one or two people on staff who know the insects in your area. Many extension offices post pest information on the Internet as well.
- **County or state departments of agriculture or health.** Same as above.
- **Entomology departments** at local colleges or universities. Entomologists study insects for a living. They can tell you lots about various kinds of bugs, but typically from a more scholarly point of view, not necessarily to help you get rid of the problem.
- **Pest-control companies.** Probably the best source of information, especially if you're simply interested in control or extermination and would rather have someone else do it. Larger pest control companies might even have their own entomologist on staff or be operated by a board-certified entomologist.

Once you've identified your bugs, you might find that they're more of a nuisance than a real pest problem. In fact, insects tend to fall into two categories:

- **Nuisance bugs**. These insects are more a bother than anything else. Many have positive aspects, such as preying on other bugs. Some are simply a pain in the butt, and serve no beneficial purpose beyond being meals for other bugs and animals.

- **Damage bugs**. As the term implies, these bugs are not only a pain in the rear (or other places they might bite), they also destroy things like food, furniture, clothing, and books. Some of them carry diseases.

As mentioned, some insects come indoors during the fall seeking protection from the elements. They squeeze in any way they can and hibernate in walls, attics, crawl spaces, and other locales. As such, you typically only have to deal with them during two seasons: the fall, when they invade your home, and the spring, when they leave.

Other bugs want to set up shop indoors and are year-round problems.

## Ladybugs

With their round red or orange bodies and their little spots, ladybugs are the symbol of cheeriness to many people. But don't let their perky looks fool you. They're carnivores, and their favorite food is aphids, a common garden pest. They also feed on such other plant pests as whiteflies, scales, and mealybugs.

There are around 400 ladybird beetles (the correct generic name for ladybugs) species in the United States. The ones that cause the most problems are multicolored Asian ladybugs, which were introduced a while back to some Southern and Eastern states to control aphids. Unlike the other species, Asian ladybugs like to hang out in groups. *Big* groups.

All ladybugs seek out safe places to overwinter. Wall voids and attics are common hibernation spots. They typically wait until spring to re-emerge, but you might see one or two walking around inside your home on a warm winter day. That said, if Asian ladybugs choose to overwinter in your home, you could be dealing with hundreds of ladybugs instead of a few.

CAUTION

**A Fine Mess**

Don't squish ladybugs. Doing so causes an orange stain that can stain carpets and fabrics. It also causes a stink—literally. Squish an Asian ladybug with your fingers, and you might get a small bite; it's harmless, but you'll feel it.

## IPM Controls

The following IPM measures are all effective controls for ladybug infestations:

- Let them live if their numbers aren't too overwhelming.
- Vacuum them up or trap them in a ladybug trap, available at home and garden stores. Regular ladybug traps aren't that effective; black light traps are expensive but do the job. Release them outdoors.
- Swat or squish them with a paper towel.
- As a long-term control, plant trees to shade the south and west sides of your house, which is where ladybugs congregate.

If you see more than 20 ladybugs in your home on a daily basis, there's a good chance Asian ladybugs have taken up residence. They will leave when the weather gets better.

## Chemical Control

Since these bugs hang out in wall voids and crawl spaces, chemical control isn't very effective. For large infestations, pyrethroid-based insecticides applied around the outside of your home may help prevent pest entry. Pay particular attention to possible entry spots—eaves, siding, window, and door trim—on the south and west sides, where ladybugs like to congregate. If you apply the chemical yourself, be sure to select a product labeled for use on ladybugs.

**Around the House**

Boxelder bugs overwinter in homes like ladybugs do and cause similar problems, including leaving small red stains when they're squished. One of the easiest ways to prevent boxelder infestations is to not plant boxelder trees around your home. However, cutting down existing trees isn't recommended, as the shade they provide vastly outweighs the nuisance the bugs cause. Indoors, control them as you would ladybugs. Swat them or squish them (carefully, so you don't stain things), or vacuum them up and dump them outside.

# Ground Beetles

There are some 12,000 different kinds of ground beetles in the United States. They're a nuisance bug that feeds on other insects. Some of the bigger ground beetles even eat slugs. They're sometimes called "stink bugs" as they can ooze out awful-smelling juices to keep predators away when disturbed. They're also often confused with cockroaches, to which they bear a startling resemblance.

Ground beetles like to overwinter in houses, and it's not uncommon to see them roaming about on basement floors when the weather turns cold.

**Around the House**

Here's a quick way to tell the difference between ground beetles and cockroaches: Ground beetles have hardened front wings; roaches either have leathery wings or none at all.

## IPM Controls

Try the following IPM controls on ground beetles:

- Round them up—a broom and dustpan work well—and herd them outside. Release them as far away from your house as you can. Otherwise, they might skitter right back in.
- Eliminate outdoor hiding places near your home, including leaves, stones, logs, and other debris.

## Chemical Controls

Chemical controls for ground beetles typically aren't necessary. If the numbers become overwhelming, treat hiding places, the foundation, and the perimeter of the building with a residual insecticide containing synthetic pyrethroids, such as permethrin, deltamethrin, or bifenthrin.

# Spiders

Another beneficial predator, spiders are some of the most feared household intruders, primarily due to such notorious species as the brown recluse and the black widow. While it's true that bites from these spiders can cause serious problems, most spiders, even ones that bite, are harmless.

**A Fine Mess**

Spiders tend to be more problematic in homes sited in wooded areas or that have naturalized landscaping, which are both ideal spider habitats.

Most spiders are accidental invaders that enter your home through cracks around doors, windows, or other openings. They play a big role in keeping flies, crickets, mites, and other pesky insects in check.

## IPM Controls

The following are effective IPM controls for spiders:

- Dust and/or vacuum areas where spiders like to hang out, such as the corners of walls and structural timber in basements and crawl spaces, on a regular basis. This will remove webs and egg sacs. Outdoors, knock down webs with a broom or spray with a hose.
- Capture and release. One way is to trap the spider under a cup, then slide a piece of paper under the spider. Release outdoors.
- Eliminate other household pests such as ants, cockroaches, and flies. They're all spider bait.
- Keep leaf debris and vegetation away from the foundation as much as possible.
- Eliminate indoor clutter. Doing so gives spiders fewer places to hide out.

Peaceful coexistence with spiders also means avoiding situations where you could get bitten. Wear gloves when handling firewood and lumber. Shake out shoes and clothing before donning. Inspect towels and bedding before use. Be careful when opening cardboard boxes—a favorite spider hideout—especially boxes stored under beds. (Better yet, don't store them there.) Don't handle spiders with your bare hands.

## Chemical Controls

Chemical control is not recommended due to the beneficial aspects of these bugs. If necessary, individual spiders can be controlled with nonresidual aerosol sprays containing pyretherin, resmethrin, or sumithrin. Dust formulations can be used in crawl spaces or to treat cracks and crevices.

# Annoying Ants

Ants are considered a beneficial nuisance insect for their role in reducing dead and decaying plant and animal organic matter. Their nests also help aerate the soil. Many ant species have a fondness for aphid honeydew—the sweet slop that aphids produce from feeding on plants.

Ants will eat just about anything, which is one reason they're such pests. All of them eat plant and animal materials. Some ants also love sweets. Others like greasy and/or protein foods.

The ants you find foraging in your kitchen are workers charged with the mission of bringing food back for their colony mates. What's more, they're also responsible for telling their buddies where food can be found. They do so by depositing a trail of pheromone, which stays in place for a long, long time.

## IPM for Ants

These non-chemical approaches are advised for ant control:

- Store all attractive food items such as sugar, syrup, and honey in closed containers.
- Rinse out soft-drink containers before placing in trash.
- Clean up grease splatters and spills as soon as they happen.
- Don't free-feed pets. Many animals find kibbled foods irresistible.
- Scrub ant entry points with soap and water. This will remove trail pheromones and make it more difficult for foragers to find previous trails.

## Chemical Controls

Toxic baits, either liquids, solids, or gels, applied in stations or broadcast as granules are effective for controlling ants. Of these, gels and liquids tend to yield faster results than solids do.

Indoors, place bait stations along ant trails. Outdoors, site them every 10 to 20 feet and at any nest openings you can find.

Insecticides labeled for indoor ant control can provide immediate infestation relief while

> CAUTION
>
> **A Fine Mess**
>
> Ants will not eat bait if food is nearby. For the best results, make sure that sinks, pantries, and other ant-infested areas are free of food particles and other ant-attractive substances.

you're employing other control measures. Outdoors, pyrethroids can be applied at entrance points. More extensive perimeter treatments, while often recommended, can disrupt baiting programs and pose more of an environmental concern than baiting does.

Professional pest control operators have access to newer, non-repellant products for ant control. For severe ant infestations, or areas where ants are a continuing problem, a professional company should be consulted for long-term relief.

## Pantry Pests

It's definitely not a pleasant thought, but many foodstuffs contain eggs laid by various beetle, weevil, borer, and moth species. Keep food long enough and provide the right conditions, and these eggs can hatch.

Many food products are breeding grounds for pantry pests, including …

- Milled grain products such as flour, cereals, and cornmeal. Badly infested flour is characterized by a sharp odor and moldy flavor.
- Dry fruit, such as raisins and dates.
- Dry dog and cat food.
- Spices.
- Chocolate, especially baking chocolate.
- Dried meats.
- Rice.
- Macaroni.

Pantry pests are fairly benign. They don't bite or sting people or pets. Nor do they spread disease or damage furniture. But they do contaminate food, and an infestation can be difficult to get rid of.

The best way to control a pantry infestation is to locate and remove the source. This means searching every stored food item wherever you find a problem—in your pantry, in cabinets, on shelves, what have you. Here are the steps to follow:

1. Set up by your sink or over a large garbage can. Have a couple of heavy plastic bags by your side as well.

2. Check opened boxes and bags first, one by one. Shake a little of the contents of each into your hand. Check the inside of the container as well. Place all infested foods in the heavy plastic bags. Seal them tightly and put them out with the trash when you're done.

3. Next, open every unopened container. Follow the same procedure as in step 2.

Until you have your insect problem under control, all food should be taken out of its original packaging and stored in glass or plastic containers with tight-fitting lids.

**A Fine Mess**

Even if a food item appears infestation-free, don't assume it is. All food stored in an area where an infestation took place is suspect. If you don't contain everything, you run the risk of another hatch, and another infestation. If a well-contained infested food hatches, the infestation remains in one place. All you have to do is throw away the infested food.

## Treating Suspect Food

To be on the safe side, you might want to treat grain products that came up negative for infestation. Heating or freezing the items will kill any eggs it might contain. Some experts prefer freezing over heating, as rising temperatures could release large numbers of insects if the food is infested.

For heat treating, place food in shallow pan. Bake it at 120°F for one hour, 130°F for 30 minutes, or in a microwave for five minutes. For freezing, place food in freezer at 0°F for four days.

## IPM for Pantry Pests

The following IPM measures are effective controls for pantry insects:

- Carefully examine all foods that could contain insect eggs—including flour, cereals, cornmeal, raisins, pet food, spices, rice, macaroni, and so on—before buying them. Check packaging date to ensure freshness.
- Don't buy foods in ripped or torn packages.
- Buy small quantities of foods that you don't use often.
- Store infestation-susceptible foods in insect-proof containers made of glass, metal, or heavy plastic, or in the freezer or refrigerator.

- Keep food storage areas clean. Vacuum up any spillage as soon as you see it.
- Avoid storing liquids with dry foods. Pantry pests are attracted to moisture. Wipe up any moisture spills as soon as you see them.

Since many foods can harbor insect eggs, complete control over pantry pests typically isn't possible. However, a little vigilance will significantly decrease the chances of battling an infestation.

### Chemical Controls

Insecticides should not be used around food products. Rely on other control methods if at all possible. Pheromone traps are available for Indian meal moths, but will not attract beetles. Still, these can be helpful for monitoring abatement efforts. Place them in areas of a previous infestation and check weekly. If you see new moths in the traps, it's time to check your food again.

For severe infestations, a residual insecticide can be used to eradicate existing bugs. Due to concerns about insecticide use around food, hiring a professional exterminator is advised.

As mentioned, all the bugs we've covered up to now are more of a nuisance than anything else. The next group of insects isn't as benign.

## Bedbugs

Dark spots on mattresses are a sure-fire indication of bedbugs. They were once a common pest in the United States; better hygiene and aggressive pest-control measures have all but eliminated them. However, they lived on in other parts of the world, and they're making a comeback here.

**Around the House**

Bedbugs can carry diseases, but they're not considered a serious disease threat. However, their bites can cause itching and inflammation. Both can be treated with topical antiseptic or antibiotic creams or lotions, which will also help prevent infections from the bites.

Bedbugs feed by biting people when they're asleep. Some people develop localized swelling or an itchy welt around these bites. Others don't react to them at all.

Bedbugs feed at night and hide during the day. Their favorite hiding spots are where people sleep. Being flat, they can easily slip into tiny crevices in bed frames and headboards. They also like to tuck into areas around mattresses and box springs. They don't nest, but they will congregate in habitual hiding places.

Since not all bites or bitelike reactions are caused by bedbugs, it's important to confirm a bedbug infestation before mounting an attack. Signs of one include …

- Dark spots and stains on mattresses, caused by dried bedbug excrement.
- Eggs and eggshells, and/or molted skins from maturing nymphs.
- Rusty or reddish blood spots on mattresses and/or bed sheets.
- A buggy or sweetish odor. This is typically associated with heavy infestation.
- The bugs themselves.

> **A Fine Mess**
>
> Unlike fleas, which typically bite ankles and lower legs, bedbugs will suck blood out of any patch of bare skin. However, since other things can cause skin irritations, bedbug infestations can go on for some time before they're detected.

Bedbugs are extremely efficient at catching a ride on luggage and clothing. Travel to a foreign country, and you just might bring back a few with you. Other bedbug transports include old mattresses, box springs, and other bedroom furniture.

Once in a home, bedbugs easily spread from room to room. Since they only feed on blood, even the most spotless home can harbor them. As such, an infestation typically requires calling a pest-control specialist.

> **In the Nick of Time**
>
> Certain types of bedbugs can also feed on birds and bats. If you find bedbuglike insects, it's not a bad idea to check for signs of a bat and/or bird infestation.

## IPM Controls

Nonchemical controls for bedbugs include:

- Regularly vacuuming mattresses, carpets, walls, and other surfaces. Pay particular attention to the edges, seams, and tufts on mattresses and box springs, and the edges of wall-to-wall carpets, which are prime bedbug hangouts.

- Steam cleaning carpets, upholstery and drapes. This will kill any bugs and eggs that vacuuming misses.
- Throwing away affected mattresses. If this isn't an option, cover mattresses with zippered cases designed for preventing dust mites.
- Thinking twice about buying secondhand bedroom furniture. If you do, examine pieces carefully before bringing them home.
- If traveling internationally, examine beds and headboards for signs of bugs. Keep luggage off the floor.

Bedbugs can't climb slippery things. Coating bed legs with petroleum jelly can keep them from climbing up. Placing bed legs in bowls of soapy water or putting the legs inside glass jars or metal cans can also keep bedbugs from bugging you.

**Tool Chest**

**Diatomaceous earth,** or fumed silica, consists of finely milled fossilized shells of minuscule organisms called diatoms. When crushed up, they break into tiny pieces of glass. The tiny particles adhere to insect bodies, where they scratch through protective wax layers and cause rapid dehydration.

## Chemical Controls

Residual insecticides containing pyrethroids or natural pyrethrins are commonly used on bedbugs. Dusts containing *diatomaceous earth* are useful in hard-to-reach places. These products adhere to the hair on pest bodies and causes death by dehydration. Application is best done by a pest-control specialist.

# Carpet Beetles

While they can also be considered beneficial as they eat dead insects like boxelder bugs and flies, carpet beetles are scavengers that feed on a variety of animal products, including woolens, hides, feathers, hair, taxidermy specimens, dried meats, and other stored foods.

**Around the House**

Adult carpet beetles, which prefer flowers to animal products, often flit around indoor light fixtures and windows. If you see them, it's a good indication of an infestation somewhere in your house. Carpet beetles can also come from bird or animal nests or animal carcasses.

Only carpet beetle larvae cause damage. They like to hang out in dark, undisturbed areas like closets and attics and inside boxes where linens and woolens are stored. They also like carpeting, upholstered furniture, and air ducts, where they feed on dust, lint, pet hair, and other debris.

Clothes moths typically take the rap when woolens turn up with holes, but carpet beetles cause more significant damage and are more often the true culprits. If you've got an article of clothing with lots of small holes, suspect moths. If the damage is more centralized but severe, it's probably carpet beetles.

Carpet beetles can be very hard to control as they're so capable of finding food in out-of-the-way places. They also tend to spread out through buildings. As such, effective control often requires insecticides, but sanitation and exclusion can go a long way, too.

## IPM Controls

Nonchemical controls for carpet beetles include the following:

- Wash or dry clean all clothing and other susceptible materials before storing.
- Store all clothing and fabrics in tight-fitting containers or space bags into which you've tucked some moth balls or flakes.
- Keep rugs, drapes, upholstered furniture, closets, and other places where carpet beetles congregate squeaky clean. Vacuum thoroughly and frequently. Dispose of the vacuum bag after you're done.
- Monitor control measures with sticky traps. Plain sticky traps are available in retail stores; sticky traps with a pheromone that attracts carpet beetles are often available through pest-control operators.
- If you have mounted animal specimens in your home, have them cleaned periodically. Alternatively (and if they're small enough) place them in a freezer for 10 to 14 days every couple of months or so.
- Annually inspect all stored woolens, linens, and furs. Air them out by hanging them in the light when you inspect them. Finish your inspection by brushing thoroughly with a soft, brass-bristle clothing brush.
- Destroy all heavily infested items.

**A Fine Mess**

Never apply insecticides to clothing. The chemicals could ruin the fabric. If you're concerned about carpet beetles and clothes moths, instead ask a dry cleaner about mothproofing your wardrobe—at least the things you're most concerned about.

### Chemical Controls

Cleaning is the best approach, as insecticides can ruin fabrics. Articles that can't be cleaned or laundered can be sprayed with products labeled for use on carpet beetles. Spot treatment is best; limit spray to known hiding spots such as the edges of floor coverings, under rugs and furniture, floors and walls of closets, floor vents, shelving, and other areas where lint accumulates.

Borate dusts can be used in attics, wall voids, and other inaccessible spots. Fumigation might be necessary for treating extensive infestations.

## Clothes Moths

Like carpet beetles, it's the larvae, not the adults, which cause problems. Clothes moth larvae are particularly attracted to beverage, urine, sweat, and skin-oil stains.

You should suspect clothes moths if you find small holes in the clothing that has been stored for a while. Other indicators are threads and fecal pellets laid by the small white larvae.

### IPM Controls

Take the following steps to control clothes moths:

- Wear your clothing. Getting it out in the open can keep moths in check.
- Clean before storage.
- Ironing. This destroys all stages of the moths.
- Periodically air clothing outside.

Chemical control is the same as for carpet beetles.

## Wood-Destroying Beetles

These nasty critters range in size from $\frac{1}{12}$- to $\frac{1}{5}$-inch long. Infestations can build for some time without notice as these beetles aren't fast workers. However, they can cause significant damage to structural wood and furniture over time.

There are a variety of wood-destroying beetles. Of them, old house borer beetles, which feed on soft woods like pine, and *powderpost* beetles, which prefer hardwoods, are fairly common.

**Tool Chest**

**Powderpost** beetles are so named because they grind the wood they feed on into a fine, flourlike powder.

Give wood-destroying beetles enough time, and they can cause more destruction than carpenter ants. Log homes are particularly vulnerable to attack from these critters, but they can bore into and destroy virtually any kind of wood.

Finding one or two beetles in your house doesn't necessarily mean you have an infestation. They could have come in with firewood or through an open window. The following are signs of an infestation:

- Rasping or clicking sounds in wood, especially in spring or summer when moisture levels are higher.
- Small holes in wood surfaces. These are exit holes made by beetles that have completed their life cycle in the wood. Sawdust or frass around or near the holes are signs of an active infestation.

Since wood-eating beetles work slowly, discovering an infestation isn't cause for panic, but you will want to end it as soon as you can.

## IPM Controls

IPM measures for wood-destroying beetles include the following:

- Remove and replace infested structural wood whenever possible. Destroy the wood by burning or taking to a landfill.
- Remove and destroy dead tree limbs around your home.
- Remove scrap lumber and wood piles.
- Paint or varnish pores, cracks, and holes where eggs can be laid.
- Inspect furniture and other objects before bringing them inside.
- If you burn firewood, only bring in what you'll burn in a day.
- Heat small wooden items in an oven at 120°F to 140°F for six hours. Or, freeze them at 0°F for three days.

## Chemical Controls

Because of the similarities between the types of beetles and damage caused by these beetles, it's a good idea to get an accurate identification of these insects before treating them chemically. Treatment may or may not be necessary, depending on whether the beetles will reinfest the wood or not. For this reason, beetle control is best done by an expert.

# Cockroaches

The stuff of urban legends, cockroach infestations are among those that homeowners fear the most. And they should. Not only are cockroaches extremely difficult to control, they're one of the leading causes of allergies, asthma, and other bronchial disorders. They can also carry bacteria and other disease organisms on their bodies and in their fecal matter.

There are about 3,500 species of cockroaches in the world. Of them, only a handful are considered major pests. They all like high humidity and high temperatures, and they tend to hang out in cellars, crawl spaces, and around kitchen and bathroom plumbing.

Food, water, and a safe place to hang out are all cockroaches need to be happy. Denying them these things plays a big role in controlling their numbers.

**Around the House**

Ultrasonic devices are frequently advertised as a nontoxic method of cockroach control; however, extensive research disproves their effectiveness as they neither kill nor repel cockroaches. Home remedies such as certain spices and herbs, salt, bran, baking soda, and so on have also proven to be ineffective.

## IPM Controls

IPM controls for cockroaches include keeping them out of structures and eliminating their food, water, and hiding places.

Other IPM controls for cockroaches include trapping. Sticky traps for cockroaches are widely available. Put them everywhere cockroaches could hang out, including garbage storage areas, under sinks, in the bathroom, in cabinets, and under and behind refrigerators.

You can make a cheap and effective cockroach trap out of an empty jar and some petroleum jelly. Any jar with a rounded inside lip will work. Coat the inner lip of the jar with the petroleum jelly. Then place a piece of bait—beer-soaked bread, dog food, apples, you name it—in the jar. Wrap a paper towel around the outside of the jar to give the critters something to grab onto, and place the traps in high-risk areas. The petroleum jelly will keep the roaches from climbing back out once they're in.

To kill trapped roaches, pour dish detergent into the jar and add hot water. Dump the contents outside or in the garbage. Wash out the jar and repeat the process every two to three days.

Two natural substances—diatomaceous earth (discussed above) and boric acid—are often recommended for indoor cockroach control. Boric acid is a stomach poison that cockroaches pick up when they walk over dusted areas. When they groom themselves, they eat the acid and eventually die.

Apply either product lightly with a squeeze-bulb duster everywhere you've seen cockroach activity—in cracks and crevices under sinks, behind fridges and stoves, along baseboards, in electrical outlets, and in cabinet and wall voids.

### Chemical Controls

IPM is the most effective approach for cockroach control. Insecticides should not be used alone as cockroaches easily become resistant to them. Many over-the-counter formulations are available. If you go this route, using products from different insecticide classes might help prevent resistance.

Inside, apply insecticides to cracks and crevices where cockroaches live. Outside, treat along foundation walls with products labeled for outdoor control.

Roach baits are an effective control and are widely available as gels, granules, pastes, and dusts. Again, rotating products between insecticide classes can help prevent resistance.

Insect growth regulators, which attack infestations by disrupting insect reproduction cycles, are an excellent control, especially when paired with baits.

## Silverfish and Firebrats

You're more likely to see the damage caused by these elusive pests than the pests themselves. Both like to feast on paper products like books and wallpaper. They can also damage clothing, especially silks and some synthetic fabrics.

Silverfish can live up to six years. They're often found near or in water sources—sinks, bathtubs, and so on—where they fall in while looking for water to drink.

Silverfish infestations start small and build. The following indicate an infestation:

- Nibble damage to book pages
- Irregular nibble patterns on coated paper
- Holes in paper (especially with heavy infestations)
- Damage to book bindings

Yellow stains, scales, and/or silverfish feces, which are small, dark, and loose, may also be evident. If you see feces, you have an active infestation.

## IPM Controls

Nonchemical controls for silverfish include the following:

- Trap them in baby food jars or other small glass containers. Wrap some tape around the outside of the jar for a foothold and set the jar upright where silverfish are likely to be. Since they can't scale smooth surfaces, they're trapped when they reach the top of the jar and fall in.
- Set out sticky boards. For the best results, combine with silverfish bait, available at hardware and home-and-garden stores.
- Heat books and other small articles to 120°F. Or freeze them.

## Chemical Controls

Use chemicals only on large infestations. Sprays and dusts containing pyrethroids can be applied to cracks and crevices along baseboards, doors, window casings, closets, and pipe openings. Diatomaceous earth or boric acid can be dusted along baseboards and beneath and behind appliances.

## The Least You Need to Know

- There are millions of insects in the world. Some are beneficial, some are pests.
- All insects can be controlled with pesticides. Integrated pest management, however, is the preferred approach.

- Natural remedies and ultrasonic devices have not been proven effective for insect infestations.
- Never rely solely on insecticides for pest control. Not only do they not work that well, they're expensive and they can cause greater problems than they solve.

Chapter 19

# Things That Go Bzzzz

## In This Chapter

- Mad as a hornet
- Knocking down nests
- Culling colonies of bees
- Face-to-face with flies

If it's summertime and you've planned an outdoor activity where food's involved, you can count on a variety of winged insects joining you at the table. Flies are standard fare, but your outdoor repast can also attract more-feared buzzers like hornets and wasps.

These insect pests stick to the outdoors most of the time, and if their nests are located far enough away from human structures, they typically don't cause much of a problem. However, many of them prefer to nest around man-made structures, and some of them can take up residence inside your home, where they can cause serious problems.

Inside or out, a couple of flies or a bee or two typically isn't much cause for alarm. Hundreds of them are.

# Flying Things in the House

If you're just dealing with a few winged things indoors, they're most likely casual intruders that came in through open doors or windows, or cracks or holes somewhere in your house. If they're flies, swatting them with a flyswatter or a rolled-up newspaper or magazine is cheap, easy, and effective.

**In the Nick of Time**

Flies can be a year-round problem around food-preparation areas. You should never use a pesticide around food, so keep a flyswatter nearby instead. They're cheap (usually around $1 or so) and easy to use, too.

Stinging insects indoors can pose a more serious problem as you want to get them outside without getting stung. Letting them leave on their own by opening windows and doors might let more in. Swatting them sets you up for a sting if you miss your mark. That said, most solitary wasps or bees inside a house will die very quickly, so there's something to be said for letting Mother Nature take its course.

## Trapping

Most flying insects are attracted to the natural light at windows. A sticky board trap placed on a windowsill will quickly trap a single invader.

## Quick Kill Via Insecticide

Many people would rather not risk getting stung. If you're one of them, this is a time when having a quick knockdown insecticide on hand makes sense. Any of the commonly available consumer products labeled for this use will work.

Most recommend spraying in closed rooms for the best results, as spot treatment only kills the insects that the product actually hits. So clear the room of pets and children, and shoot the product into the air, following label directions. Then get out of there and let the insecticide do its stuff.

When you come back, your insect nemeses should be dead. Sweep them up so they don't turn into food for insect predators, and throw them away in the garbage.

Quick knockdown insecticides don't have much of a residual effect, but they will take care of immediate infestation problems. If you keep finding insects inside your house, however, it's time to forego the instant bug death and implement other controls.

# Calling in IPM

As detailed in Chapter 18, Integrated Pest Management (IPM) is the most effective way to deal with animal pests of all kinds, and you'll find IPM steps detailed throughout this chapter. The strategies all emphasize approaches other than insecticide use. When it comes to stinging insects, however, you might have to get more aggressive with insecticides if nests are located in areas where they can cause problems for people and animals, or to minimize stinging risks while you're implementing other parts of the program.

Insecticides are considered the last step when battling housefly infestations. There are simply too many places that can serve as harborage for flies, and you'd have to use a lot of chemicals for effective control.

# Stinging Things

Just about everyone treads cautiously around bees, wasps, and other stinging insects, and for good reason. Even if you're not allergic to their venom, no one likes to get stung.

**Around the House**

Many people call all stinging insects bees regardless of what they look like. But there are differences between the species. Some live alone, most live in colonies. Some are aggressive, others aren't.

## Risk Factors

All stinging insects pose a potential health threat to anyone who's allergic to their venom. However, some are more aggressive than others, and they pose a more serious risk. As a rule, wasps, hornets, and yellow jackets are more dangerous than honeybees, and their behavior is more unpredictable. Always treat them with respect when they're around.

If you decide to take on any of these insects by eliminating their nests, be sure you know what you're doing before you start. Approaches vary depending on the type of insect, and it's a good idea to identify what you're dealing with before you go on the attack.

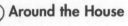

**Around the House**

If you have been stung in the past and had a strong allergic reaction to it, there's a 60 percent chance of having a more severe reaction the next time you're stung. Reactions can be localized and range from slight pain and redness to swelling and enlargement of the entire limb. Generalized reactions will affect the entire body, the most serious would be anaphylactic shock. Anyone experiencing more than localized reactions should always call an expert to eliminate stinging insect nests.

## Should They Go or Should They Stay?

If insect nests are visible but they're not near your home or near parts of your yard where you and your family hang out, you might want to think twice about treating them. While it may seem obverse, stinging insects are considered beneficial, as they prey on other nuisance insects. It's a good idea to let them live if possible.

Any nests located in areas where insects could feel threatened should be removed, as the occupants will sting to protect their nest. Inside nests should also be eliminated. We'll start with some of the big, bad stingers and work our day down to the fairly benign ones.

# Bald-Faced Hornets

The old saying "mad as a hornet" definitely describes these stinging insects. They can be extremely aggressive when their nests are disturbed, so much so that pest controllers typically garb up in special suits called wasp suits, sealed at the wrists, ankles, and collars, to protect themselves when battling these angry little critters.

Bald-faced hornets build inverted teardrop-shaped nests that can contain thousands of insects. They typically attach them to out-of-the-way spots on trees, bushes, and the sides of buildings, which can make removal difficult. This, coupled with the feisty nature of these bugs, is enough for most people to want to call in the experts to remove these nests.

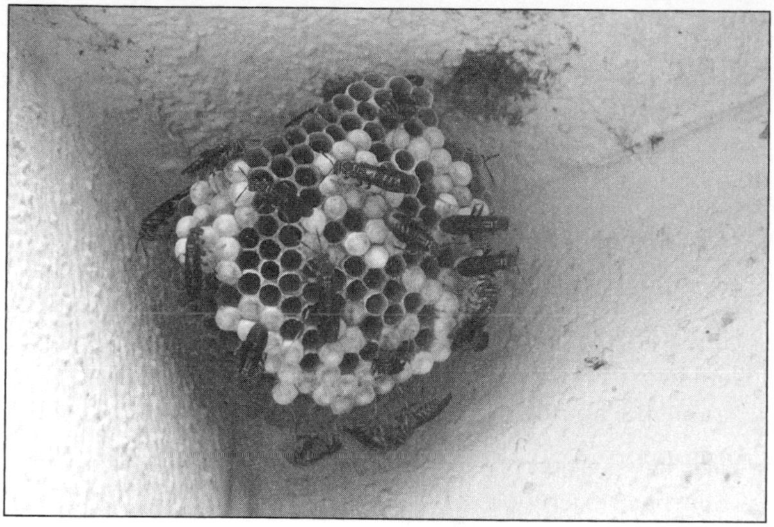

*This bald-faced hornet colony decided to attach its nest high on the side of a building. Note the classic, teardrop shape and the bottom opening.*

### A Fine Mess

Do some research and you might come across suggestions for "kind and gentle" nest removal. This entails slipping a plastic garbage bag over the nest, sealing the bag, and detaching the nest from its anchor spot. The bagged nest is then frozen or left in the sun, where the combination of heat and lack of oxygen kills the insects. This approach probably will kill them, but it also exposes you to lots of stings if you don't get the bag around the nest in time. Plus, the wasps could chew a hole out of the bag. The best advice: Find another way to remove the nest.

## DIY Hornet Nest Removal

We recommend leaving these nests to the experts, but you can eliminate them yourself if you want to. You'll have to plan for a night attack. This is when the hornets will be in their nest, which will minimize the chances of getting stung.

Wearing protective gear is highly recommended. A wasp or bee suit is ideal, but pricey if you're only going to use it once. At a minimum, wear a long-sleeved shirt, long pants, a bee hat, veil, and gloves. You might find the latter items where professional pest-control products are sold. If you know someone who keeps bees, see if you can borrow a set.

Here's what you'll do:

- Be sure you can get close enough to the nest for effective insecticide application. You might need a ladder. If so, put it near the nest on the day you intend to go after it.
- Buy some wasp and hornet freeze. This stuff comes in aerosol containers. You might want to buy two cans, just to be on the safe side.
- Recruit a friend to hold a flashlight so you can see what you're doing.
- Wait until the sun goes down. When it's dark, move your ladder into position. Have your friend illuminate the area with the flashlight. Don't aim it right at the nest—this will irritate the hornets.
- Apply a couple of quick shots of the freeze to the outside of the nest first. This will knock down any hornets hovering around the opening. Then attack the opening of the nest. Aim the freeze directly into the opening, and make sure it gets in there. But be careful. You don't want to break the paper coating around the nest. Doing so will release irritated hornets in all directions, and make your life very miserable.
- After you're done, climb down, turn off the light, and run like heck. Leave the ladder. You can retrieve it later.

Check the nest in a day. If you still see hornets hovering, you'll have to repeat the application. If you don't, it's still a good idea to do a final application before you take the nest down. Doing so will take care of any hornets that might have decided to spend the night elsewhere.

When you're sure all activity has ceased, cut the nest down, seal it in a heavy plastic bag, and throw it away.

## Yellow Jackets

"Yellow jacket" is an umbrella term for a number of different wasp species. They often nest underground in old rodent burrows or underneath landscape timbers, but they'll also set up housekeeping in wall voids and rock walls. Their nests start small but can swell to thousands of inhabitants by the end of the summer.

Most yellow jackets are predators and feed on other insects. Some start out as predators and develop a preference for human food. As their natural food supply thins out in late summer and early fall, all yellow jackets can be a big problem. They need to eat, and they'll tackle just about anything to satisfy their hunger for proteins and carbohydrates. This includes human food, and they're particularly fond of things like soft drinks and hamburgers, which makes them huge pests at late-summer picnics.

## Playing "Keep Away"

The best way to avoid confrontations with yellow jackets is to avoid areas where they nest. Since they tend to tuck their nests into out-of-the-way places, they can be hard to find. One sure indication is lots of yellow jackets flying in and out of a single hole.

> **In the Nick of Time**
>
> Once yellow jackets find food in a certain place, they'll keep coming back to that spot long after the food is gone. You can prevent them from doing so by keeping food and beverages away from them. Wait until the last minute to serve outdoor meals, and keep all food-storage containers tightly sealed.

## IPM for Yellow Jackets

There are a number of approaches to yellow jacket control. The most benign is knocking down newly started nests in early spring. This should encourage the founding female to look for another nesting spot—hopefully, far away from you—or to give it up and join another colony as a worker.

> **In the Nick of Time**
>
> Trapping in early spring can save you lots of headaches in the summer. Every female you capture in the spring will eliminate anywhere from 500 to 5,000 yellow jackets.

If you can't find nests, trapping is another effective nonpesticidal control. However, it can be time intensive, as you have to keep doing it for the best results. And you have to remember to start early every spring. This is when you're most likely to trap the queens. Doing so will keep yellow jacket numbers down for the entire season.

If you forget, you can start trapping anytime during spring or summer, but it won't be as effective as the colony will already be established.

Most yellow jacket traps are variations on one design theme: a funnel-shaped device that leads to some sort of a containment or catch center. Traps also come in two basic configurations: disposable and reusable. Disposable traps make it easy to get rid of

**A Fine Mess**

Be careful when emptying traps. You might come across a few live yellow jackets that survived their containment. If you need to empty a trap that contains live yellow jackets, place the trap in the freezer or an ice chest. The cold will kill them.

**A Fine Mess**

If you're using protein to attract yellow jackets to a trap, be sure to change it regularly. Yellow jackets don't like rotten meat and will stay away from it.

trapped yellow jackets—all you have to do is seal them up (if they aren't self-sealing) and throw them away. If you select a reusable trap, you'll have to empty it yourself. Buy at least one trap per acre of land. If you're trapping in the fall, you'll need to buy at least double that amount to trap all the scavengers.

Not all yellow jackets like the attractant chemicals used to lure them to traps. For this reason, some manufacturers suggest adding a protein-based bait to increase the effectiveness of traps during the early summer. Yellow jacket nutritional needs change to carbohydrates in the late summer, necessitating a switch to fruit or fruit juice at this time.

Be sure to check the traps regularly, empty reusable traps when they get full, and replenish the bait, if you're using it, when necessary.

## Hitting Them Where They Nest

If you can locate the nest, you can eliminate it by shooting a wasp freezer or a desiccant dust into the nest opening. If you're going to do this, be very careful. Like hornets, yellow jackets can be extremely aggressive when their nest is disturbed. Follow the steps outlined for treating a hornet's nest.

For yellow jacket nests in the ground, try pouring a soap and water mixture into the hole. You can use virtually any kind of soap for this. If this doesn't work, you can shoot a liquid or dust insecticide into the opening. Be sure to choose one that's formulated for use on lawns or soil. Watch the entrance for a couple of days; if it's devoid of action, cover it with soil.

The last option is to wait and do nothing, especially if the nest isn't near high-traffic areas. Cold weather will kill them.

## Yellow Jackets in Walls

Yellow jackets will often build nests in attics and wall voids. Once again, getting rid of them is best left to professionals, but you can do it yourself by puffing insecticide powder or desiccant dust into the entrance hole. Over time, workers will carry the dust back to the queen and the other workers, and they'll all die off. Don't use wasp and hornet freeze—it could send them into the house.

**A Fine Mess**

Never plug the opening to a wall nest after you treat it. The insects could try to chew their way out to escape their fate.

# Paper Wasps

Paper wasps can be identified by their unique, umbrella-shaped nests, which they typically build under eaves and ledges. They're not as aggressive as yellow jackets or bald-faced hornets, which makes them fairly easy to get rid of. Over-the-counter wasp and hornet spray works fine for this.

Again, it's best to attack paper wasp nests at night, but you can also do it during the day. Just don't stand right under the nest when you spray it, as the wasps will drop right out and possibly sting you. Wait a day to make sure the colony is destroyed, then knock or cut down the nest.

Because paper wasps aren't as aggressive, you might be able to skip the spray if it's a small nest. Just slip a large, heavy plastic garbage bag around it. Seal it up, cut the nest from the tree, and freeze it or let it sit out in the sun. The wasps will die in a day or two.

**In the Nick of Time**

Nests should always be taken down after colonies are destroyed. Doing so will keep away other scavenger insects, such as ants and carpet beetles.

# No-Worry Wasps

Mud daubers are a type of wasp that rarely stings, so they typically aren't a problem. They build nests that look like mud tubes—hence the name—on the sides of buildings, under decks, in garages, and in other spots. If you see a mud dauber nest, check for holes in the chambers. If you see them, you definitely don't need to do anything because the adult wasps have already left.

Mexican honey wasps, also called Mexican bees, store honey like honeybees do but build paper nests. These wasps are very docile and typically won't cause a problem unless their nest is in a high-traffic area. Then you might want to consider removing the nest.

# Hard-to-Hate Honeybees

It's hard not to love honeybees. They're cute, they're the epitome of industriousness, and they make honey, one of nature's tastiest foods. But it's best to love them at a distance. Fortunately, doing so isn't a problem most of the time.

A bee or two will sometimes forage for food inside human dwellings. If you leave them alone, they'll go about their business and eventually leave. These foragers aren't much of a threat, as there's nothing for them to defend.

Swarms of honeybees, on the other hand, can be a real problem. Most of the time, swarms will end up in a new home far away from yours. But not always. They can also take up residence in wall voids, attics, or chimneys.

If a swarm happens to cluster on something in your yard—a fence, a tree, your mailbox, whatever—it's typically not a cause for concern. They'll usually move along when their scouts find a suitable relocation spot. However, if you're concerned about them deciding that your home is where they want to live, you may want to eliminate them.

Beekeepers will sometimes collect swarms. Calling your county extension office or local police department might put you in touch with someone who does it in your area. If you do locate a local beekeeper, don't be surprised if you have to pay to have the bees removed. If you live in an area where African bees have put down roots, you might be told that you're on your own.

If you can't find someone to collect the bees, you've got a couple of options. You can take defensive measures to keep them out of your house, or you can kill them.

## Going on the Defensive

Bees like to nest in protected locations or cavities. To keep them from coming in, you'll have to block every possible entryway, including …

- Cracks and crevices around window frames, doorframes, etc.
- Access holes for pipes or electric wires.
- Weep holes in bricks.

Swarms that haven't found a home can be controlled with soapy water. To do so, mix 1 cup of liquid soap or detergent in 1 gallon of water. Load the mixture in a hand sprayer or a hose-end applicator designed for spraying trees and shrubs. Apply quickly, and soak the swarm thoroughly. This will drown them. Only use this approach if you feel sure you can completely and thoroughly cover the swarm. If you can't, it's not worth taking the risk of getting stung.

**A Fine Mess**

If bees have already established a nest inside a wall, don't attempt to suffocate them by blocking their entrance. Doing so might make them search for an alternative exit. If they find one and make their way into living areas, they'll sting to protect their nest.

## Chemical Control

Bees can be killed with any number of insecticides labeled for this use. If you do it yourself, be sure to wear protective clothing. If you're spraying a nest, apply a second treatment about a week after the first, or before you go after the nest.

## Bees in the House

Bees that have taken up residence inside a wall must be killed as soon as possible, as they'll quickly build combs for raising their young and storing honey. Injectable dusts are recommended for doing this. Also recommended: hiring a professional.

If the bees have been in the wall longer than a week or so, you can count on having to open up the wall to remove the nest and the dead bees. Leaving it in place will not only attract other pests, the comb and honey will stain your walls.

# On the Fly

Houseflies are such danged nasty pests that it's hard to believe that they are considered beneficial bugs in nature, but they are. As decomposers of dead and decaying vegetation and organisms, they perform a vital function. They're also an important part of the food chain, serving as a food source for birds, reptiles, fish, and even some kinds of plants.

**Around the House**

Houseflies are often called "filth flies," and for good reason. They chow down on nasty things—garbage, manure, dead animals, and the like. These also serve as breeding and egg-laying sites.

Because flies often feed on filth, they can harm people and animals by spreading diseases such as dysentery or typhoid fever. They can also contaminate food and cause food poisoning and/or diarrhea. When feeding, some flies—most notably stable flies and mosquitoes, which fall into the same order—can also inflict painful bites.

Most flies prefer to spend their time outdoors, but a handful of species have found human structures preferable to living in the wild. There are two categories of these pests:

- Household-infesting flies, which breed and complete their life cycles indoors when they can find favorable breeding spots.
- Household-invading flies. These flies breed and develop outdoors, but come inside during certain times of the year.

**A Fine Mess**

Think a few flies aren't that big of a deal? Think again. One fly can carry more than 4 million bacteria on its body and over 28 million in its stomach.

Experts recommend identifying the species that is invading your home. Doing so is key to figuring out what's causing the infestation and helps pinpoint IPM measures. This is a good idea and will put you in control faster, but simply following a good IPM plan will accomplish the same goals. It just might take a little longer.

Here's a quick description of the different categories and the species in each, just in case you do want to take the focused approach. The ones you're most likely to encounter lead off each list:

House-infesting flies:

- Housefly. The most common fly pest around homes. They lay eggs on wet decaying organic matter, on animal manure, and in rotting plant debris.
- Blow fly. Shiny, metallic flies. They lay their eggs on dead animal carcasses, decaying meat, and garbage that contains meat scraps. Called blow flies because their larvae develop inside dead animals, causing the carcasses to bloat.
- Fruit fly. Tiny tan flies with red eyes. More of a problem during the fall, they reproduce and develop on overripe and rotting fruit, vegetables, and other moist plant material. They'll also feed in drains where organic debris has been allowed to accumulate.

- Phorid fly. Very small fly that flies with its back legs hanging down. They like to lay eggs on rotting vegetables, fruit, or meat; potted plants; wet organic soil and cut flowers; and in garbage disposals and floor drains.
- Drain fly. Also called moth, sewer, or filter flies. They breed in the organic material that can build up inside drainpipes. If you have flies in your bathroom, they're probably these.

House-invading flies:

- Cluster fly. Not filth flies, but a common indoor pest. Dark gray flies, about the same size as blow flies. They're slow flyers and smell like honey when swatted. Adult flies overwinter in the top floors or attics of homes, typically choosing the south- and west facing walls where they can stay warm. On warm days they'll invade indoor spaces and collect en mass at windows, often in rooms that aren't used regularly.
- Face fly. These flies resemble houseflies. They pester cattle during the summer and overwinter in wall voids. Adults will emerge from attics and walls during warm days. They're typically more of a problem in rural areas, especially in homes near pastures or where cattle are kept.
- Flesh fly. These flies are gray with black stripes. They feed on animal carcasses, compost piles, and garbage dumpsters.
- Stable fly. Also called biting houseflies, they feed on the blood of warm-blooded animals, including humans. Their bite is painful, most often incurred around the ankles, and they'll even bite through clothing in their quest for blood. Adults lay eggs in decaying vegetation, including rotting straw, grass clippings, compost piles, and decaying fruit and vegetables.
- Fungus gnat.These flies resemble tiny mosquitoes. They feed on fungi, which they find in over-watered plants and pigeon feces. Light attracts them, and they'll come inside at night through open doors and windows.

# IPM for Flies

Three IPM approaches—sanitation, inspection, and exclusion—are most effective when battling flies. Mechanical measures are also helpful; however, if you do a good job with the first steps, you may not need to do much more.

As mentioned, chemical control is the last resort for flies. It works, but it simply isn't as effective as other measures.

## Sanitation

As previously detailed, almost all flies are attracted to filth, which they both eat and lay eggs in.

Most sanitation efforts are pretty obvious. It's always a good idea to manage garbage, yard, and garden wastes appropriately and to remove animal carcasses from your yard as soon as you see them.

Some sanitation approaches aren't as obvious. Cleaning household drains on a regular basis, for example, is the best way to battle drain and phorid flies.

> **In the Nick of Time**
>
> Having a hard time figuring out where fruit flies are coming from? Check your drains. Put some tape over the opening, leaving a little space for airflow. If you find flies on the tape, they're coming from the drain.

Other sanitation approaches include …

- Using garbage cans with tight-fitting lids. Line them with garbage can liners to keep waste from accumulating in the bottom or clinging to the sides. Clean the cans when they get dirty.
- Covering compost piles with black plastic sheeting. House flies, stable flies, fruit flies, blowflies, and gnats all breed in them. Covering piles not only keeps flies out, it helps organic matter decompose faster.
- Picking up animal waste regularly. It's best to pick up after your pets right after potty time. If you can't, don't let waste sit for too long, especially when it's warm out.
- Don't let fruit and/or vegetables rot in your garden. Harvest everything promptly and remove all decaying plant material regularly.

## Inspection

If fly problems continue, you'll need to look for fly-breeding sites that sanitation didn't eliminate. Knowing the species you're battling can be a big help here, as you'll only have to look for the substances that attract those flies.

Inspect your home and your grounds thoroughly. Be sure to check attics and crawl spaces for dead animals. Also, check eaves and rafters for bird activity. If you see evidence of it, turn to Chapter 21 for more help.

## Exclusion

You can do everything possible to manage fly-breeding sites indoors and out and still have problems with housc-invading flies, as some of them are attracted to things other than filth.

> **Around the House**
>
> House-invading flies typically come indoors when the seasons change, and especially when there's a big difference between indoor and outdoor temperatures. Hot air lures them indoors when it's cold outside; cold air lures them indoors when it's hot.

House invaders will come inside anywhere they sense a temperature difference. The only way to prevent them from doing so is to eliminate those differences. Here's how:

- Install screens on all doors and windows, and use them. Make sure all screens fit tightly and are free of tears and holes. Inspect them regularly to make sure they stay that way.
- Screen all exterior vents. Screening with 14 to 16 strands per inch is effective for most flies, but may not keep out smaller species.
- Seal all cracks and crevices on the outside of your home with caulking or foam.
- Make sure all weather stripping around doors is in good shape. If it isn't, replace it. If you can see the light around a door, a fly will be able to sense the temperature difference.

If there are lots of flies around, keep chimney flues closed as well.

## Mechanical Controls

Swatting is one of the best-known ways to eliminate flies, but it's not very efficient. Trapping them on flypaper is another time-tested mechanical approach. While flypaper isn't pretty, it does do the job. Hang strips where flies are peskiest. A standard rule of thumb is one 10-inch strip for 1,000 cubic feet of space. There's a product similar to flypaper that you can mount on glass doors and windows. Since it's clear, it isn't as obvious as flypaper, and it does a good job of attracting and trapping all light-loving insects.

Outdoor flytraps are also available. These devices contain an attractant that lures the flies. For best results, hang them in full sun and low to the ground away from your house.

Ultraviolet light traps can be very effective for controlling some flies, especially those that fly at night. Proper placement is key for these traps. They need to be positioned where they can't be seen from outside, and in the fly zone—no more than 5 feet above the floor. Place away from food-preparation areas and other light sources.

## Chemical Controls

As previously mentioned, insecticides are the last resort when battling flies. If necessary, use one or more of the following:

- Hang fly strips with pesticides in attics and/or small, unoccupied rooms where flies are a problem.
- Place fly bait outdoors where flies gather. You'll have to replace these if they come into contact with water.
- Spot-treat outdoor congregation areas with an over-the-counter spray. This will provide quick relief, but no residual effect.
- Apply a residual spray outdoors, again where flies hang out. You might need to hire a pest-control expert to do this, as the best chemicals are only available to licensed pest-management professionals.

> CAUTION
>
> **A Fine Mess**
>
> Fly baits should only be used in hanging stations, as they can be very toxic to pets and children. A pet that ingests fly bait will not live long enough to get to the vet.

The last approach is especially useful if done before house-invading flies look for places to stay for the winter.

## The Least You Need to Know

- IPM is the most effective way to deal with flying and stinging insects.
- When controlling stingers, sometimes rely more heavily on insecticides to protect people and animals from bites.

- Never take on a hornet or wasp nest without wearing protective clothing. Better bets: Hire a pest-control expert or leave the nests alone if they're in out-of-the-way areas.
- Sanitation, inspection, and exclusion are the best IPM measures for flies.

# Chapter 20

# Out, Out, Damn Flea!

## In This Chapter

- Life and death of a flea
- Where fleas are found
- Pet controls
- Environmental controls

All dogs and cats scratch. Some more than others. However, if your pet is scratching more than normal, or you're seeing odd little bumps on your ankles or lower legs, fleas might be the culprit.

There are more than 2,000 species of fleas in the world—that we know about, anyway. Of them, only about a dozen or so cause problems for humans and their pets. But they can cause *lots* of problems. Just ask anyone who has ever had to deal with a flea infestation.

## Flea-Bitten?

Many things can make your pet—and you—itchy. But fleas are a common itch producer, so it's easy to conclude that they're the cause of the problem. You may very well be dealing with this particular critter, as they're extremely common, but you need to know for sure.

Here's the fastest way to make this diagnosis: Comb or brush your pet. As you do, look for tiny dark dots or comma-shaped objects. This is "flea dirt"—flea excrement to you and me.

If you've never seen flea dirt before, or you're not sure that what you're seeing is flea dirt (it could be plain old dirt), here's a simple test: Put a damp paper towel under your pet as you comb. If it's flea dirt, you'll see little red dots where the dirt hit. They're from the blood in the dirt.

**A Fine Mess**

Not seeing flea dirt? Don't rule out fleas yet. Bumps on your ankles and lower legs can also point to a flea problem. Bites typically turn into small, red, slightly raised hard spots. Each bite will have a single puncture point in its center, which is how you can distinguish it from ant and spider bites, which have two punctures. Bees, wasps, bedbugs, and mosquitoes also make single-puncture bites, but they raise larger welts.

# Quick to the Kill

Although fleas are one of the peskier infestations you'll ever deal with, it's one that, thanks to modern chemistry, you can attack quickly.

Until fairly recently, insecticide dusts and sprays were the only ways to control fleas. Today, pet owners can choose from several new products that are vastly safer and more effective. If you start using them before flea season begins, you greatly reduce the chances of your having to deal with a flea infestation. If you use them to combat an existing infestation, they can help cut the problem down to size extremely quickly, especially when paired with other eradication efforts.

**A Fine Mess**

For your flea-abatement efforts to be most effective, you'll also need to treat your home and, if you keep your pet outside, your yard. Here's why: Adult fleas aren't your only problem, so killing the ones that are on your pets is only part of the solution. You also have to kill the fleas in their other stages of development. If you don't, you'll have an ongoing infestation that will never quite go away.

## Spot-On Insecticides

Spot-on insecticides (brand names Advantage, Frontline, Top Spot, Revolution) are so-named as they are applied to a single spot on the animal's skin. The best products are available from veterinarians. They contain insecticides that have been found safer than those found in some other flea control products. Some also offer protection against other pet pests, such as heartworms. Using these products is less expensive than dosing with separate flea and heartworm preventatives.

You can also buy these products from national pet pharmacies. This can be convenient, but the costs are typically similar, if not more, than what you'll pay in most vet clinics.

Some spot-on products are available at pet stores, home stores, and other retail outlets. These products contain older insecticides that can cause problems in both animals and humans, such as numbness, tingling and burning sensations on the skin, and asthmalike reactions in hay fever sufferers. They've also been classified as possible carcinogens.

> CAUTION
>
> **A Fine Mess**
>
> Always ask your vet's advice before buying or using any flea control products. Some are definitely safer than others. And never use products on cats that are designed for dogs, and vice versa. A product that's safe for Rover might not be for Miss Kitty.

Although these products are significantly cheaper than the others, toxicity concerns make them a poor choice. They're also not as effective as other products.

If you've never used a spot-on product, it's a good idea to talk to your vet about the one that's right for your pets. You may want to have your vet administer the first treatment, as effectiveness depends on getting the product on your pet correctly.

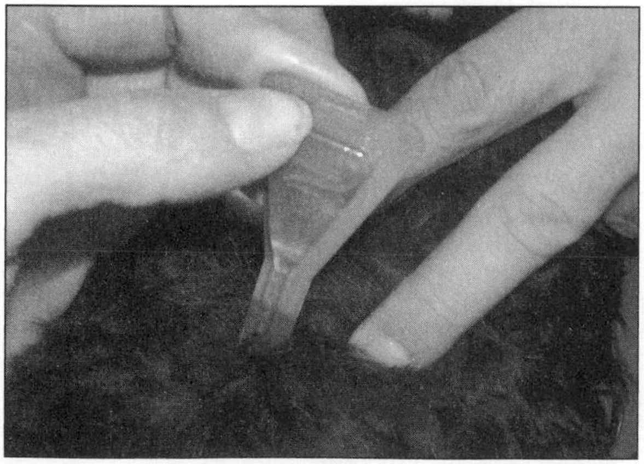

*Applying a spot-on flea killer is as easy as parting your pet's hair in between its shoulders and squeezing a vial of liquid directly onto its skin. Make sure the tip of the vial makes good contact with the animal's skin. Be sure to apply the entire contents of the vial to your pet.*

## Insect Growth Regulators

Insect growth regulators (IGRs) interrupt flea life cycles by messing with their hormones. They make the eggs of female fleas sterile and prevent flea larvae that haven't entered their pupae stage from maturing into adult fleas. As such, they'll prevent the next generation of fleas from developing, but they won't kill fleas that are already on your pet or around your house.

IGRs are available from veterinarians as sprays, spot-ons, or in collars. They are also available though pest control operators for indoor and outdoor application. Some operators also carry IGR products that can be used on pets.

## Insect Development Inhibitors

Similar to IGRs, insect development inhibitors also disrupt egg and larval development. When adult fleas chomp down on your pet, they ingest a substance that essentially acts as birth control for fleas. It won't stop you from seeing adults, but it does stop new generations from being born. They're available from vets as a once-a-month treatment administered in pill or liquid form.

## Washing the Problem

Other flea-control products such as shampoos and dips also get rid of fleas. However, some of these products contain insecticides that have been linked to certain health and toxicity concerns.

CAUTION

**A Fine Mess**

Studies show that flea-control products containing organophosphate insectides and carbamates are potentially toxic and can produce unwanted side effects in pets. It's a good idea to avoid any products with labels listing the following: chlorpyrifos, dichlorvos, phosmet, naled, diazinon, tetrachlorvinphos, malathion, carbaryl, and propoxur).

These products will kill the majority of the fleas on your pet and help quell the itching. However, most of them have no residual effect, which means you'll have to do something else to control the fleas. Oftentimes, this means applying a flea dip every few days or so.

These products also take longer to be effective, and, over time, end up costing more than newer products do. If you have multiple pets, you'll also end up spending a considerable amount of time bathing and dipping them.

If you feel you must go this route, talk to your vet and get his or her recommendations for the appropriate products to use and how to apply them.

# Treating Your Environs

As mentioned, the best way to deal with flea infestations is to prevent them from happening, which is something that many pet owners realize a little too late. One of the most effective preventive measures is to start using preventive products before flea and tick season starts.

All is not lost if treatment begins after fleas and ticks become a problem. However, since the critters have had a chance to gain a foothold, they'll be all around. As such, most vets—pest-control specialists, too—recommend taking additional steps to bring the infestation to an end.

## Cleaning Up

It's always a good idea to clean pet bedding and resting areas on a regular basis. Doing so is especially important if you're battling a flea infestation. You won't need any special equipment for this beyond a good multipurpose cleaner, a washer and dryer, clothes detergent, and your vacuum. Toss all washable bedding into your washer, and wash it in warm to hot water. When clean, stick it in the dryer. Do not air dry.

If bedding isn't washable, vacuum it thoroughly.

**Around the House**

If your animals sleep on your bed or your kids' beds, wash all bedding materials from them, too. Fleas can't survive the wash cycle.

Next, clean the hard surfaces where your pet sleeps or rests. If they're carpeted, vacuum them thoroughly. If they're not, wash them down with your all-purpose cleaner, applied with rags or mop. If you use rags, wash them with the bedding. If you use a mop, discard the mop head after you're done.

## Insecticide Control

Infestations also call for treating your home with an insecticide. The most effective also contain an IGR. Given the expense involved and concerns over handling chemicals, many people prefer to have a professional apply insecticides both indoors and outdoors, but you can do it yourself. If you decide to hire a professional, make sure you specify that your home needs to be treated for fleas. The approach for doing so is very different than spraying for other pests.

> **A Fine Mess**
>
> Insecticides can be toxic to people; all products should be handled with care. Always follow label instructions and avoid direct contact with skin; wear gloves and a mask when mixing and spraying. Keep all products out of the reach of children.

> **In the Nick of Time**
>
> Steam cleaning and applying borates to carpets are two environmentally safe and effective approaches for controlling fleas indoors. Steam cleaning not only destroys fleas, even those that haven't hatched, it also removes the partially digested blood that's the food source for flea larvae. Borates—boric acid and borax—are worked deep into carpet fibers, where they create an unfavorable environment for fleas. Choose products registered for fleas, and be sure to test a small area first as boric acid can discolor some carpets.

If you decide to do it yourself, choose an aerosol or spray product over a bomb or fogger. Coverage can be spotty with the latter, and they're not as effective if they don't contain an IGR.

Before you spray—whether you do it or hire someone else—arrange to have all people and animals out of the house. They'll need to stay out for at least one to two hours—possibly more—after treatment as well. Vacuum your house before you start. This will pick up about 60 percent of the flea eggs, about 27 percent of the flea larvae, some adult fleas, and flea dirt. After you're done, immediately take the vacuum cleaner outside and discard the bag. Don't do it indoors. The tiniest spill can redeposit everything you're trying to get rid of.

If you're treating the house yourself, don gloves and your facemask. Follow all the label directions. Spray everywhere, but pay particular attention to the areas where your pet spends the most time. Also spray any pet bedding that you didn't wash.

Don't reenter the house until the insecticide is dry. When it's dry, vacuum again to remove any fleas that have hatched. They'll keep emerging for about two weeks after treatment as the insecticide won't kill fleas in their pupae stage.

Depending on the product, you might have to retreat. Follow the label directions for doing this.

## Outdoor Control

To be on the safe side, it's also a good idea to spray the area surrounding your house. Again, you might want to hire a professional exterminator for this, especially if you have a large yard or are battling a severe infestation. These people are specially licensed to use insecticides that aren't available to homeowners, and will have the necessary equipment to do a thorough treatment.

If you do this step yourself, be sure to don your protective equipment. Long pants, a hat, and a long-sleeved shirt will protect you from any sprayback or drifting that might occur. Again, your best choices are products that contain IGRs. Spray thoroughly everywhere, with particular emphasis on where your pet or other animals hang out, as well as under porches, crawl spaces, inside garages or sheds, or under pet homes. All are areas where fleas typically hang out. Follow the label directions carefully. Depending on the product you use, a repeat treatment might be necessary in a few weeks.

If you don't want to spray, or simply want an easier option, look for granular insecticides labeled for outdoor use against fleas and ticks.

If it's growing season, cut down weeds and trim your shrubs. This will better expose flea eggs and larvae to sun and water, which are both effective flea desiccants. If you aren't under watering restrictions, give your lawn and any shrubs around your house a good dousing, which will drown some of the fleas in these areas.

Wash down any hard surfaces where your pet hangs out with a mild detergent. If there is bedding outdoors, vacuum it or wash it (bring it in before you tackle the indoors to avoid recontamination).

If you're dealing with a heavy infestation, treat your yard as above.

Now that your immediate problem is on its way to being solved, let's take a closer look at why it happened. Gaining a better understanding of fleas and their behavior will help you be more vigilant about dealing with them in the future. And that's a good thing for you, your pets, and everyone else who comes to your home.

# Meet the Flea

**Around the House**

People spend more than $1 billion annually controlling fleas.

Like most pests, fleas are something that typically don't occupy a huge space on our radar screens until they become a problem. However, if you're a pet owner, chances are good that you'll have to deal with fleas at some point during the course of your ownership.

Fleas are often the butt of jokes and unkind remarks. As such, they often seem more of an irritation than anything else—but they can cause big problems.

## Scratching the Itch

Scratching is a customary aspect of pet behavior and grooming, and fleas make pets scratch, so it might not seem like they're that big of a deal. But they are. Although flea bites themselves are fairly innocuous—many pets and their owners don't even feel them when they occur—the irritation that results from the bites can be a real problem.

Everyone reacts to flea bites a bit differently. Depending on how sensitive the skin is, a single bite can cause immense discomfort or none at all.

Some people, and pets, suffer greatly when bitten and develop severe reactions, such as rashes and inflammation, which can escalate into secondary infections from scratching.

Inflammation and infections are nothing to take lightly. Unfortunately, they're the least of your concerns when fleas are hopping around.

## More Serious Health Concerns

Fleas can also cause more serious problems for pets and their owners, including:

- Dog tapeworms, which can infest dogs and cats. Humans can get it, too, by accidentally consuming parts of an infested flea. How could this happen? Let's say your little nipper played with a flea-infested cat and didn't wash her hands after playtime was over. You can take it from here. Dog tapeworms cause intestinal discomfort and diarrhea but are easily treated.

- Bubonic plague. Rat fleas can transmit it from rodent to rodent, and to humans. If you're a history buff, you might remember how this disease periodically ravaged populations, especially during the 14th, 15th, and 16th centuries. If you think it's a thing of the past, think again. The World Health Organization reports 1,000 to 3,000 cases of plague every year.

- Typhoid fever. Another ancient rodent-transmitted disease, but still a problem today. An estimated 16 million cases of typhoid fever cause 600,000 deaths annually around the world.

Those itches and scratches don't seem like such a small thing now, do they?

# Why Fleas Happen

Fleas are always around. They're part and parcel of our environment. But they like certain surroundings and conditions better than others. People and pets who live in certain parts of the United States, such as the desert Southwest, don't have as many problems with fleas as do those who live in the Midwest or the Deep South, where conditions are ripe for flea infestations. Why? Because fleas love humidity and warm temperatures.

**Around the House**

Adult cat fleas, which are the most common fleas that infest pets (both dogs and cats), spend virtually their entire lives on their hosts and can lay as many as 30 eggs a day.

Give fleas the right environment—humidity levels above 70 percent, temperatures ranging from 65 to 80 degrees—and they can be extremely prolific breeders. When conditions are favorable in the flea kingdom, they can complete an entire reproductive cycle in as few as 16 days. Couple prolific breeding with the fact that an adult flea can live for several months without a meal, and you've got a recipe for infestation.

One other factor has to be in place for that infestation to happen. Although fleas can go for months without eating, female fleas have to eat before they lay their eggs. Their favorite food? Blood.

**A Fine Mess**

Fleas prefer meals from cats or dogs. They typically can't complete a life cycle on human blood. This doesn't mean they won't go for it, though, especially if other hosts are in short supply.

As mentioned, the best way to control fleas is to prevent them from gaining a foothold in the first place. But this isn't always possible. Take a midwinter trip to somewhere warm with Fido, and he could come back with fleas. Let

Ms. Kitty stay with Grandma (who doesn't believe in flea-control products and would never use them on her babies) while you're away, and she could come back with them, too.

# Defensive Measures

As previously mentioned, the best way to deal with a flea infestation is to prevent it from happening. The following tips will help protect your pets and your home.

Pet defenses:

- Use spot-on insecticides and IGRs during flea season. This is the best approach you can take for both cats and dogs.
- Minimize exposure to fleas by having your pets sleep indoors. Keep them in one area instead of letting them roam about. This will help keep the flea population in one place, and make control efforts easier.
- Spray your pet's sleeping area with a flea repellent. You can find these products at veterinarian clinics, home stores, and other retailers.

Environmental defenses:

- Vacuum pet areas at least twice a week. Discard vacuum bag promptly.
- Exclude pets from carpeted areas so fleas are not a problem there from the start.
- Keep grass mowed and shrubs trimmed. If neighborhood animals tend to hang around your house, remove items and substances that can attract them as much as possible. This can be difficult if your pets spend most of their time outdoors. Consider an enclosed kennel for dogs. Keep cats indoors.

# Questionable Control Measures

Do a little checking around on fleas, and you'll probably come across a bunch of suggestions for products and approaches that don't involve chemicals, or that use minimal amounts of them. A few are somewhat effective. Most aren't. They include …

- Flea traps. There's no evidence to show that flea traps do anything to control flea populations. However, they can be an effective tool for monitoring adult flea levels.

- Ultrasonic pest-repelling devices. Shown to be completely useless. Don't waste your money.
- Natural dietary supplements such as brewers yeast, thiamin, sulfur, garlic, etc. None are scientifically proven for flea control, although lots of pet owners swear by garlic.
- Plants and the oils derived from them, including fresh bayberry, pennyroyal, eucalyptus, tea tree, rosemary, and citronella. Again, there's little to no scientific support for any of them.

Flea collars—the old-fashioned ones that don't contain IGRs—are another questionable control measure that, sadly, many people rely on as they're cheap and readily available. They contain an insecticide that pets distribute through their fur when they groom themselves. Most don't contain enough of the insecticide to do much good, and they don't last very long.

## The Least You Need to Know

- There are more than 2,000 species of fleas in the world. Of them, a dozen or so cause problems for humans and pets.
- Newer flea-control products do an effective job of keeping fleas under control without the harmful side effects of older products.
- The best way to avoid flea problems is to prevent them from happening.
- IGRs are effective flea eradicators but can take up to several weeks to destroy all fleas.

## Chapter 21

# Bats (and Birds) in the Belfry

### In This Chapter

- Winged worries
- Going bats
- Scare tactics
- Net effects

Winged things—birds and bats—play a major role in just about every story or movie about a haunted or abandoned house. But their love for human abodes isn't just the stuff of fiction. And they don't limit their invasions to creepy or unoccupied buildings.

Both birds and bats can, and do, take up residence where they're least welcome—in attics, under eaves, and in other favorable nesting and roosting spots. And they can cause lots of problems when they do.

If you're dealing with one winged intruder—or lots of them—this chapter is for you.

# Solo Intruders

Although bats and birds are in two completely different biological classes—bats are mammals and birds aren't—the problems they cause and the approaches for dealing with them are similar in many ways, which is why we're addressing them together.

> **A Fine Mess**
>
> All bats and birds can be carriers of diseases and other organisms that are best not to come into contact with. Never touch any of them with your bare hands. If you have to handle one for any reason, wear thick gloves, preferably made of leather.

The occasional bird or bat that gets trapped in a house typically isn't a big deal, and it usually isn't a disaster. However, it can be a little alarming and more than a little frightening, for both you and the animal.

As such, it's important to get the animal out of your house as soon as you can and with the least amount of trauma to it, your home, and its occupants.

## Corralling a Bird

Birds typically get trapped in houses in one of two ways—either they fly in an open door or window, or they come in through a fireplace or roof vent. Here's what to do if you see one flapping around your house:

- Close all exits to the room except one. Leave that one open. Darken the room by covering all windows and doors except the one you're leaving open. The bird will eventually fly toward the light source and out of your home. If necessary, keep the bird moving by throwing small, soft objects at it or nudging it with a stick.
- If you're trying to evict a bird during the night, put a bright light—car headlights or a strong flashlight will work—outside the exit door or window to attract it.
- If you can't open an exit, and the bird is still flying, try knocking it down with something—a broom, a tennis racket, a fishing net, anything that you can reach it with. Once the bird is down, put an empty bucket, can, or wastebasket over it. Slide a piece of cardboard under to contain it.

Most birds can be driven to an exit with an inexpensive laser pointer light. An extra bonus: these lights work day or night.

If you find a bird lying on the floor of a room in your house, and you can provide an exit for it, do so and leave the room. Keep children and pets away. If it's able to fly, it eventually will. If it can't, follow the same containment approach as outlined in the previous list.

If the bird appears sick or injured, don't take matters into your own hands. Call a wildlife rehabilitator immediately. This individual will either help the bird or destroy it. A good source of information is the Wildlife Rehabilitation Information Directory, on the web at www.tc.umn.edu/~devo0028/#aa.

If the bird is dead, and you live in an area where *West Nile virus* is a concern, DO NOT TOUCH IT WITH YOUR BARE HANDS! Contact your local health department to report it, and ask them for instructions on disposing it. There is a handy chart for finding these departments at the Centers for Disease Control website, www.cdc.gov/ncidod/dvbid/westnile/city_states.htm.

**Around the House**

Wild birds can get sick, but most bird diseases can't be transmitted directly from birds to humans. As such, the chance of contracting a disease from handling a wild bird is remote, but it's still a good idea to take precautions, especially if the bird is dead.

**Tool Chest**

West Nile virus (WNV) is a potentially fatal disease that is transmitted by mosquitoes that have fed on birds infected with the virus. Symptoms of the disease include headache, fever, tiredness, body aches, and occasionally a skin rash. The illness can be as short as a few days or last as long as several weeks. Some people develop no symptoms when infected with WNV.

## Birds in the Chimney

Chimneys are a common entry point for some birds. If there's one in yours, you'll hear flapping wings during the day as the bird tries to fly toward the light at the top of the structure. If there's something there to impede its exit, however, you have a trapped bird, and you'll need to get it to come out through the fireplace.

To capture a bird caught in a chimney:

1. Open the damper.
2. Place a large box or clothes basket in the chimney opening. You might have to place something under it to get the box close enough to the opening.
3. Keep the room quiet.

4. When the bird enters the box, slip a piece of cardboard over the top. Take the box outdoors and release the bird.

**Around the House**

Birds can safely be released after capture. However, in accordance with federal laws under the Migratory Bird Act of 1918, it's illegal to destroy them unless they're a non-native species, such as house sparrows, European starlings, and pigeons. It's also illegal to relocate or possess them, their nests, or their eggs.

## Battling a Bat

Like single birds, a solitary bat isn't that much of a concern. However, you'll want to get it out of your house as soon as you can. Although rare, bats can carry rabies, which is transmitted through bites and scratches.

**A Fine Mess**

If nothing knocked a bat to the ground, but you find one there, there's a good chance that it's sick or injured. Do not handle it with your bare hands. A healthy bat is far less likely to bite or scratch than a sick one is, but never take a chance. Always handle them with care.

Young bats occasionally enter homes in the early evening when they're seeking shelter or a hiding place. Once inside, they will do their best to escape. The best thing you can do is help them along. Simply leave open only those doors and windows that lead outside. The bat will be attracted to the fresh air and will eventually wing its way out.

Keep in mind, however, that bats are usually asleep during the day and active during the evening. If you want the bat to leave on its own, you'll need to leave it alone during the day and make sure the room it's in gets dark enough so the bat will know it's time to leave.

If the first method didn't work, you can try to trap or net the bat and release it outdoors. There are a couple of different ways to do this:

- Use a small container such as a box or can. Place it over the bat and carefully slide a piece of hard cardboard under it. Take the trapped bat outside and release it.
- Throw a light blanket or sheet over the bat. Do this gently; bats are fragile and should be handled with care. Gather up the sheet with the bat inside and take it outside for release.

- Get a tube from a roll of paper towels. Seal one end with heavy tape. Leave the other end open. Place the tube horizontally next to the bat. Bats like to hide in dark places; the idea here is that the bat will embrace the tube as a cozy little bat cave. If it does, put a heavy piece of cardboard over the opening and take the tube and bat outside.

As mentioned, a single bat or bird isn't much of a concern. However, both species can take up residence in your home and cause some serious problems.

# Bats—Good and Bad

For the most part, bats are a good thing. They eat bugs—many of them of the noxious or pest variety—and their feces, or guano, makes wonderful fertilizer. However, there aren't too many people who would want to share their living quarters with these little creatures. And there are some good reasons for not doing so.

It is possible to contract diseases from bats. Rabies, of course, is the best known, but is actually a rare concern with bats, as very few carry the disease and they typically won't bite unless they're royally pissed off. That said, cats and dogs do risk infection if they pick up diseased bats, so it's a good idea to keep their rabies vaccinations up to date.

Histoplasmosis, a fungal disease that can be transmitted by inhaling the dust from dried bat manure (bird manure can contain the pathogens, too), is more of a concern, especially for people with immune disorders.

Bats—or, better put, the large amount of urine and feces they produce—can also cause odor problems and can damage wood. And young bats can drive you batty (sorry for the pun) as they will squeak without stopping if the females are away from the nest.

Bats are also secondary pest transmitters. Most bat colonies harbor bat bugs, an insect that is so similar to bedbugs it takes an expert to distinguish between the two. Where large bat colonies exist and then are forced to leave, the bat bugs will often invade the house, looking for a blood meal from the human occupants.

There are approximately 900 bat species in the world, with about 40 of them found in the United States and Canada. Most prefer natural roosts like hollow trees and cracks in rocks, but some species, especially in urban areas, will make their homes in attics, the areas behind shutters, and even downspouts. Because bats are loyal to their birthplaces, they'll return to the same roosting site year after year. Since they can live more than 10 years, this can be a real problem if allowed to continue.

Like most other pests, the best long-term solution for dealing with bats is keeping them out of your home and in the wild where they belong. With bats, however, it's about the only solution. Chemicals only work when they can be applied in small areas where their fumes can accumulate. Even then, their effect is temporary at best. As the fumes weaken, the bats will come back.

Other remedies, such as scattering mothballs where bats roost or installing ultrasonic devices, have not proven to be effective. It can take up to 5 pounds of mothballs to create a strong enough odor to keep bats from returning to their roost, and you have to keep on refreshing your supply for the best success. Ultrasonic devices may actually attract them.

**In the Nick of Time**

Bat-to-human transmission of rabies is extremely rare but not entirely unheard of. If you spend a lot of time working in attics or exploring caves where bats hang out, consider being immunized against rabies.

# Bat-Proofing Your Cave

To keep bats out of your home, you first have to determine where they're coming in. Bats can squeeze into very small spaces—literally the size of your thumb—which is why it can be difficult to exclude them, but it isn't impossible if you can locate their entry spots.

The following areas are common bat-entry sites:

- Chimneys, including the flashing around them
- Flashing and fascia on other parts of structures
- Window frames
- Roofing, including ridge caps and roof vents
- Soffits and soffit vents
- Electrical and plumbing conduits

One way to detect bat entrances is by their feces. If you find musty-smelling droppings on the ground or stuck to the outside of your house, there's a good chance bats left them there. Look up from the guano spot, and you'll probably spot the entrance to their roost. If it's been in use for even a little while, the edges of the opening should have turned dark brown from the oil and dirt that rubs off the bats' bodies as they enter and exit their roost.

**Around the House**

Bat and bird problems are considered infestations. As such, they aren't covered by most homeowner's insurance policies. If defects in construction or products allowed the animals to enter your home, you could be protected under a new home or existing home warranty. Check with your builder or the policy issuer.

If you don't see openings marked like this, the droppings might be from birds or mice. If you want to know for sure, crush the droppings (not recommended, by the way, unless you're wearing a face mask, as you could inhale harmful microorganisms from the dust). If you find undigested insect parts, you have bats. Unlike mouse droppings, bat droppings are soft and crush easily. They're always dark and never look white like bird droppings can.

**In the Nick of Time**

One of the easiest and quickest ways to find bat entrances is by watching for them at night (you might lose a little shut-eye, though). Since they're nocturnal, they'll leave their roosts just before dark and return just before dawn. Pick the time that's best for you, and go on bat watch for a few days. It should tell you what you need to know.

Indoors, listen for squeaks and rustles in suspect areas. Baby bats will squeak nonstop when mama bats leave the nest.

# Ruling the Roost

Once you've figured out where bats are roosting, you can take steps to eliminate them. There are two optimum times for doing so: in the spring before migratory bats return to roost, and in the fall as they leave for the winter. Timing is important here; you don't want to trap baby bats inside your home, as they'll die. When they do, their carcasses will cause odor and insect problems.

Because bats don't chew through materials, you can use just about anything you have as barriers. However, anything you use must be anchored securely as bats will push aside shoddy workmanship.

No matter what you use, be sure to give the bats one escape route until you're sure they've all flown the belfry. Why? Not all bats leave the roost every night. If you were to seal off all entrances, you'll trap some of them inside. Not only is this the kiss of death, especially for baby bats, but trapped bats will typically seek alternative exits and come out inside of buildings.

However, you do want to make sure all bats that left can't get back inside. Building a one-way bat door will do it. Here's how:

1. Choose your material. Polypropylene netting, also called bird netting, is simple to use, widely available, and very effective. You can buy it at a hardware or home-improvement store. A heavy plastic garbage bag is another option. Just remember: You want a pretty decent length of either material, enough so it will drape down under its own weight but not so long that the bats can't come through.
2. If you're using a bag, cut both ends away. If you're using netting, tape or staple the edges together to make a tube.
3. Install the bat door by taping or stapling it in place around the entrance to the roost.

> CAUTION
>
> **A Fine Mess**
>
> Never try to eliminate a bat colony during the summer. This is prime baby bat–rearing season, and you run the risk of trapping youngsters who can't fly yet.

The material will open wide enough for bats to crawl out, but they won't be able to reverse direction and climb back through. Watch the door for several nights. After three to four days, you shouldn't see any more bats coming out. At this point, you can remove the door and seal the entrance.

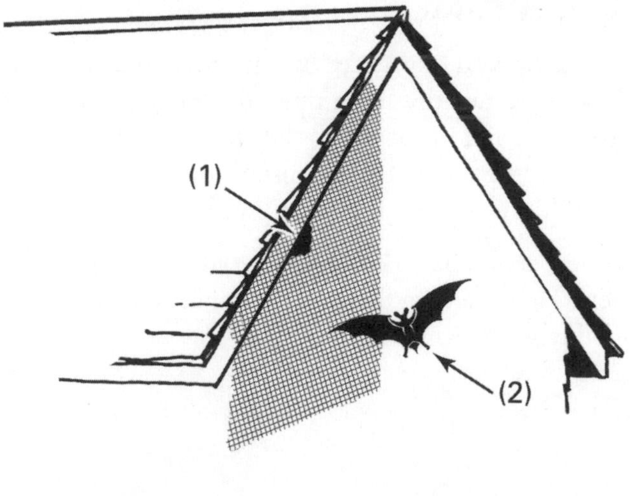


*A one-way bat door. Bats can get out but they can't get back in.*

If you want to hasten their departure, you can apply naphthalene-based chemical repellent to the roosting area. This substance makes it difficult for bats and other small animals to breathe, and will typically make them seek fresh air.

## Caulk It Up

Seal up all small cracks and holes with caulk. Choose a high-quality product that will last a while. You don't want to do this more often than necessary. Be sure to pay special attention to joints and other areas where materials come together.

While you're at it, nail down any loose shingles or facings you come across, since bats can also squeak in under these.

**In the Nick of Time**

You'll need to match the caulk you use with the surface you're applying it to. Some caulks don't adhere to stain or paint that contains silicone, wax, stearate, or paraffin-based oil. Clear silicone caulk doesn't bond well with unfinished cedar siding or shingles. If you're going to paint over the caulk, choose a paintable caulk.

## Screen Shots

Mesh hardware cloth is the material of choice for closing up cracks or holes that are too large for caulk, and for protecting vents that must be kept open. Buy 6-millimeter (0.2-inch) screen and cut it to size—at least 2 inches bigger than the opening you're covering. Nail it into place.

Sheet metal can also be used to cover larger openings, especially those that let the elements in. Again, cut to size, leaving at least a 2-inch margin all around. Nail into place.

## Lights, Camera, Action!

As bats shun light, shining some into an infested attic may motivate them to seek darker digs. This approach works best in early spring when bats return from their hibernation sites, not after they've established a roost.

Lights must be kept on 24/7 and moved regularly to eliminate dark corners and shadows. If you don't, the bats will simply move to these areas.

### Gimme Shelter

Perhaps the kindest, gentlest approach to bat control is to provide alternative housing for them. Installing bat houses on your property will not only encourage them to roost somewhere else than your house, it keeps the bats in the area where they can continue to hunt for yard and garden insect pests. It's a win-win for you and the bats.

Bat houses can be purchased at hardware stores and garden centers. The Organization for Bat Conservation, a national nonprofit dedicated to preserving bats and their habitats, offers ready-made houses and plans for building your own. You'll find more information on them in the resources appendix.

If you decide to give your bats an alternative roosting site, you'll want to buy more than one bat house, as they need to be installed at various heights. It can take up to one year and sometimes longer before the bats will take up residence.

## Battling Bunches of Birds

Nuisance or pest birds are typically more of a problem than bats are, both in urban and rural settings. Three species in particular—English sparrows (also called house sparrows), starlings, and pigeons—cause the most problems, due to their roosting preferences. All of them like to roost or nest on rafters, window sills, and ledges.

Many people take somewhat of a cavalier attitude about bird infestations, but they really shouldn't. Here's why:

- Birds are known transmitters of a bunch of diseases, as well as of parasites and insects. Since pest birds live in close association with humans and they can travel great distances, they're perfect mechanisms for spreading all sorts of nasty stuff by contamination, direct contact, or inhalation.

- They nest in the most inopportune places—gutters, drainpipes, machinery housings, chimneys … you name it. All are potential problem spots. Clogged gutters and drainpipes can cause extensive water damage. Nests in machinery housings can catch fire. Nests in chimneys and air vents can block airflow and cause carbon monoxide poisoning.

**Around the House**

The big three pest birds—pigeons, house sparrows, and starlings—are all introduced species that have done very well in their adopted country. All are well-established, numbering into the millions. These species, along with other bird pests like woodpeckers and crows, rack up tens of millions of dollars in damage annually to structures, automobiles, crops, and more.

- Bird droppings are acidic and will eat away at anything they hit. Tar-based roofing materials are especially vulnerable. Let droppings accumulate on your asphalt-shingle roof, and you open yourself up to leaks, as the acid eats into the material.

Now those sweet little sparrows and those cute, cooing pigeons don't seem so innocuous, do they?

# Banishing Birds

Like other wildlife pests, pest birds can be effectively controlled using Integrated Pest Management (IPM). Of the various IPM approaches, physical controls are the ones most often employed with pest birds. There aren't many effective chemical controls; those that are available are mostly designed to repel birds, not kill them. Be-sides, eliminating birds doesn't really get rid of the problem. It just paves the way for other birds to take up residence.

**In the Nick of Time**

Pest-bird experts recommend using a variety of different control methods and changing them often, as birds get accustomed to them. If you're not getting the level of control you want, don't get discouraged. Try other approaches.

Good sanitation—in this case, limiting or eliminating access to food and water—is an important first step in controlling pest bird populations.

Birds don't come into houses to eat, but they will spend more time in yards that offer good eats than those that don't. If they know your yard is hospitable, they'll assume they're welcome in or on your house, too.

While yanking out plants and trees that bear edible fruits, berries, and seeds will go far to eliminate a bird infestation, you don't have to take this drastic of a measure to get rid of your chirpers. Covering fruit-bearing trees with bird netting as fruit ripens will make it less accessible to the birds and more accessible to you.

If you have bird feeders in your yard, consider removing them. If you have to have them, do some research and find out what the pest birds like to eat. Then change the food to something that they don't care for. It's also a good idea to empty all birdbaths and other pools of water where birds can bathe.

## Saying Boo!

Scaring devices are a proven approach for controlling birds. There are hundreds of different deterrents, ranging from bird-scaring balloons to devices that deliver a harmless electrical shock when birds land on them. Many, like hanging aluminum pie plates, you can make yourself. Others, such as toy pinwheels to reflective tape, are about as cheap and easy as you can get. They'll all work if you use them correctly, which means …

- Changing locations often. Obviously, scare tactics depend on an element of surprise. Putting up a scarecrow or hanging a couple of scare balloons is a good start, but they'll soon become a part of the landscape if they stay in one place. Experts recommend moving things around as often as possible. Even daily isn't too often.
- Using more than one scare device. A single device might work at first, but it will quickly lose its effectiveness.
- Using more than one type of scare device. A combination of different scare tactics works better than one. Combining visual devices with sound repellers—there are even species-specific sound devices available—enhances the effectiveness of both.

For the best results, relocate scare devices at night so birds get a fresh look at them in the morning. Buy or make enough items so you can put some of them away every so often, and store them away from bird sight when they're not in use. Maintaining an element of surprise is essential.

> CAUTION
>
> **A Fine Mess**
>
> Many repellent approaches work best in the early stages of a bird infestation. If you wait too long, they'll nest and become an established population.

Chemical repellents that discourage roosting are also effective against some bird populations. They fall into a couple of different categories, including …

- Scented repellents. These products contain naphthalene, which makes it hard for birds to breathe. They need to be reapplied on a regular basis, and they typically cause only temporary relocation.
- Sticky repellents. As the name suggests, these products contain a sticky substance that irritates birds when they land on it. They don't work for all birds—house sparrows, for example, only cling to a small area so they don't

pick up much repellent. Sticky repellents can be a bit messy to apply and they attract dirt and other substances. For the best effectiveness, put a base of masking tape down first on the areas you're going to treat, then apply the repellent. This makes the product more effective on porous surfaces and makes it easier to remove.

## Barriers for Birds

This IPM method will keep birds off or out of all existing and future nesting sites. These are permanent control methods and can be more costly than other approaches, but they're the most effective in the long run:

- Installing a board or metal covering at a 45-degree angle on ledges where birds roost. Birds can't get a grip on angled surfaces.
- Installing bird spikes or wires. These are devices with short, heavy wire prongs that stick out at various angles. Sometimes called porcupine wires, they typically come in strips that can be glued or nailed on ledges. They don't work for all birds; some will happily build their nests inside the clusters of wires.
- Blocking off rafters, ledges, and other exposed areas with bird netting. Farmers have used this stuff for years to protect their crops from pecking damage. It's also effective for screening areas where birds could nest. It's easy to install—just cut it to size and anchor with nails or clips designed to work with the product.

If all else fails, birds can be trapped. However, it's time-intensive and not for amateurs. Baiting is tricky and traps must be checked daily. They also must have food and water in them at all times. If they're in areas where birds are exposed to the elements, the traps should be covered and protected from the wind. Pest species of birds should be destroyed after trapping or they will only return to their roosts.

A chemical called Avitrol can be used to kill certain bird species. However, licensed pest control specialists are the only people who can purchase and use it. If you need to take either approach, it's a good idea to consult with a wildlife or pest-control specialist to map out an effective plan.

## The Least You Need to Know

- Single bats and birds aren't in your house to stay. The best thing you can do is give them a quick way out by closing off the area they're in and opening a door or window so they can fly out.
- Never touch a bat or bird with your bare hands. While the chances of contracting a disease by doing so are relatively small, it's still risky.
- The best way to eliminate bat and bird problems is to keep them out of your home. Established roosts are more difficult to remove, but not impossible.
- Chemical repellents are not effective for battling bat infestations, but can work well with birds, especially when paired with other controls.

# Part 5 Third-Party Issues: Insurance, Contractors, and Service People

So much about dealing with disasters boils down to two things: making sure you're covered in case they happen and finding the right people to assist you, both in averting disasters and in coping with their aftermath. Having a good, comprehensive insurance policy in place takes care of the first concern. Finding people you can trust to work on what's probably your most valuable asset can be a bit trickier.

If you're looking for advice on hiring the right contractor for the job, or wondering if your homeowner's insurance needs to be cranked up a notch, this Part is for you.

Chapter 22

# Finding, Hiring, and Working with Contractors, Repairpersons, and Service People

## In This Chapter

- Finding good help
- Working the referral network
- Soloist or franchisee?
- Questions you should ask

Throughout this book, we've discussed situations where it's necessary to call in outside help. Now it's time to talk about how to find trustworthy, qualified people to work on your house.

This might seem like a no-brainer, but it isn't as easy as you may think. You don't want to trust your biggest investment to just anyone, nor should you. Especially on large jobs, hiring help isn't something you want to rush into or take lightly. Depending on the scope of the work you need done, you might even have to interview more than one person to find the one that you want to work with.

There are plenty of good companies and people out there, and a whole lot of others that aren't. In this chapter, you'll learn how to tell the good from the bad, and how to work with the ones you hire.

## Finding the Talent

Even if you're fairly handy with home repairs, chances are pretty good that you'll have to hire someone for repairs or other services somewhere along the way. You might not have the time or proper equipment, or the size or difficulty of the job might be more than you want to take on.

**Around the House**

The majority of complaints received by consumer protection agencies like the Better Business Bureau are related to home builders, home contractors, and home repairpersons. Sometimes, the problems are related to communication issues. More often, it's because homeowners don't hire qualified people to do the work, often because they don't know what questions to ask.

Regardless of what you need done, you want to make sure the company or individual you hire is capable of doing the job. You also want to make sure that you can trust whomever you end up hiring. The first step in the process is finding possible candidates for the job.

No matter where you live, there are probably at least a couple of people or companies that do the work you need done. There are also probably at least a couple of people or companies that claim they can do the work, but can't. Your first job is to find the good contractors and weed out the bad. How do you do it? Most people use one or more of a variety of proven approaches.

How many candidates should you check out? It depends. If it's a big job, such as running a new sewer line or replacing a damaged brick facade, it's a good idea to have at least three companies on your short list. For smaller jobs, such as minor repairs, pest-control services, and whatnot, you can let your gut instincts and your comfort level guide you a bit more.

## Word of Mouth

Just about the best way to find qualified people is to ask around. Maybe your neighbor had to hire a roofer after the last rainstorm and was happy with that person. Or maybe Aunt Sally's cats had fleas last year, and she had to hire a pest-control specialist to get rid of them.

Talk to friends, neighbors, relatives … even other contractors or repairpersons. Qualified people and companies float to the top. Chances are if you ask enough people, you'll start getting some consensus. Even if you don't, you should still come up with a good list of potential candidates.

## Let Your Fingers Do the Walking

Yellow pages listings and/or ads aren't cheap. Companies that spend money on them are usually pretty serious about being in business, whether they're well-established concerns or start-ups.

## Chambers of Commerce

Chambers of commerce are also pricey little organizations. Again, any company that ponies up the money for membership is serious about being in business and interested in building a clientele.

**A Fine Mess**

The Better Business Bureau (BBB) where you live can provide reports on any complaints they have received about a company. However, not having any complaints on file doesn't necessarily mean that the company in question is a good one. It simply means that the BBB hasn't received any complaints about them.

## Professional Organizations

Many trades—including plumbers, electricians, restoration specialists, and exterminators—have professional organizations at the local, state, and/or national levels. If you can't find a contractor through other means, checking with these organizations is worth a shot. Some have websites that list members or allow searches for members located in your area.

## Special Considerations—Disasters

If your home disaster is part of a larger disaster—say, a major storm that hit your community—you'll probably be one of many seeking the help of a qualified contractor. These situations are prime targets for individuals who overcharge, perform shoddy work, or skip town without finishing—or in some cases, even starting—the job.

Many communities have enacted emergency ordinances to protect their residents against these individuals. However, such ordinances don't offer 100 percent protection. Plus, if you're desperate to get repairs done, it can be easy to let desperation rule your emotions and decide to take a risk.

In situations like these, it can be tough to wait, but it's usually the best approach. Not waiting can cost you more money in the long run, especially if you end up spending a lot of money on temporary repairs.

Follow the suggestions in this chapter regardless of the situation. Try not to let your emotions color your decisions.

## Hiring the Talent

Once you have some prospects lined up, it's time to determine whom you'll give the work to. This calls for a certain amount of vetting or scrutiny to determine this entity's ability to do the job.

If you're thinking about hiring a nationally recognized franchise to do things like pest control or smoke- and/or water-damage cleanup, some of this work is already done for you. Franchise businesses have to maintain a certain level of standards to fulfill their obligations to the parent company. What's more, many of these companies require their franchisees to take classes or continuing education to keep current in their field of expertise.

This isn't to say that you're assured of a trouble-free transaction if you use a franchise. It's still a good idea to check them out, and maybe talk to a few people who have used them. But having a parent company to bring your complaints to might give you more recourse if things don't go well.

Questions you should ask of any entity that's unfamiliar to you:

- Do you work full- or part-time? Preferably, you want full-timers, as this means they're doing this kind of work for a living, not as a sideline. However, don't rule a part-timer out if you're otherwise impressed with the person or company. Keep in mind, though, that a part-time contractor might not be able to get the job done when you need it, and may not be quite as up on skills as someone who does it full time.

- How long have you been in the business? You want to see someone who's been around for at least five years. According to statistics, business failures are most likely to happen within the first five years.
- Are you licensed? Licensing requirements vary between states and sometimes even among local municipalities. As an example: South Dakota licenses or certifies only asbestos abatement, electrical, and plumbing contractors. In New York, all construction work, except for asbestos abatement work, is regulated at the local level, and you have to contact the licensing board in the contractor's community to see if he or she is licensed. Colorado also doesn't license general construction contractors, which means you have to check local licensing requirements. In Washington state, anyone wanting to do construction work must register with the Washington Department of Labor and Industries. If licensing is required, ask to see proof of the license.

**Around the House**

To get and keep a license, contractors must be able to do the work they are licensed for and typically have to prove they have a certain level of training and experience. In some cases, they have to take a certain number of continuing education courses every year or meet other requirements.

With the exception of plumbers and electricians, tradesmen who are paid by the hour typically don't need a license. Contractors who bid on jobs worth more than a few hundred dollars must be licensed in most states.

All states that license tradesmen maintain lists of license holders, which can be obtained by calling the licensing board in your state. If you're not sure what the requirements are where you live, check out the Contractor's License Reference Site at www.contractors-license.org.

- Do you carry liability insurance and worker's compensation insurance? Accidents can happen, even to the most experienced contractor, and the contractor's liability insurance should cover such occurrences. This is especially important for worker compensation. If a worker who doesn't have this coverage is injured on your property, you could be liable for his injuries. If the company you're considering can't provide this information, talk to someone else, as it means that you might have to assume the risks, which is never a good position to be in. It's also best to hire a company that uses a third-party insurer instead of being self-insured.

- How many similar projects have you completed? No two projects are exactly alike, but whoever you use should have some experience with similar projects.
- Who will do the work? If they plan to use subs, ask who will manage or oversee the work, and ask to see license information on these individuals as well. It can be a good thing, by the way, if a contractor works alone (if it's appropriate to the scope of work that needs to be done); it means fewer people coming in and out of your home, and possibly lower costs and fewer delays. If they use subs, demand to see evidence of workman's compensation for all workers on your property.
- If there are any environmental risks to the project, how will you handle the abatement, cleanup, and disposal of hazardous materials?
- Can you supply the names and phone numbers of at least three clients? Satisfied customers are the best reflection of quality work. A reputable contractor will give you this info. If a contractor won't, call an end to the interview. If possible, visit one or two clients to inspect the quality of the work. At the very least, call a couple of them. Ask if they're pleased in general and if there were any problems at any point during the project.
- Do you warranty your work? If so, for how long and under what circumstances? Is the guarantee in writing?
- How much will it cost? Ask for a rough estimate at least. For big jobs, it might take more than one meeting to arrive at a solid figure.

**In the Nick of Time**

It's not a bad idea to do a little research on your own when it comes to costs. Doing so can help you determine whether the bids you're getting are reasonable. Shop around at hardware stores or building-supply stores to get a feeling for retail prices on materials, and don't forget to factor in the cost of labor; some of this information is available online.

- Do you provide a written contract? Most do. If not, offer to have one prepared. You can find preprinted forms online. For a large job, have an attorney review the contract. Many contracts are written primarily to limit the contractor's liability. Arbitration clauses can save a significant amount of time and money in the case of a dispute.
- On large jobs, ask for credit references—typically, where the contractor banks and a few trade references—and verify them.
- How long will the job take? When will you do the work?

Reputable people won't be offended by any of these questions.

Finally, be sure you get along with the contractor. It's important that you're able to communicate well with this individual. If you feel like he's talking Greek and you're talking English, things could get tense when you ask questions and don't get answers that you can understand.

## The Skinny on "Underground" Contractors

Underground contractors are people who work a little beyond the pale. They might be freelancing—taking on additional work on top of their usual jobs—or they might simply like to be renegades. As such, they're usually part of an underground economy that trades in cash, doesn't pay taxes, and adheres to as few rules and regulations as possible.

These individuals surface in a variety of ways. Some of them take advantage of disaster situations and prey on homeowners when they're most vulnerable. Others surface via word of mouth; someone will tell you about a guy (or gal) that does great work for a great price. This may very well be true, but more often than not, there's a price that comes along with getting things done cheap. More than one homeowner has had to fix problems caused by an underground contractor, and ended up spending more than he or she would have if they had bought aboveground talent in the first place.

How can you tell if an individual is an underground contractor? The following are good tip-offs:

- They are not able to provide a permanent address or other permanent contact information.
- They do not want to put things in writing.

- They want cash payments, or offer a discount if you pay cash.
- They tell you that it's not necessary to get permits or have inspections on their work, or that things will be cheaper and go faster without them.

> **A Fine Mess**
>
> The old saying "there's no such thing as a free lunch" definitely applies to contractors who like to do things their way, with little or no regard to licenses, building codes, or good practice. Most of the time, it's risky to deal with these people. Their preference for operating on the fringe typically colors every aspect of how they do business. Many refuse to be licensed or carry insurance. They might ignore safety concerns and local ordinances, or refuse to get permits or inspections. All of this causes risks for anyone who hires them. The best advice: Stay far, far away.

## More on Estimates

No matter what kind of work you need done, it's important to get an estimate of costs before work begins. On large projects, it can take weeks for a contractor to prepare a full estimate, especially if drawings are involved. If this is the case, you can expect to be billed for the drawings whether or not you hire this particular company to do the work.

When you get the estimates, ask to have them submitted in person so you can discuss them. Compare the estimates from each contractor to make sure they're describing the same scope of work and using the same materials. Make sure everything you asked for is in the estimate. It should also include everything necessary to complete the job. If something isn't listed, don't assume it's included in the price. Generally, it's not. Some contractors will offer fixed price quotes. These include all the materials, equipment, labor, and fees necessary to complete the job. Also factored in is the contractor's cost of doing business—his overhead and profit. Others will offer cost-plus contracts. With these, you pay the actual cost of materials, labor, and equipment plus a set percentage for overhead and profit. If you're working with a cost-plus contract, be sure to specify cost limits up front so the contractor has a good idea of how much you want to spend.

Just about every house project goes over budget. As such, it's a good idea to figure that yours will as well. Typically, it's a good idea to set aside between 5 and 20 percent of your overall budget to cover "unplanned for" expenses that aren't included in the estimate. The complexity of the project will have some effect on how much you set aside.

You can expect to see some variations in estimates, but they should be fairly close. An estimate that's substantially higher or lower than the others doesn't necessarily mean that it should be dismissed out of hand, however. The contractor who submitted it might be seeing something the others missed, or might have some cost-saving ideas that the others don't. If you're interested in using this contractor, talk things over and see if there are good reasons for the discrepancies.

Always choose the contractor you feel will give you the best overall value for the money after you've taken everything into consideration, including the company's reputation and how things have gone with them to date. This doesn't mean hiring the company that submits the cheapest bid, although it might.

> CAUTION
>
> **A Fine Mess**
>
> Don't just choose the company that prepares the lowest estimate. It might be unrealistically low, in which case you could end up with lots of additional costs. Worse, you might end up with a job that is less than satisfactory because the contractor used shoddy materials or cut other corners as a result of underbidding the job.

# Getting It in Writing

When you've determined who you want to use and you've come to an agreement on price, it's time to sign a contract. These instruments protect both you and the contractor from misunderstandings by specifying exactly what the scope of the job is, what it entails, and how much it will cost. You should always have a contract, regardless of the size of the project, and you should understand the terms before you sign it. Some firms use preprinted contracts. This is okay; just be sure to fill in any blank spaces with "n/a" (not applicable) or "nil" (nothing).

Small jobs really don't require lengthy contracts, but you should at least have a written (and signed) document detailing the scope of work, the materials required, costs, start and completion dates, and warranties.

For larger projects, contracts should include the following:

- Names, addresses, and phone numbers of the involved parties.
- Copies of licenses and insurance certificates.

- Drawings (if necessary) and specifications.
- Who's responsible for obtaining permits, if necessary. Oftentimes, this is the contractor, although some contractors prefer homeowners to do it.
- Total price for the job, including an hourly rate for extras.
- Start and completion dates. There should also be language detailing provisions for delays and penalties if work isn't done on time.

> CAUTION
>
> **A Fine Mess**
>
> Again, steer clear of any contractor who wants you to pay cash. These deals leave you with no legal recourse if things aren't done to your satisfaction.

- Payment schedules. Many contractors will require a deposit of one third of the total price before they start work. Depending on the scope of the project, interim payments may also be required. Don't make the final payment until the work is completed to your satisfaction.
- Who will clean up the site and remove the construction debris when the job is finished.
- List of subcontractors (if any).
- Warranty details, both from the contractor and from manufacturers of products used by the contractor (the contract should state that the contractor will provide this information). Most reputable contractors will offer a warranty on their work, which states that they'll come back to fix things if something goes wrong within a certain period of time.
- How disputes will be settled.
- Contingency clauses for unexpected problems.
- A termination agreement that specifies the costs for canceling the contract at various stages of the project.

Read the contract over carefully to make sure you understand what it says and that it accurately reflects your understanding of what the project is all about. Don't sign it until you're satisfied with it. If it doesn't include everything you've discussed, write the missing information into the contract. Both you and the contractor should initial all changes.

If you're contracting for a major project, have your attorney review the document before you sign it.

# Mechanic's Liens

Mechanic's liens are legal claims on your property that give a contractor or another individual the right to keep or sell your property as security for an unpaid debt. On large projects, suppliers and/or subcontractors sometimes file mechanic's liens against properties to ensure payment by the main contractor.

Usually, paying your contractor in full will release all of these liens, as he will then pay all of his subs and suppliers. However, if he fails to do this, subs and suppliers could go after you for the money if the liens are still in place.

# Working with Contractors

On large projects, it's a good idea to talk to your contractor on a regular basis. Keep the lines of communication open. When you have questions, be as specific as you possibly can about your concerns.

On small jobs—even little things like spraying for bugs—it's always a good idea to be on hand if it's the first time you've used the company. How someone goes about doing the job will tell you a lot about whether or not you want to use them again. Don't hover unnecessarily, but keep an eye on how the job is done. Again, ask questions if you don't understand things.

If you've followed the steps in this chapter on hiring a contractor, you should have a good experience as the job unfolds. However, problems can and do arise. When they do, deal with them as soon as they become known. Don't let small problems become big ones over failures to communicate. Talk directly to the contractor, not to his subs. Give the contractor reasonable time to respond and remedy the situation. There could be issues that aren't obvious to you that the contractor is trying to work out without involving or upsetting you.

If problems worsen and you're not receiving satisfactory answers, send a letter to the company outlining the problems. Copy your attorney on the letter. Depending on the severity of the problems, you might need to take additional steps, including contacting the appropriate authorities.

CAUTION

**A Fine Mess**

Most states have some type of home improvement laws that protect consumers when dealing with contractors. These laws vary from state to state, so it's a good idea to know what the law is in yours.

If problems can't be resolved, you might have to terminate the contract, and possibly sue the contractor. As such, it's always a good idea to communicate in writing if problems aren't solved to your satisfaction.

If you believe you've been ripped off, call the consumer division of your state attorney general's office.

## When the Job Is Done

When the job is complete, you'll typically be asked to sign something that signifies acceptance of the work. On larger projects, this could be a completion certificate. On small jobs, you might just be asked to sign a statement on the contract stating that the work was done to your satisfaction.

If it's a big job and mechanic's liens have been filed on your property, the contractor should provide proof that all liens are paid off and removed.

### The Least You Need to Know

- Problems with home builders, contractors, and repairpersons make up the majority of complaints received by consumer protection agencies.
- Hiring qualified people to do the work and keeping the lines of communication open with them are two of the best ways to avoid problems with contractors and other repairpersons.
- Never rush into signing a contract. Always make sure it says what it needs to say, and that you understand it in its entirety.
- Think twice about hiring anyone who wants to be paid in cash, wants all the money up front, or otherwise seems a bit shady.
- Always ask questions if you don't understand something. The old saying "there's no such thing as a stupid question" definitely applies here.

Chapter 23

# Covered Or Not: Homeowner's Insurance and Home Warranties

## In This Chapter

- Protecting your most valuable investment
- Policy parts
- Levels of coverage
- Protecting new and old construction

Years ago, a wise person came up with some sage advice about disasters: Prepare for the worst, and hope for the best. Protecting your property by carrying homeowner's insurance or a home warranty is one of the best things you can do in anticipation of the worst that could happen.

For most of us, our home is our most valuable investment and the thing we spend the most money on. Unfortunately, we don't always pay as much attention as we should to the legal instruments available to protect that investment.

Sadly, it sometimes takes a disaster to learn that you don't have enough coverage.

Are you wondering if you have enough insurance? Unsure of your responsibilities should a disaster strike? Don't know if the crack in your foundation is covered by a new or existing home warranty? This chapter answers these questions and more.

## Protection from the Unexpected

As the name implies, homeowner's insurance is insurance that homeowners take out to protect their home and everything in it from the unexpected.

Homeowner's insurance came about in the late 1950s, pretty much as a result of the homeownership boom following World War II. Although various forms of insurance coverage had long been available, the concept of having one policy that covered all the bases was new back then. Homeowners were quick to embrace the ease and convenience of these comprehensive coverage policies, and homeowner's insurance is now one of the most popular forms of personal insurance.

**Around the House**

Virtually every lender requires that borrowers have homeowner's insurance before they'll underwrite a mortgage. If you pay cash for your home, you pay off your mortgage, or you live in a rental property, no one is going to force you into carrying homeowner's insurance (or renter's insurance), but it's simply a good idea to do so. Why risk everything you've invested in your home and your personal property?

The typical homeowner's policy provides coverage in two areas. Part I covers property; Part II covers liability. Both types are discussed in the following sections.

## Property Protection

There are hundreds of different insurance companies, and virtually all of them offer some type of homeowner's insurance. Policy specifics do vary, but the basics are pretty much the same wherever you go.

To begin with, they all provide coverage for the following:

- Dwelling. This is your home plus its attached structures, fixtures, appliances, plumbing, heating, permanent air conditioners, and wiring.

- Other structures. This includes detached structures—garages, storage sheds, fences, driveways, patios, sidewalks, and retaining walls.
- Personal property. This includes the contents of your home and other personal items owned by you or family members who live with you.
- Loss of use. This provision covers your expenses if you can't live in your home while repairs are being made.

# Protection from Peril

Homeowner's policies cover your property for some or all of the following 17 disasters:

- Fire or lightning
- Windstorm, including hurricanes and tornadoes, and hail
- Explosion
- Riot or civil commotion
- Damage caused by aircraft
- Damage caused by vehicles
- Smoke
- Vandalism or malicious mischief
- Theft
- Breakage of glass that is part of the building and damage caused by that breakage
- Volcanic eruption
- Falling objects
- Weight of ice, snow, or sleet
- Accidental discharge or overflow of water or steam from a plumbing, heating, air-conditioning, or automatic protective sprinkler system, or from a household appliance

- Sudden and accidental tearing apart, cracking, burning, or bulging of a steam or hot-water heating system, air-conditioning, or automatic fire-protective system
- Freezing of a plumbing, heating, air-conditioning, or automatic fire-protective sprinkler system, or of a household appliance
- Sudden and accidental damage from artificially generated electric current

## Levels of Protection

Which policies cover what? Here's a rundown on the most commonly offered policies, and the protection they provide:

- HO-1 covers only the first 11 disasters on the previous list. This bare-bones option is no longer available in most states.
- HO-2 provides basic protection against all 17 disasters.
- HO-3 takes HO-2 up a notch. It covers houses and other structures for all perils—including the named disasters above. The only exceptions are perils that the policy specifically excludes—typically earthquakes and floods.
- HO-4 is for renters. It protects personal belongings and any part of the dwelling that you own—say, for example, you had bookcases built in the den of your apartment—against all 17 disasters.
- HO-6 covers people who live in condominiums or co-ops. Like HO-4 policies, it covers belongings and structural elements inside the dwelling.
- HO-8 is a special policy that's designed for older homes. Since older homes typically contain more costly materials and construction methods, these policies reimburse for damage on an actual cash value basis—replacement cost less depreciation.

For homeowners, HO-3 is the most popular and the one most commonly written. Not only does it provide better coverage than HO-2 does, it usually costs only a bit more.

**In the Nick of Time**

Many homeowner's policies cover damage that ranges above and beyond the 17 disasters listed here. In fact, most cover damage from just about anything unless it's specifically excluded. Because of this, it's important to know what your policy does and doesn't cover.

## Homeowner's Insurance, Texas Style

Things are a little different in Texas when it comes to homeowner's insurance. There, the State Insurance Board permits the sale of the following policy forms:

- HO-A, which provides limited actual cash value coverage for only the types of damage specifically listed in the policy.
- HO-A amended policies. These provide more-extensive coverage than HO-A policies but less coverage than the next level.
- HO-B, which covers a home for all perils (unless excluded) against all risks. It also covers contents against named perils. This policy covers replacement cost up to the policy limit on a house; its contents are covered for actual cash value unless additional replacement cost coverage is purchased.
- HO-C, which provides house and contents coverage for all risks not specifically excluded by the policy. Again, the dwelling is insured for replacement cost up to the policy limit; contents are covered for actual cash value unless additional coverage is purchased.

Policies are also available for renters and people who own condominiums, townhomes, mobile homes, and so on.

HO-A, HO-B, and HO-C are all standardized policies. They must be worded exactly the same and offer the same coverage regardless of who offers them. HO-A amended policies are not standardized. Companies can also offer alternatives to the policies listed here if they're approved in advance by the commissioner of insurance. These policies also are not standardized.

# What's Not Covered

As mentioned, most homeowner's policies are amazingly comprehensive and cover things you'd never think would happen. A meteorite falling from the sky? You're covered. A fire that you caused when you used a faulty extension cord? Covered again.

That said, what policies typically don't cover is pretty important. Just about all of them exclude damage caused by the following:

- Floods
- Earthquakes
- Not taking care of your home properly

You can buy separate policies for flood and earthquake coverage, and if you live in an area prone to either, it's a good idea to do so. The extra $50 or so you'll pay annually for each is more than worth it. But there's no policy to cover what you, as a homeowner, are responsible for maintaining.

Other common exclusions include the following:

- Sewer and septic backups. As mentioned in Chapters 2 and 3, sewer and septic backup coverage typically isn't part of a standard homeowner's policy and must be added. Some municipalities offer this coverage and will bill you as part of your monthly utilities bill.
- Damage due to neglect.
- Intentional loss.
- Earth movement.
- General power failure.
- Damage caused by war.
- Rot, mold, or mildew.
- Losses resulting from not protecting your property after a loss.
- Insect and rodent infestations. Insurance companies regard infestations as home maintenance issues and typically don't cover pest-related damage. Many policies also contain exclusions for animal losses, meaning damage caused by birds, vermin, rodents, insects, or animals owned or kept by the policy owner. However, damage caused by a wild animal in your home might be covered, as long as the animal isn't a rodent.

Depending on where you live, things like wind and hail damage can also be excluded. Another interesting exclusion relates to changes to building codes. As an example, say your pipes freeze, and your local building code requires replacing them with a different material than what was originally used. The difference in cost between the old materials and the new product would be your responsibility.

## Understanding Loss and Recovery

What you stand to recover if you sustain a loss depends on the kind of policy you buy. Here, it's important to make sure you have enough coverage to both rebuild your home and replace your possessions.

For your home, you have the following options:

- Replacement cost. This covers repairing or replacing damaged property with the same or similar materials.
- Guaranteed or extended replacement cost. This is the highest level of protection. Guaranteed replacement cost coverage will repair or replace anything that's covered, no matter how much it costs. Extended replacement cost coverage will pay a set amount—typically 120 to 125 percent—above the policy limit.

**A Fine Mess**

Unless your homeowner's policy specifies replacement-value or guaranteed replacement coverage, you probably only have actual cash value coverage. If you have a loss, the payoffs with these policies can be minimal—as little as pennies on the dollar.

Homeowner's policies typically provide coverage for possessions at between 50 to 70 percent of the amount of insurance that's on your home. If, for example, your home is insured for $200,000, you'd be covered for $100,000 to $140,000 of personal property.

Your belongings can be insured for the actual cash value, which will pay for replacing them minus a deduction for depreciation for age and/or use. A better option is a replacement cost policy, which reimburses you for exactly what it costs to replace things.

Many policies will exclude certain types of property, and most only offer limited coverage on certain types of property, such as fine art, jewelry, furs, and so on. Many homeowners take advantage of *endorsements* or *floaters*, and buy additional coverage for these items.

**Tool Chest**

**Endorsements** are add-ons to standard insurance policies that provide additional coverage for such things as jewelry, fine art, secondary residences, and so on. These provisions are also called riders. **Floaters** are separate policies that provide coverage on anything not specifically excluded by your policy.

# Living Away from Home

Finally, the property protection part of a homeowner's policy covers the costs of living somewhere else if you can't occupy your home due to an insured loss. You'll be reimbursed for such things as hotel bills, meals, and other living expenses above and beyond what you'd normally incur.

## Liability Coverage

Homeowner's insurance also provides personal liability protection should you, your family, your pets, or your property injure someone else or damage their property. This can happen on your own property or elsewhere. However, this coverage does not extend to auto or business-related accidents.

> **Around the House**
>
> Liability coverage also pays should you be sued for damages, and will cover both the costs of defending you and court awards, up to your policy limit.

Standard homeowner's policies typically cap liability limits at about $100,000, which is pretty low in this day and age. For this reason, most experts recommend purchasing a rider that will increase your coverage to at least $300,000. If you have a home office where you see clients, bumping up your coverage is highly recommended. Depending on the type of work you do, you might have to buy a separate business insurance policy.

## Buying the Right Policy

As mentioned, it's important to buy a homeowner's policy with enough coverage to allow you to recover as fully as possible from disasters. There are lots of factors that you'll need to consider, starting with …

- How much personal property you have to insure. This includes the value of your home and the value of your personal property. If you own a lot of nice jewelry, or you work out of your home, you should count on buying additional coverage.
- How much personal liability insurance you feel you need. As mentioned, standard levels are pretty wimpy, and it doesn't cost that much to bump up this coverage.
- Additional endorsements for things like boats, aircraft, vans, etc.

> **In the Nick of Time**
>
> Insuring for 100 percent of replacement costs should completely cover you in case of a loss, but it may not. For this reason, consider adding excess dwelling coverage to your policy. This will pay from 120 to 150 percent of the face value of your policy should you have to replace your home. It also covers building cost increases.

In general, experts recommend that you buy enough insurance to allow you to completely rebuild your home. This amount is your home's replacement value. While it can be based on your home's market value or what you paid for it, it doesn't have to be and typically isn't. Insurance companies will sometimes require inspections to determine this value.

Homeowners typically underestimate the value of their personal belongings. This can really hurt should you lose everything in a fire or other disaster. For this reason, experts recommend doing a complete and thorough inventory of all household items and personal belongings. This should include the following:

- Written description of each item. This should include what you paid for it, what you think it's worth, or how much you think it will cost to replace it. Keep a copy of this list stored somewhere else, such as a safe deposit box at your bank.
- Photographs or videotape of all items. This is pretty easy in the digital age. Save everything to a memory card and store it off-site.
- Receipts for all major purchases. Again, keep them somewhere else—a safe deposit box is ideal.

Doing this should also convince you to buy replacement-cost coverage. It does cost more, but it will replace items at their current cost, not at their depreciated value.

You can buy homeowner's insurance through an agent or directly through an insurance company. If you have questions about coverage, you might want to work with an insurance agent who can answer your questions and walk you through various policies and what they cover.

## Upholding Your End of the Deal

Homeowner's insurance is a contract between the insurance company and the policyowner—you. These contracts are known as conditional contracts, as they require policyowners to perform certain duties if a covered loss occurs. Failing to carry out these duties could result in not recovering for losses or recovering less than you should.

As a policyowner, you're required to do the following:

- Notify your insurance company or agent as soon as a loss occurs.
- Protect the property from further damage.

CAUTION

**A Fine Mess**

Don't wait for a disaster to strike to take inventory of what you own. Doing so will not only help you determine how much insurance you need, it will also simplify the claims process should you incur a loss.

- Prepare a detailed list of all items damaged. This should include a full description and actual cash value or replacement cost (depending on your policy) for each item.
- Allow the insurance company or agent to inspect the damaged items.
- Write a detailed statement that describes the events that led to or caused the loss.

## Existing Home Warranties

These are specialty policies that insurers offer to people buying existing homes. There are a variety of different products available. If you're in the market for a new house and you're looking at existing properties, you'll probably be told about them sometime during the buying process, as they can be included in the offer you make on a home.

These policies can be purchased by buyers or sellers and typically cost around $300. They usually cover things like appliance failures and some systems, such as plumbing, heating, and air conditioning.

We can't recommend for or against these products. What we can say is that they can be worth looking into, especially if you're buying an older home or if you're concerned about something going wrong during the year or so after you buy it. That said, don't buy a home warranty or agree to one without first having the home inspected.

## New Home Warranties

Every state has building codes and permit processes to ensure that new homes are safe and livable when they're sold. Most states and/or municipalities also require homebuilders to provide certain warranties on the homes they build.

Typically, these warranties guarantee that homes will be free from defects in materials and workmanship for one year. Longer coverage is provided on other defects, such as in electrical, plumbing, and heating and cooling mechanical systems, and major structural elements like foundations, walls, and roofs.

The warranty periods and what builders are required to warranty can differ a bit from state to state. To find out what is and isn't covered where you live, check with city or state officials. If you don't know whom to call, try the state department of insurance or division of consumer affairs.

## The Least You Need to Know

- Homeowner's insurance is the best way to protect your assets should a disaster strike.
- How much coverage you need depends on what it will cost to replace your home and its contents.
- If you work out of your home or own expensive things, you'll probably need to purchase additional coverage.
- Existing home warranties might be worth looking into if you're buying an older home.
- Homebuilders are typically required to warranty their work and the materials they use for a certain period of time after homes are sold.

# Appendix A

# Glossary

**angle stop** A valve that shuts off water to appliances, faucets, washing machines, toilets, and so on.

**attic vents** Screened openings that ventilate attic space.

**awl** Small, pointed tool used for making holes in wood and other materials.

**backfill** Replacing excavated earth in a trench around or against a basement or crawl space foundation wall.

**ball valves** Main water valves that have single handles. When the water is on, the handle will be in line with the pipe it's located on.

**baseboard** Trim that's placed on the wall next to the floor around a room.

**beam**s Structural pieces that support building weight. Also called *girders.*

**borates** Chemicals derived from boron, a naturally occurring mineral. They're used to treat wood to protect it from rot and boring insects.

**brick tie** Small, corrugated metal strips that hold brick veneer to the wall behind it.

**brick veneer** A facing layer of brick that's fastened to sheathing over a framed or tile wall.

**brown rot** Fungi that causes wood to become dark brown.

**building codes** Community ordinances that govern how homes can be built or modified.

**caulking** Flexible material used to seal gaps between two surfaces.

**closet bolts** The bolts that hold a toilet to a closet flange.

**closet flange** The metal piece that a toilet sits on.

**combustion spillage** The unwanted flow of combustion gases into a home.

**commensal animals** Animals that live on, in, or in close association with other animals, but are not parasitic on them.

**composition shingles** Shingles that consist of a base covered by asphalt and granules. Also called *composite* or *asphalt* shingles.

**compression nut** Part of a compression fitting, which consists of a threaded body, a compression nut, and a compression ring. When the body and nut are tightened, they squeeze the ring around the pipe and form a watertight seal.

**crawl space** The shallow space under the living area of a house.

**creosote** A flammable, tarlike substance that's created when hot smoke flows up into the chimney.

**dampwood termites** Termites typically found in buried wood or fallen logs in forests.

**desiccant dust** Insecticide that eradicates insects by causing them to dry out.

**diatomaceous earth** An organic product consisting of finely milled fossilized shells of minuscule organisms. Also called *fumed silica*.

**drain tile** Perforated plastic pipe placed at the bottom of foundation walls that drains excess water away from the foundation. Sometimes called *perimeter drains*.

**dry rot** Erroneous term for brown rot, which, in its advanced stages, causes wood to turn dry and powdery.

**drywall** Manufactured panels used to make interior walls, made of gypsum plaster encased with thin cardboard. Also called *gypsum wallboard*, *wallboard*, *Sheetrock*, or *plasterboard*.

**drywood termites** Termites that attack dry wood above soil level.

**ducts** Round or rectangular metal pipes that distribute warm or cold air to rooms in the house.

**eaves** The edge or edges of a roof that project beyond the sides of a building.

**endorsements** Add-ons to insurance policies that provide additional coverage.

**fascia** Horizontal boards attached to rafters or truss ends along eaves. Gutters are attached to fascia.

**felt** Tarpaper that's installed under roof shingles.

**fixed wiring** The wiring in the walls of a structure that leads up to wall sockets and light fixtures.

**flashing** Sheet metal or other material used to protect a building from water seepage.

**floaters** Separate insurance policies that provide coverage on anything specifically excluded in insurance policies.

**flue** Pipes through which fumes from a fireplace, furnace, or gas water heater escape to the outside.

**flue liner** Material used to form a flue.

**flue pipe** A pipe used to connect a fireplace to a chimney.

**footing drain** A pipe or piping system that captures and redirects water that collects around a foundation. Also called *drain tiles.*

**foundation** The supporting portion of a structure below the first-floor construction.

**frass** The trash and debris—fecal pellets, wood powder, and so on—that accumulates in the nests of carpenter ants.

**galleries** Long nests that carpenter ants create in wood.

**gate valves** Main water valves with round handles that must be turned a number of times to close the valve.

**grade** Ground level, or the elevation at any given point.

**ground-fault circuit interrupter** An electrical device that senses potential shock hazards caused by moisture or a damp floor. When it detects a problem, it shuts off power to the circuit in question.

**gutter** A channel or conduit of metal or wood set below and along the eaves of a house that catches and carries off rainwater from the roof.

**humidistats** Devices that measure relative humidity.

**integrated pest management (IPM)** A pest-control program that relies primarily on nonchemical means, such as controlling food, climate, and entry points, to prevent and manage pest infestations.

**joint** Where two surfaces or components come together and are held in place with cement, mortar, nails, glue, or other materials.

**joint cement or joint compound** The product used to seal joints on drywall. Also called *drywall mud* or *spackle.*

**joists** Wooden 2 × 8s, -10s, or -12s that run parallel to one another and support a floor or ceiling.

**lateral line** Underground trench that provides such services as sewer, water, electricity, gas, telephone, and so on to houses.

**level** A device used to determine a flat or tilted surface. It contains a sealed, liquid-filled tube with an air bubble. The bubble moves to the center of the tube when the instrument is on an even plane. Also called a *spirit level.*

**masonry** Stone, brick, concrete, hollow tile, concrete block, or other similar building units or materials.

**metal lath** A thin strip of metal used to create supports for plaster, tiles, slate, shingles, and so on.

**mortar** The mixture of cement (or lime), sand, and water used in masonry work.

**nuisance animals** Wildlife that cause property damage.

**pheromone** A chemical produced by an organism that signals its presence to other members of the same species.

**perimeter drain** Perforated plastic pipe around the perimeter of a foundation wall that collects and diverts groundwater away from the wall.

**pipe clamps** Hinged devices used to repair burst pipes.

**pointing** Applying a small amount of mortar in the openings around bricks. In new brickwork, it's done to add extra protection from the weather. In old brickwork, pointing is done to repair eroded or damaged mortar.

**powderpost beetles** Beetles that turn wood into a fine, flourlike powder when they feed on it.

**pressure-treated wood** Lumber that has been saturated with a preservative to ward off wood-destroying fungi and insect borers.

**primer** A substance applied to seal raw surfaces or prepare surfaces for painting.

**PVC** Abbreviation for polyvinyl chloride, a type of white or light gray plastic pipe used in plumbing.

**pyrethrins** The poisonous chemicals contained in pyrethrum.

**pyrethroids** Synthetic versions of pyrethrum, an insecticide made from chrysanthemums.

**relative humidity** The amount of water vapor present in the air divided by the amount of water vapor the air can hold.

**rodding** Inserting a long rod through a sewer or similar plumbing line to clear clogs.

**rodenticides** The formal name for rodent poisons.

**roofing membrane** The material that lies under shakes, shingles, and other roofing materials.

**sanitary sewer** A sewer system that collects wastewater from bathroom, kitchen, and laundry drains.

**scum** The technical term for the lighter waste that floats to the top of septic tanks. Also called *buoyant waste*.

**sealer** A clear or pigmented finishing material usually applied over raw wood to seal it.

**septic system** A private, on-site water-treatment system, consisting of a septic tank, drain pipes, and a drain field.

**shake** A wood roofing material, normally cedar or redwood, produced by splitting a block of wood along its grain.

**sheathing** The layer of boards applied to the studs and joists of a building to strengthen it and serve as a foundation for a weatherproof exterior.

**sill** A piece of wood laid horizontally to form the bottom of a window or door frame, or the lowest part of the frame of a structure that rests on the foundation and supports floor joists and wall uprights.

**soft rots** Wood-destroying fungi that can attack wood shingles in wet climates.

**spalling** Describes brick that is shedding its topmost layer.

**spot-on** Topical flea killers are so named as they are applied to a single spot on the animal's skin.

**stop valve** A device installed in a water-supply line, usually near a fixture, that allows water to be shut off to one fixture without interrupting the flow to the rest of the system.

**storm sewer** A sewer system that collects storm water.

**stud** A vertical piece of framing wood. Also called a *wall stud.*

**subfloor** The framing components of a floor over which the finish layer is placed.

**subterranean termites** As the name suggests, these termites live in the ground, where they build large nests and long tubes, called "mud" or "shelter" tubes, through which they travel. They're the most common type in the United States, making up about 90 percent of all termite populations.

**sump pump** A submersible pump, either electric or water-driven, in a sump pit that forces any excess groundwater to a drain or pipe for removal to the outside of the home. Sump tanks capture the water collected from drain tile.

**termiticides** Insecticides developed to exterminate termites.

**vapor barrier** A building product—typically, polyethylene plastic sheeting—installed on exterior walls and ceilings under drywall and on the warm side of the insulation. It retards the movement of water vapor into walls and prevents condensation in them.

**vent** Pipe or duct that allows air and gases to flow outside.

**wasp suits** Special suits, sealed at the wrists, ankles, and collars, worn as protection from stinging insects.

**wax gasket** Simple, ring-shaped piece of wax that provides a watertight seal on the base of a toilet.

**weep holes** Small holes that allow accumulated water to escape.

**West Nile virus** A potentially fatal disease that is transmitted by mosquitoes that have fed on birds infected with the virus.

**white rots** Wood-destroying fungi that cause the affected wood to take on a whitish appearance.

**window frame** The stationary part of a window.

**window sash** The operating or movable part of a window.

Appendix B

# Annual House Checklist and Maintenance Schedule

Giving your house a once-over on a regular basis and following a home maintenance schedule are two of the best ways to prevent household disasters of all types.

The checklist here breaks down what you should look at and for on a regular basis. It's organized by subject, and matches each part of the book. In each area, we start on the outside of the house and work our way in. We also keyed the list to take you back to the chapters that cover each task.

Following the checklist is an annual maintenance schedule, organized by season.

## Water, Water Everywhere

### Roof

**Outside:**

- Inspect for signs of water and wind damage, including curled, damaged, loose, or missing shingles (Chapter 1).
- Examine edges for damage to roof sheathing (Chapter 1).

- Check flashing around chimney, vent stack, skylights, roof edges, dormers, etc. (Chapter 1).
- Inspect vents and louvers to make sure they're clear and operating correctly (Chapter 1).
- Inspect and clean screens on vents and louvers (Chapters 1 and 6).
- Examine chimney cap and clean if necessary (Chapter 9).

**Inside:**

- Check attic for signs of water damage (Chapter 1).

## Plumbing and Drainage

**Outside:**

- Check grading around your house to assure proper water drainage (Chapter 5).
- Check hard and soft surfaces (soil and asphalt or concrete) for depressions and settling (Chapter 5).
- Inspect gutters and downspouts for damage and clogs (Chapters 1 and 5).

**Inside:**

- Check main water supply handle to make sure it's working properly (Chapter 2).
- Check pipes for signs of leaks/cracks (Chapter 2).
- Check faucets, hoses, toilets, etc., for leaks. Also inspect shutoff valves for sinks, toilets, laundry, and main water shutoff valve (Chapter 2).
- Check basement and foundation walls for dampness or water marks (Chapter 5).
- Examine caulking around sinks, bathtubs, and showers (Chapter 6).
- Examine tubs, showers, and sinks (in and around) to make sure they're draining properly (Chapter 6).

# House on Fire!

**Outside:**

- Inspect chimney for signs of damage (Chapter 9).
- Check chimney cap to make sure it's clear of debris, nests, etc. (Chapter 9).

**Inside:**

- Check all smoke alarms to make sure they're in working order (Chapter 10).
- Have furnace inspected to make sure it's in proper working order (Chapter 10).

# Rock Solid? Maybe Not!

**Outside:**

- Check foundation walls for cracks and termite tubes, as well as other indications of termite and/or wood borer problems (Chapters 12 and 15).
- Check masonry, siding, etc., for holes and cracks (Chapter 13).
- Inspect wood surfaces—decks, porches, etc.—for signs of wood damage/rot (Chapter 14).

**Inside:**

- Inspect foundation walls for cracks and termite tubes, as well as other indications of termite and/or wood borer problems (Chapters 12 and 15).
- Check all wood beams, joists, etc., for signs of rotten wood (Chapter 13).

# Uninvited Guests

**Outside:**

- Check all materials and structures—siding, roof, foundation, vents, louvers, etc.—for damage and signs of entry, including cracks and holes (Chapters 17, 18, 19, and 21).

- Look for bird and insect nests under eaves, along ledges, and so on (Chapters 19 and 21).

**Inside:**

- Check attic for signs of entry by pests and/or nests (Chapters 17, 18, and 21).

# Maintenance Schedule

## Spring

**Outside:**

- Clear leaves and other debris from around outside air conditioner. Remove cover if used.
- Clear debris out of window wells, storm drains, gutters, downspouts, and downspout extenders.
- Inspect gutters for signs of sagging or damage. Fix as necessary. Check downspout extenders to make sure they're firmly attached.
- Trim back overhanging limbs on trees. Trim back shrubs if overgrown around house.
- Check weather stripping on windows and doors for fit and condition. Repair as necessary.
- Clean screens on roof vents and louvers.
- Clean chimney cap if necessary.
- Seek and destroy early signs of bird and stinging insect nests in key spots—eaves, ledges, etc.
- Repair any weather damage/holes/cracks on the following: roof, siding, trim, and windows.
- Have chimney cleaned and checked (if you don't do it in the fall).
- Remove insulation from outdoor faucets, pipes in unheated garages, pipes in crawl spaces, etc.

- Turn on water to outdoor faucets. Turn on sprinkler system; check sprinkler heads. Make repairs as necessary.
- Clean and inspect all window and door screens. Make repairs/replacements as necessary.
- Have air conditioner checked and serviced if necessary.
- Check bricks or blocks for cracked mortar or loose joints.
- Check painted surfaces for paint failure, water damage, or mildew.
- Examine all trim for fit, damage, and condition.
- Check caulking where two different materials meet, where wood siding joins the foundation wall, at inside corners, and where the window and door trim meets the siding.
- Check for broken or cracked glass and damaged screens or storm windows.

**Inside:**

- Test smoke alarms (at onset of daylight saving time). Replace weak batteries.
- Clean out sump tank and clear screen on sump pump.
- Remove hair from drains in sinks, tubs, and showers. Use a drain cleaner approved for the materials in your plumbing system if necessary.
- Check for loose putty around glass panes.
- Test all ground-fault circuit interrupters, especially after electrical storms.

## Summer

**Outside:**

- Check sludge and scum level in septic tank (if you have a septic system). Have system serviced if necessary.
- Have lateral sewer line inspected and cleared, or apply a root killer.

**Inside:**

- Test all ground-fault circuit interrupters, if you don't do it monthly (on outside circuits, too).
- Inspect all electrical cords for wear.
- Inspect washer hoses and dryer vent system (both indoors and out).
- Remove hair from drains in sinks, tubs, and showers. Use a drain cleaner approved for the materials in your plumbing system if necessary.
- Check pressure levels on fire extinguishers. Service if necessary.

## Fall

**Outside:**

- Remove garden hoses from spouts. Drain and store for the winter. Wrap spouts in insulation.
- Drain in-ground sprinkler systems.
- Clear debris out of window wells, gutters, downspouts, and storm drains.
- Check weather stripping on windows and doors for fit and condition. Replace as necessary.
- Check windows, doors, and siding for holes and cracks. Caulk as necessary.
- Check and clean chimney (if you don't do it in the spring).
- Inspect all soffit vents and other venting systems to make sure they're clear of debris.
- Check bricks or blocks for cracked mortar or loose joints.
- Check painted surfaces for paint failure, water damage, or mildew.
- Examine all trim for fit, damage, and condition.
- Check caulking where two different materials meet, where wood siding joins the foundation wall, at inside corners, and where the window and door trim meets the siding.
- Check for loose putty around glass panes.

- Check for broken or cracked glass and damaged screens or storm windows.
- Insulate outdoor faucets, pipes in unheated garages, and pipes in crawl spaces with materials such as rags or newspapers.

**Inside:**

- Have furnace checked and serviced if necessary.
- Remove hair from drains in sinks, tubs, and showers. Use a drain cleaner approved for the materials in your plumbing system if necessary.
- Test all smoke alarms (when standard time resumes). Replace batteries as necessary.
- Test all ground-fault circuit interrupters, especially after electrical storms.

## Winter

**Outside:**

- Check roof for damage and/or icicles indicating potential ice dams.

**Inside:**

- Check basement for leaks and seepage during thaws.
- Remove hair from drains in sinks, tubs, and showers. Use a drain cleaner approved for the materials in your plumbing system if necessary.
- Test all ground-fault circuit interrupters, especially after electrical storms.
- If leaving the house for an extended period, avoid frozen pipes by opening the cabinet doors to allow heat to reach the pipes. Don't turn the heat completely off.

# Appendix C

# Resources

## Websites

American Institute for Conservation (AIC)
**http://aic.stanford.edu/disaster**
*Information on disaster resources and a conservation professionals locator.*

**American Institute for Conservation of Historic and Artistic Works**
1717 K Street NW, Suite 301, Washington, DC 20035, 202-452-9545
*For assistance in cleaning and restoring valuables damaged by water and fire.*

**American Red Cross**
www.redcross.org
*Helpful tips for getting life back to normal after major disasters like fires and floods.*

**Association of Specialists in Cleaning and Restoration**
www.ascr.org
*Can't find a restoration specialist in the yellow pages? Check here for referrals.*

**Chimney Safety Institute of America**
www.csia.org
*Information on avoiding chimney fires and other chimney-related information. Locator for CSIA-certified chimney sweeps.*

**Federal Emergency Management Agency (FEMA)**
www.fema.gov
*General information on disaster preparedness. Also specific information on saving water-damaged items.*

**Heritage Emergency National Task Force**
www.heritageemergency.org
*Guidelines for salvaging water-damaged books, photographs, textiles, and other heirlooms.*

**National Association of Waterproofing and Structural Repair Contractors**
http://nawsrc.org
*Good resource for water and structural questions.*

**National Centers for Disease Control**
www.cdc.gov/ncidod/dvbid/westnile/city_states.htm
*Information on the West Nile virus and other communicable diseases that can be passed from animals to humans.*

**National Chimney Sweep Guild**
www.ncsg.org
*General information on the benefits of professional chimney cleaning. Directory listing of certified chimney sweeps.*

**Organization for Bat Conservation**
www.batconservation.org
*Information on plans for building bat houses and buying ready-made bat houses.*

**Wildlife Rehabilitation Information Directory**
www.tc.umn.edu/~devo0028
*Information on wildlife rehabilitation, what to do when you find injured wildlife, and who to contact.*

**The Wildlife Society**
www.wildlife.org
*Information on wildlife stewardship and compassionate approaches to controlling wildlife.*

**The Old House Web**
www.oldhouseweb.com
*Lots of good information, including how-to articles, for old-house enthusiasts and others looking for help with their homes.*

**Insurance Information Institute**
www.iii.org
*Articles and other information on all types of insurance.*

**Hometime.com**
www.hometime.com
*The online version of the long-running public television show. Good source of advice and information on projects and repairs.*

# Books

Better Homes and Gardens. *New Complete Guide to Home Repair and Improvement.* Des Moines, IA: Meredith Publications, 2001.
*Comprehensive book full of illustrations and descriptions detailing many common home repairs.*

Bohdan, Michael. *What's Buggin' You?: Michael Bohdan's Guide to Home Pest Control.* Santa Monica, CA: Santa Monica Press, 1998.
*Humorous and helpful guide on treatments and techniques for getting rid of household pests.*

Fagerlund, Richard, and Johnna Lachnit. *Ask the Bugman!: Environmentally Safe Ways to Control Household Pests.* Albuquerque, NM: University of New Mexico Press, 2002.
*Suggestions for controlling some 50 pests in and around the home. Good information on Integrated Pest Management (IPM) controls.*

Hufnagel, James A., and Edward R. Lipinski. *The Stanley Complete Step-By-Step Revised Book of Home Repair and Improvement.* New York: Free Press, 2000.
*Thorough and wide-ranging guide for beginning do-it-yourselfers. Covers both interior and exterior projects.*

McClintock, Mike. *Home Book: The Ultimate Guide to Repairs and Improvements.* Upper Saddle River, NJ: Creative Homeowner Press, 2000.
*Large, comprehensive book on home improvement and repairs. Lots of step-by-step instructions and diagrams, information about materials and tools, and more.*

# Index

## A


ABC label (fire extinguishers), 95-96
absorption field (drainage systems), 36
acceptance of work (professionals), 296
aftermath of a fire, 125
  cleanup process, 126-128
  locating valuables, 126-128
  removing smoke and smell, 128-132
aluminum wiring, electrical fires, 116
amp products, house fires, 123
angle stops, 16
animal damage, roof leaks, 7
ants, 224
  chemical controls, 225-226
  IPM controls, 225
arcing, electrical fires, 116
areas of origin, house fires, 113
artwork, cleaning up water-related disasters, 86
ash clean-up (fireplace), 106
attics, removal of wild animals, 212-214
Avitrol, 281


## B


backup-flow valves, 31
bacterial infections, rodent carriers, 190
bait systems
  carpenter ants, 182
  flies, 254
  termites, 178
baking soda, extinguishing small fires, 90
bald-faced hornets, nest removal, 242-244
ball valves, 16
barbecue charcoal, 123
basement flooding, 47
  causes, 49-50
  drain systems, 53-54
  fixes, 52
  foundation cracks, 56
  gutter problems, 53
  prevention, 51
  sump pump maintenance, 54-56
  window-well water, 57
bat intrusions, 270
  eradication, 275
    alternative shelter, 278
    lighting, 277
    screens, 277
    sealing cracks and holes, 277
  prevention, 274-275
  pros and cons of bats, 273-274
  trapping or netting, 272-273
bathtub leaks, 65-66
BBB (Better Business Bureau), 286-287
bedbugs, 228
  chemical controls, 230
  IPM controls, 229-230
bees, honeybees, 248
  chemical control, 249
  prevention, 248-249
  wall infestation, 249
beetles
  carpet, 230
    chemical controls, 232
    IPM controls, 231
  ground, 222
    chemical controls, 223
    IPM controls, 223
  wood-destroying, 232-233
    chemical control, 234
    IPM controls, 233
Better Business Bureau. *See* BBB
bird intrusions, 270-279
  chimney birds, 271-272
  corralling birds, 270-271
  eradication, 279
    chemical repellents, 280-281
    IPM controls, 281
    scaring devices, 280
bites
  fleas, 264
  houseflies, 251
blockages, sewage systems, 25-27
blow flies, 250
books, cleaning up water-related disasters, 84-85
Bora-Care, 163
borates, 163, 178
boric acid, cockroach control, 235
boxelder bugs, 222

brick crumbling (exterior surface problems), 146
cracks, 147-148
repairs, 148
brick veneers, 150
mortar replacement, 149
water damage, 148
spalling, 147
broken pipes
causes, 17
cleanup, 21-22
prevention, 20-21
repairs, 19-20
stopping the flow, 15-17
thawing pipes, 18-19
brown rats. *See* Norway rats
bubonic plague
fleas, 264
rodent carriers, 191
building a fire, 104-105
buoyant waste, 36-37

## C

carbamates, 260
carbon monoxide poisoning, 118
carpenter ants, 167-169, 180-182
diagnosing problem, 180
extermination, 181-182
identification, 169
immediate fixes, 168
preventing infestation, 181
repairing damage, 182
carpet beetles, 230
chemical controls, 232
IPM controls, 231
carpets, water damage, 79
causes
basement flooding, 49-50
broken pipes, 17
electrical fires, 117
flea infestation, 265-266
foundation faults
clay soil, 137-138
settling houses, 137
house fires, 112-113
amp products, 123
dryer lint traps, 121-122
electric blankets, 121
exceeding light fixture wattage limit, 121
flammable products, 122-123
foul-smelling appliances, 123-124
light fixtures, 120
spontaneous combustion, 120
sun rays, 121
kitchen fires, 90-92
roof leaks, 6-8
septic system problems
chemicals and substances, 40
compaction, 40
excessive water usage, 39
overloading the system, 38-39
wet walls, 61
dishwasher leaks, 67
humidity/condensation, 67-69
leaky bathtubs/showers, 65-66
leaky toilets, 62-65
pipe cracks, 62
wood rot, 159-160
chambers of commerce, 287
charcoal, flammable products that cause house fires, 123
chemical control
ants, 225-226
bedbugs, 230
bird eradication, 280-281
carpet beetles, 232
cockroaches, 235
firebrats, 236
flies, 254
ground beetles, 223
honeybees, 249
IPM (Integrated Pest Management). *See* IPM
ladybugs, 222
pantry pests, 228
silverfish, 236
spiders, 224
wood-destroying beetles, 234
Chimfex Fire Suppressors, 99
chimney birds, 271-272
chimney fires, 97
ash cleanup, 106
creosote, 101-104
extinguishing, 106
fire maintenance, 105-106
prevention, 107-109
roaring sound, 98-99
starting a fire, 104-105
structure of a chimney, 100
Chimney Safety Institute of America, 107
chimney sweeps, 107
chimney-fire suppressors, 99
chimneys, removal of wild animals, 210-212
cholecalciferol, rodent poisoning, 202
city rats. *See* Norway rats
clay soil, foundation faults, 137-138
clean-outs, 24
cleanup
chimneys, 107-109
fire aftermath, 126-128
septic systems, 44
sewage problems, 32

water-related disasters, 73
broken pipes, 21-22
cleaning and disinfecting, 78
decision to hire professional, 74-76
dry vacs, 76-77
floors/floorcoverings, 79
mold and mildew, 80-84
possessions and valuables, 84-86
walls, 78-79
wet vacs, 76-77
clean-water supply systems, broken pipes
causes, 17
cleanup, 21-22
prevention, 20-21
repairs, 19-20
stopping the flow, 15-17
thawing pipes, 18-19
closet bolts, 62
clothes moths, 232
cluster flies, 251
cockroaches
chemical controls, 235
IPM controls, 234-235
colony elimination, termite treatment, 177-178
combustion gas fires, 117-118
combustion spillage, 118
commensal rodents, 188-189
compaction, septic systems, 40
condensation
wet walls, 61, 67-69
wood rot, 159
Consumer Product Safety Commission, 122
contractors, 295-296
underground contractors, 291-292
contracts, hiring professionals, 293-294
control of entry points, IPM (Integrated Pest Management), 219
copper wiring, electrical fires, 116
cord length, sump pumps, 55
corralling birds, 270-271
cost-plus contracts, 292
county extension offices, insect identification, 220
cracks
brickwork, 147-148
broken pipes, 17, 62
foundations, 135
causes, 137-138
prevention, 138
repairs, 139-141
signs of shifts, 136
crawl spaces, removal of wild animals, 212-213
creosote, 101-104
buildup, 102
chimney fires, 102
formation, 102
crumbling brick (exterior surface problems), 146-148

## D

damage bugs, 221
damper assembly (chimneys), 100
dampwood termites, 171-172
de-rooting, preventing sewage problems, 29-30
defensive measures, flea infestation, 266
dehumidifiers, cleaning up water-related disasters, 75
Department of Natural Resources, 210
departments of agriculture, insect identification, 220
diatomaceous earth, 182, 235
dietary supplements, flea control, 267
dips, flea eradication, 260-261
dirt fixes, basement flooding, 52
discharge pipes, 54
disease carriers, rodents, 190-191
dishwashers, leaks, 67
disinfection, cleaning up water-related disasters, 78
disposable traps, yellow jackets, 245
distribution boxes (drainage systems), 36
diversion valves, 37
documentation of damage, water-related disasters, 76
dog tapeworms, 264
drain field (drainage systems), 36
drain flies, 251
drain tiles, 53
drainage systems, 36, 53-54
droppings, sign of rodent infestation, 191
dry rot versus wet rot, 157-158
dry wells, 37
dryer lint traps, house fires, 121-122
dryer sheets, as rodent repellent, 197
drying out water-related disasters, 73
cleaning and disinfecting, 78
decision to hire professional, 74-76
floors/floorcoverings, 79
mold and mildew, 80
enhancement of growth, 81
protection from, 81-84

possessions and valuables
artwork, 86
books, 84-85
furniture, 86
photographs, 85
walls, 78-79
wet/dry vacs, 76-77
wood, 162
drywall repairs, 70
drywood termites, 171, 178-179
dump rats. *See* Norway rats
dwelling coverage, homeowner's insurance, 298


## E


efflorescence, 148
EIFS (exterior insulation and finish systems), 153
electric blankets
house fires, 121
thawing frozen pipes, 18
electric heat tape
preventing broken pipes, 21
thawing frozen pipes, 18
electric space heaters, 18
electrical fires, 114
alternative wiring products, 116
causes, 117
fixed wiring, 115-116
warning signs, 117
electrical shock, rodent extermination, 202
electrician's tape, fixing pinhole leaks (pipes), 19
electricity safety, water-related disasters, 75
endangered animal species, 210
endorsements (insurance policies), 303
English sparrows, 278
entomologists, 217
entomology departments, insect identification, 220
Environmental Protection Agency, 26
environmental treatment, flea eradication, 261
cleaning, 261
insecticide control, 262
outdoor control, 263
epoxy resin, LiquidWood, 164
eradication. *See also* extermination
bat intrusions, 275-278
alternative shelter, 278
lighting, 277
screens, 277
sealing cracks and holes, 277
bird infestations, 279
chemical repellents, 280-281
IPM controls, 281
scaring devices, 280
fleas, 258
environmental treatment, 261-263
IGRs (insect growth regulators), 260
insect development inhibitors, 260
shampoos and dips, 260-261
spot-on insecticides, 259
erosion, effect on grade, 51
escape plans (house fires), 119
estimates, 292-293
evaporative coolers, 69
excessive water usage, septic systems, 39
exclusions, homeowner's insurance, 301-302
existing home warranties, 306
exterior construction, 146
exterior insulation and finish systems. *See* EIFS
exterior surface problems
crumbling brick, 146
cracks, 147-148
spalling, 147
finding the break, 145
repairs
brick repairs, 148-150
stucco, 151-153
vinyl and metal siding, 153
wood siding, 150-151
understanding exterior construction, 146
water damage, 143-145
extermination. *See also* eradication
carpenter ants, 181-182
rodents, 194
disposal, 203-204
population reduction, 199-202
rodent-proofing, 198-199
sanitation, 195-198
termites, 174
colony elimination, 177-178
drywood termites, 178-179
quality pest-control companies, 175-177
soil barriers, 177
wood treatment, 178
extinguishers (fire), ABC label, 95-96
extruded plastic lumber, preventing wood rot, 160

## F


face flies, 251
faults (foundations), 135-136
  causes, 137-138
  prevention, 138
  repairs, 139-141
  signs of shifts, 136
Federal Emergency Management Agency. *See* FEMA
FEMA (Federal Emergency Management Agency), 112
fiberglass batt insulation, water damage, 78
fiberglass-resin tape, fixing hairline cracks, 19
field guides, insect identification, 220
filter flies, 251
filth flies. *See* houseflies
fire-fighting equipment, 95-96
fireboxes (chimneys), 100
firebrats, 235-236
fires
  aftermath, 125
    cleanup process, 126-128
    locating valuables, 126-128
    removing smoke and smell, 128-132
  chimney, 97
    cleaning, 107-109
    creosote, 101-104
    roaring sound, 98-99
    structure of, 100
    understanding how wood burns, 104-106
  kitchen, 89
    causes, 90-92
    extinguishing small fires, 90
    prevention, 92-96
  residential, 111
    areas of origin, 113
    causes, 112-113, 120-124
    combustion gas fires, 117-118
    electrical fires, 114-117
    gas shut-off valves, 119
    homeowner's story, 113-114
    prevention, 118-119
fixed wiring, electrical fires, 115-116
fixes. *See also* repairs
  basement flooding, 52
  bathtub leaks, 66
  broken pipes, 18-19
  carpenter ant damage, 182
  exterior surface problems
    brick repairs, 148-150
    stucco, 151-153
    vinyl and metal siding, 153
    wood siding, 150-151
  foundation faults, 139-141
  insect intrusions, 218
  roof leaks, 10-13
  termite damage, 179-180
  toilet leaks, 63-65
  wet walls, 69-71
  wood rot, 162-165
  wood-destroying insects, 168
flammable products, 122-123
flashings, 7
flea collars, 267
flea infestation, 257
  causes, 265-266
  defensive measures, 266
  eradication efforts, 258
    environmental treatment, 261-263
    IGRs (insect growth regulators), 260
    insect development inhibitors, 260
    shampoos and dips, 260-261
    spot-on insecticides, 259
  health concerns, 263
    bites, 264
    bubonic plague, 264
    dog tapeworms, 264
    typhoid fever, 265
  identification, 257-258
  questionable control measures, 266-267
flesh flies, 251
flies
  chemical controls, 254
  IPM controls, 251-253
  mechanical controls, 253-254
floaters (insurance policies), 303
flooded basements, 47
  causes, 49-50
  drain systems, 53-54
  fixes, 52
  foundation cracks, 56
  gutter problems, 53
  prevention, 51
  sump pump maintenance, 54-56
  window-well water, 57
floor drain plugs, 31
floors/floorcoverings, drying out water-related disasters, 79
flues (liners and pipes), 99-100

flypaper, 253
foam pipe insulation, 21
food sanitation, rodent extermination, 195
footing drains, 53
formation of creosote, 102
Formosan subterranean termite, 170
foul-smelling appliances, house fires, 123-124
foundation faults, 135-136
  basement flooding, 56
  causes, 137-138
  prevention, 138
  repairs, 139-141
  signs of shifts, 136
frass (carpenter ants), 180
freeze-treating suspect food (insect intrusion), 227
freezing weather and broken pipes, 17
fruit flies, 250
fumed silica, 230
fumigation, rodent extermination, 202
fungi
  mold, 80
  poria incrassate, 160
  sap stain fungi, 158
  wood rot, 157
fungus gnats, 251
funnel-shaped devices (yellow jacket traps), 245
furniture, cleaning up water-related disasters, 86

## G

gallons per hour. *See* GPH
gallons per minute. *See* GPM
gas shut-off valves, 119
gate valves, 16
glue traps, trapping rodents, 201
gnaw marks, sign of rodent infestation, 193
GPH (gallons per hour), sump pump capacity, 55
GPM (gallons per minute), sump pump capacity, 55
grade (ground slope)
  dirt fixes, 52
  maintenance, 51
  pavement fixes, 52
grease fires, 90
grease marks, sign of rodent infestation, 193
green wood, chimney fires, 103
ground beetles, 222-223
ground-fault circuit interrupters, wet/dry vacs, 76
Guardian, 163
gutter problems, basement flooding, 53

## H

hair dryers, thawing frozen pipes, 18
hairline breaks, 17-19
Hantavirus pulmonary syndrome. *See* HPS
Hantaviruses, rodent carriers, 191
health concerns, flea infestation, 263
  bites, 264
  bubonic plague, 264
  dog tapeworms, 264
  typhoid fever, 265
heat guns, thawing frozen pipes, 18
heat lamps, thawing frozen pipes, 18
heat-treating suspect food (insect intrusion), 227
hiring help (professionals), 288-291
  acceptance of work, 296
  contractors, 295-296
  contracts, 293-294
  estimates, 292-293
  locating talent, 286-287
  mechanical liens, 295
  special consideration disasters, 288
  underground contractors, 291-292
Histoplasmosis, 273
HO-1 homeowner's insurance, 300
HO-2 homeowner's insurance, 300
HO-3 homeowner's insurance, 300
HO-4 homeowner's insurance, 300
HO-6 homeowner's insurance, 300
HO-8 homeowner's insurance, 300
HO-A amended homeowner's insurance, 301
HO-A homeowner's insurance, 301
HO-B homeowner's insurance, 301
HO-C homeowner's insurance, 301
home warranties, 306-307
homeowner's insurance
  choosing a policy, 304-305
  exclusions, 301-302
  home warranties, 306-307
  levels of protection, 300
  liability coverage, 304
  loss and recovery, 302-303
  owner responsibilities, 305
  property protection, 298-299

protection from perils, 299-300
Texas, 301
honeybees, 248-249
hornets, bald-faced hornets, 242-244
horsepower. *See* HP
house borer beetles, 233
house fires, 111
areas of origin, 113
causes, 112-113
amp products, 123
dryer lint traps, 121-122
electric blankets, 121
exceeding light fixture wattage limit, 121
flammable products, 122-123
foul-smelling appliances, 123-124
light fixtures, 120
spontaneous combustion, 120
sun rays, 121
combustion gas fires, 117-118
electrical fires, 114
alternative wiring products, 116
causes, 117
fixed wiring, 115-116
warning signs, 117
gas shut-off valves, 119
homeowner's story, 113-114
prevention, 118-119
house mouse (*Mus musculus*), 189
house sparrows, 278
houseflies, 249
chemical controls, 254
house-infesting flies, 250
house-invading flies, 251
IPM controls, 251-253
mechanical controls, 253-254
HP (horsepower), sump pump capacity, 55
HPS (Hantavirus pulmonary syndrome), 191
humidity, wet walls, 61, 67-69
hydraulic cement, 139
hygrometers, 68

## I

ice-dam–related roof leaks, 5-6
identification
fleas, 257-258
insects, 169, 220
IGRs (insect growth regulators), 260
IMPEL Rods, 163
in-ground foundation watering systems, 138
indoor sanitation, rodent extermination, 196-197
infestations
fleas
causes, 265-266
defensive measures, 266
eradication efforts, 258-263
health concerns, 263-265
identification, 257-258
questionable control measures, 266-267
insects
ants, 224-226
bedbugs, 228-230
carpet beetles, 230-232
clothes moths, 232
cockroaches, 234-235
damage bugs, 221
firebrats, 235-236
fixes, 218
ground beetles, 222-223
ideal conditions, 218
identification, 220
IPM (Integrated Pest Management), 218-220
ladybugs, 221-222
nuisance bugs, 221
pantry pests, 226-228
silverfish, 235-236
spiders, 223-224
wood-destroying beetles, 232-234
rodents
droppings, 191
gnaw marks, 193
grease marks, 193
holes in food packages, 193
nests, 192
nibble marks, 192
pet excitement, 193
squeaks, 192
tracks, 193
urine pools, 192
insect development inhibitors, flea eradication, 260
insect growth regulators. *See* IGRs
insect intrusions, 217
ants, 224-226
bedbugs, 228-230
carpet beetles, 230-232
clothes moths, 232
cockroaches, 234-235
damage bugs, 221
firebrats, 235-236
fixes, 218
ground beetles, 222-223
ideal conditions, 218
identification, 220
insecticides, 240
IPM (Integrated Pest Management), 218-220
ladybugs, 221-222
nuisance bugs, 221

pantry pests, 226-228
silverfish, 235-236
spiders, 223-224
winged insects, 239
honeybees, 248-249
houseflies, 249-254
IPM controls, 241
mud daubers, 247-248
quick kill versus insecticides, 240
stinging insects, 241-247
trapping, 240
wood-destroying insects, 167
beetles, 232-234
carpenter ants, 180-182
identification, 169
immediate fixes, 168
termites, 169-180
inspection
roof leaks, 8-10
septic systems, 41
Institute of Medicine of the National Academies, 80
insulation, 20-21, 146
insurance, homeowner's, 298
choosing a policy, 304-305
exclusions, 301-302
home warranties, 306-307
levels of protection, 300
liability coverage, 304
loss and recovery, 302-303
owner responsibilities, 305
property protection, 298-299
protection from perils, 299-300
Texas, 301
Integrated Pest Management. *See* IPM
intruders
attraction to indoors, 190
bats, 270
eradication, 275-278
prevention, 274-275
pros and cons of bats, 273-274
trapping or netting, 272-273
birds, 270-279
chimney, 271-272
corralling, 270-271
eradication of, 279-281
carriers of disease, 190-191
commensal rodents, 188-189
extermination, 194
disposal, 203-204
population reduction, 199-202
rodent-proofing, 198-199
sanitation, 195-198
fleas
causes, 265-266
defensive measures, 266
eradication efforts, 258-263
health concerns, 263-265
identification, 257-258
questionable control measures, 266-267
insects, 217
ants, 224-226
bedbugs, 228-230
carpet beetles, 230-232
clothes moths, 232
cockroaches, 234-235
damage bugs, 221
firebrats, 235-236
fixes, 218
ground beetles, 222-223
ideal conditions, 218
identification of, 220
IPM (Integrated Pest Management), 218-220
ladybugs, 221-222
nuisance bugs, 221
pantry pests, 226-228
silverfish, 235-236
spiders, 223-224
winged insects, 239-254
wood-destroying beetles, 232-234
signs of infestation, 191-193
wild animals
attraction to indoors, 208-209
getting animal outside, 206-207
nuisance animals, 208
preventing intrusion, 214-215
problems animals cause, 209
remaining calm, 206
removal, 209-214
trapping, 207
IPM (Integrated Pest Management), 218-220
ants, 225
bedbugs, 229-230
bird eradication, 279-281
carpet beetles, 231
clothes moths, 232
cockroaches, 234-235
firebrats, 236
flies, 251-253
ground beetles, 223
ladybugs, 222
pantry pests, 227-228
silverfish, 236
spiders, 224
winged insects, 239-246
wood-destroying beetles, 233

## J-K


Jecta, 163

kick holes, 171
kickouts, 171
kitchen fires, 89
  causes, 90-92
  extinguishing small fires, 90
  prevention, 92
    fire-fighting equipment, 95-96
    food preparation basics, 93-94
    tuning-up kitchens, 94-95


## L


ladybugs, 221-222
landscaping, effect on grade, 51
lateral lines (sewage systems), 24-26
leach field (drainage systems), 36
leak-detection systems, 21
leaks
  bathtubs, 65-66
  broken pipes, 15-17
  dishwashers, 67
  roofs, 4
    causes, 6-8
    diagnosis, 8-10
    ice-dam–related leaks, 5-6
    permanent relief, 11-13
    storm-related leaks, 4
    temporary relief, 10-11
  showers, 65-66
  toilets, 62-65
leptospirosis, rodent carriers, 190
levels of protection, homeowner's insurance, 300
liability coverage, homeowner's insurance, 304
licensing requirements, professionals, 289
light bulbs, thawing frozen pipes, 18
light fixtures, house fires, 120-121
lighting, bat eradication, 277
lightning protection systems, 117
lightning strikes, house fires, 117
lint traps (dryers), house fires, 121-122
LiquidWood, 164
live traps
  rodents, 201
  wild animals, 207
loss and recovery (homeowner's insurance), 302-303
loss of use coverage (homeowner's insurance), 299


## M


main lines (sewer systems), 25-26
main water valves, 16
maintenance
  grade (ground slope), 51-52
  septic systems
    inspection, 41
    minimizing water flow, 43
    pumping out, 42-43
  sump pumps, 54-56
Masonite, 151
mechanical controls, 253-254
mechanical liens, 295
metal siding repairs, 153
Mexican bees, 248
mice. *See* rodents
microwave fires, extinguishing small fires, 90
Migratory Bird Act of 1918, 272
mildew (cleaning up water-related disasters), 80
  enhancement of growth, 81
  protection from, 81-84
minimizing water flow, septic systems, 43
modifying internal plumbing, preventing sewage problems, 30
  backup-flow valves, 31
  floor drain plugs, 31
  overhead sewers, 32
  standpipes, 31
moisture meters, wood rot, 161-162
mold
  cleaning up water-related disasters, 80
    enhancement of growth, 81
    protection from, 81-84
  versus rot, 158-159
mortar replacement, 149
moth flies, 251
mounting bolts (toilets), 63
mud daubers, 247-248
mud-jacking, 52
multiple-dose rodenticides, 202
municipal water systems, 16
*Mus musculus* (house mouse), 189

## N


National Chimney Sweep Guild, 107
National Fire Protection Association, 115
National Pest Management Association, 175
natural controls, IPM (Integrated Pest Management), 219
nests
  insects, 242
    bald-faced hornets, 243-244
    yellow jackets, 245-246
  sign of rodent infestation, 192
nesting bats, 272-273
new-home warranties, 306-307
nibble marks, sign of rodent infestation, 192
nonporous materials, mold growth, 83
Norway rats (*Rattus norvegicus*), 189
nuisance animals, removal, 208
  chimneys, 210-212
  crawl spaces and attics, 212-213
  protected species, 209-210
  under the porch, 213-214


## O


one-way bat doors, 276-277
open systems, sewers, 25
organizations, locating professional help, 287
organophosphate insecticides, 260
outdoor sanitation, rodent extermination, 196
outflow pipes (drainage systems), 36
outlet drains, 54
oven fires, extinguishing small fires, 90
overflow, sewage systems, 26-27
overhead sewers, 32
overloading septic systems, 38-39
owner responsibilities, homeowner's insurance, 305


## P


pantry pests, 226
  chemical controls, 228
  IPM controls, 227-228
  treating suspect foods, 227
paper wasps, 247
parent colonies, carpenter ants, 180
passive controls, IPM (Integrated Pest Management), 219
patches, foundation cracks, 139-141
pavement fixes, basement flooding, 52
pedestal sump pumps, 56
perforated pipes (drainage systems), 36
perils, homeowner's insurance, 299-300
permanent fixes, roof leaks, 11-13
personal property, homeowner's insurance, 299
pest-control companies
  insect identification, 220
  termite extermination, 175
    colony elimination, 177-178
    drywood termites, 178-179
    soil barriers, 177
    warranties, 176-177
    wood treatment, 178
pheromones, 179
phorid flies, 251
photographs, cleaning up water-related disasters, 85
pigeons, 278
pinhole leaks, broken pipes, 17-19
pipe clamp repair kits, 19
pipes
  broken pipes
    causes, 17
    cleanup, 21-22
    prevention, 20-21
    repairs, 19-20
    stopping the flow, 15-17
    thawing pipes, 18-19
  cracks, 62
  discharge pipes, 54
  flue, 99-100
plaster patches, 70
plumbing systems
  broken pipes
    causes, 17
    cleanup, 21-22
    prevention, 20-21
    repairs, 19-20
    stopping the flow, 15-17
    thawing pipes, 18-19
  wastewater problems
    blockages, 25-27
    breakdown, 27
    cleanup, 32
    overflow, 26-27
    prevention, 27-32
    sanitary sewers, 25
    sewage flow, 23-25
pointing, 145
poisons, rodent extermination, 201-202
policies, homeowner's insurance, 304-305

Polypropylene netting, one-way bat doors, 276
polyurethane caulk, repairing foundation cracks, 139
population reduction, rodent extermination, 199
electrical shock, 202
fumigation, 202
poisoning, 201-202
trapping, 199-201
poria incrassate (fungi), 160
porous materials, mold growth, 82
possessions, cleaning up water-related disasters
artwork, 86
books, 84-85
furniture, 86
photographs, 85
powderpost beetles, 233
pressure-treated lumber, preventing wood rot, 160
prevention
basement flooding, 51
bat intrusions, 274-275
broken pipes, 20-21
carpenter ant infestation, 181
foundation faults, 138
honeybee intrusions, 248-249
kitchen fires, 92
fire-fighting equipment, 95-96
food preparation basics, 93-94
tuning-up kitchens, 94-95
residential fires, 118-119
sewage problems, 27
de-rooting, 29-30
keeping extra water out, 32
keeping systems clean, 28-29
modifying internal plumbing, 30-32
termite infestation, 172
elimination of wood-ground connections, 173
moisture-abatement efforts, 173-174
screen installation, 174
wild animal intrusion, 214-215
wood rot, 160-161
private wells, 16
professionals
acceptance of work, 296
contractors, 295-296
contracts, 293-294
drying out water-related disasters, 74-76
estimates, 292-293
hiring, 288-291
locating talent, 286-287
mechanical liens, 295
pest-control, 175-179
special consideration disasters, 288
underground contractors, 291-292
property protection, homeowner's insurance, 298-299
protected species, wild animals, 209-210
public works departments, 17
pumping out septic systems, 42-43

## Q-R

raccoons
preventing intrusion, 215
removal
chimneys, 210-212
crawl spaces and attics, 212-213
rainwater runoff (gutters), 53
rat-bite fever, 191
rats. *See* rodents
*Rattus norvegicus* (Norway rats), 189
*Rattus rattus* (roof rats), 189
relative humidity, wet walls, 61, 67-69
removal. *See also* eradication; extermination
smoke and smell (aftermath of a fire), 128-132
wild animals
chimneys, 210-212
crawl spaces and attics, 212-213
protected species, 209-210
under the porch, 213-214
repairs. *See also* fixes
bathtub leaks, 66
broken pipes, 19-20
carpenter ant damage, 182
exterior surface problems
brick repairs, 148-150
stucco, 151-153
vinyl and metal siding, 153
wood siding, 150-151
foundation faults, 139-141
termite damage, 179-180
toilet leaks, 63-65
wet walls, 69
drywall, 70
plaster patches, 70
water stains, 70-71
woodwork damage, 71
wood rot, 156, 162-165
repellents, rodent extermination, 197-198
re-pointing, 145
residential fires, 111
areas of origin, 113
causes, 112-113
amp products, 123
dryer lint traps, 121-122

electric blankets, 121
exceeding light fixture wattage limit, 121
flammable products, 122-123
foul-smelling appliances, 123-124
light fixtures, 120
spontaneous combustion, 120
sun rays, 121
combustion gas fires, 117-118
electrical fires, 114
alternative wiring products, 116
causes, 117
fixed wiring, 115-116
warning signs, 117
gas shut-off valves, 119
homeowner's story, 113-114
prevention, 118-119
reusable traps, yellow jackets, 245
rhizomorphs, 160
rodding sewer lines, 24
rodenticides, 201
rodents, 187-188
attraction to indoors, 190
carriers of disease, 190-191
commensal rodents, 188-189
extermination, 194
disposal, 203-204
population reduction, 199-202
rodent-proofing, 198-199
sanitation, 195-198
rodent-proofing, 198-199
signs of infestation
droppings, 191
gnaw marks, 193
grease marks, 193
holes in food packages, 193
nests, 192
nibble marks, 192
pet excitement, 193
squeaks, 192
tracks, 193
urine pools, 192
roof leaks, 4
causes, 6-8
diagnosis, 8-10
ice-dam–related leaks, 5-6
permanent relief, 11-13
storm-related leaks, 4
temporary relief, 10-11
roof rats (*Rattus rattus*), 189
roosting areas, bats, 275
alternative shelter, 278
lighting, 277
screens, 277
sealing cracks and holes, 277
root clogs, 29
rot (wood rot)
causes, 159-160
dry rot versus wet rot, 157-158
drying out wood, 162
fungi, 157
moisture meters, 161-162
prevention, 160-161
repairs, 156, 162-165
versus mold, 158-159
safety
electrical devices and water, 75
mold and mildew clean-up, 81-84
salmonellosis salmonella, 190
sanitation
IPM (Integrated Pest Management), 219, 252
rodent extermination
food sanitation, 195
indoor sanitation, 196-197
outdoor sanitation, 196
repellents, 197-198
sewers, 25
sap stain fungi, 158
satellite colonies, carpenter ants, 180
scaring devices, bird eradication, 280
scented repellents, bird eradication, 280
screens
bat eradication, 277
preventing termite infestation, 174
scum, 36-37
seepage pits, 37
septic systems, 35
causes of problems, 38-40
cleanup, 44
drainage systems, 36
maintenance
inspection, 41
minimizing water flow, 43
pumping out, 42-43
septic tanks, 36
stopping the flow, 36
settling houses, foundation faults, 137
sewage problems
blockages, 25-27
breakdown, 27
cleanup, 32
overflow, 26-27
prevention, 27
de-rooting, 29-30
keeping extra water out, 32
keeping systems clean, 28-29
modifying internal plumbing, 30-32
sanitary sewers, 25
stopping the flow, 23-25
sewer flies, 251

sewer rats. *See* Norway rats
sewer-relief caps, 24
shampoos, flea eradication, 260-261
Shell-Guard, 163
shingles (roofs), 7
shower leaks, 65-66
signs of shifts (foundation cracks), 136
silica gel dusts, 178
silverfish, 235-236
single dose rodenticides, 202
sistering, 179
skunks
  preventing intrusion, 215
  removal, 213-214
sludge, 36-37
smoke
  alarms, 118-119
  chamber (chimneys), 100
  fire aftermath, 128-132
snap traps (rodents), 200
snow and ice shields, 5
snow roof rakes, 5
soft rots, 158
soil
  barriers, termite treatment, 177
  compaction, 51
  erosion, 51
spalling, 147
spiders, 223-224
spirit levels, 51
splashguards, 53
spontaneous combustion, house fires, 120
spot-on insecticides, flea eradication, 259
spring-loaded traps (rodents), 200
squirrels
  preventing intrusion, 214
  removal
    chimneys, 210-212
    crawl spaces and attics, 212-213
stable flies, 251
Stachybotrys atra (mold), 80
standing water, electrical precautions, 75
standpipes, 31
starlings, 278
starting a fire (fireplace), 104-105
sticky repellents, bird eradication, 280
stinging insects, 241
  bald-faced hornets, 242-244
  nests, 242
  paper wasps, 247
  risk factors, 241
  yellow jackets, 244
    IPM controls, 245-246
    nests, 245-246
    walls, 247
stink bugs. *See* ground beetles
stopping water flow (broken pipes), 15-17
storm-related roof leaks, 4
structure of chimneys, 100
stucco repairs, 151-153
submersible sump pumps, 55
subsurface drainage systems, 53
subterranean termites, 170
sump pumps, 54-46
sump tanks, 53
sun rays, house fires, 121
super termites, 170
surge protection devices, 117
swarms of honeybees, 248
switches, sump pumps, 55
synthetic pyrethroids, 223

## T

t-handles, 17
tarpaper, 7
temporary fixes, roof leaks, 10-11
termites, 167
  dampwood, 171-172
  drywood, 171
  extermination, 174
    colony elimination, 177-178
    drywood termites, 178-179
    quality pest-control companies, 175-177
    soil barriers, 177
    wood treatment, 178
  identification, 169
  immediate fixes, 168
  preventing infestation, 172
    elimination of wood-ground connections, 173
    moisture-abatement efforts, 173-174
    screen installation, 174
  repairing damage, 179-180
  subterranean, 170
  termiticides, 178
testing smoke alarms, 119
thawing pipes (broken pipes), 18-19
ties, 146
Tim-bor, 163
toilet leaks, 62-65
traps
  bat, 272-273
  flea, 266
  rodent, 199
    glue, 201
    live, 201
    snap, 200
  yellow jacket, 245
  wild animal, 207
  winged insect, 240
tree damage, roof leaks, 8
trisodium phosphate. *See* TSP
TSP (trisodium phosphate), 71, 83, 148
typhoid fever, fleas, 265

typhus, rodent carriers, 191
Tyvek, 146

## U

U.S. Fire Administration, 91
ultrasonic devices
  flea control, 267
  rodent repellents, 197
ultraviolet light traps (flies), 254
underground contractors, 291-292
urinating pillars (rodents), 192
urine pools, sign of rodent infestation, 192

## V

valuables
  cleaning up water-related disasters
    artwork, 86
    books, 84-85
    furniture, 86
    photographs, 85
  locating after a fire, 126-128
valves
  angle stops, 16
  backup-flow, 31
  main water, 16
vinyl siding repairs, 153
vinyl wallcoverings, water damage, 79
vitamin $D_3$, rodent poisoning, 202

## W

walls, wet, 59-60
  causes, 61-69
  repairs, 69-71
warning signs, electrical fires, 117
warranties
  home, 306-307
  pest-control companies, 176-177
wasps, 247-248
wastewater systems
  septic systems, 35
    causes of problems, 38-40
    cleanup, 44
    drainage systems, 36
    maintenance, 41-44
    septic tanks, 36
    stopping the flow, 36
  sewage flow, 23
    blockages, 25-27
    breakdown, 27
    cleanup, 32
    overflow, 26-27
    prevention, 27-32
    sanitary sewers, 25
water damage
  brick repairs, 148
  broken pipes, 21-22
  drying out tips, 73
    cleaning and disinfecting, 78
    decision to hire professional, 74-76
    dry vacs, 76-77
    floors/floorcoverings, 79
    mold and mildew, 80-84
    possessions and valuables, 84-86
    walls, 78-79
    wet vacs, 76-77
  exterior surface problems, 143-145
  flooded basements, 47
    causes, 49-50
    drain systems, 53-54
    fixes, 52
    foundation cracks, 56
    gutter problems, 53
    prevention, 51
    sump pump maintenance, 54-56
    window-well water, 57
  wet walls, 59-60
    causes, 61-69
    repairs, 69-71
water leaks, broken pipes, 15-17
water stains, 70-71
watering systems, in-ground foundation watering systems, 138
wax gaskets, 63
wax seals (toilets), 62
weep holes, 148
Weil's disease. *See* leptospirosis
West Nile virus. *See* WNV
wet rot versus dry rot, 157-158
wet walls, 59-60
  causes, 61
    bathtub leaks, 65-66
    dishwasher leaks, 67
    humidity/condensation, 67-69
    pipe cracks, 62
    shower leaks, 65-66
    toilet leaks, 62-65
  repairs, 69
    drywall, 70
    plaster patches, 70
    water stains, 70-71
    woodwork damage, 71
wet/dry vacs, drying out water-related disasters, 76-77
white rots, 158
wild animal intrusions
  attraction to indoors, 208-209
  nuisance animals, 208

preventing intrusion, 214-215
problems animals cause, 209
remaining calm, 206
removal, 206
chimneys, 210-212
crawl spaces and attics, 212-213
protected species, 209-210
under the porch, 213-214
trapping, 207
window-well water, basement flooding, 57
winged insects, 239
honeybees, 248-249
houseflies, 249
chemical controls, 254
house-infesting flies, 250
house-invading flies, 251
IPM controls, 251-253
mechanical controls, 253-254
IPM controls, 241
mud daubers, 247-248
quick kill versus insecticides, 240
stinging insects
bald-faced hornets, 242-244
nests, 242
paper wasps, 247
risk factors, 241
yellow jackets, 244-247
trapping, 240
WNV (West Nile virus), 271
wood rot
causes, 159-160
dry rot versus wet rot, 157-158
drying out wood, 162
fungi, 157
moisture meters, 161-162
prevention, 160-161
repairs, 156, 162-165
versus mold, 158-159
wood sheathing, 146
wood siding repairs, 150-151
wood treatment, termites, 178
wood-burning appliances, chimney fires
cleaning chimneys, 107-109
creosote, 101-104
roaring sound, 98-99
structure of chimneys, 100
understanding how wood burns, 104-106
wood-destroying insects, 167
beetles, 232-234
carpenter ants, 180-182
identification, 169
immediate fixes, 168
termites, 169
dampwood, 171-172
drywood, 171
extermination, 174-179
preventing infestation, 172-174
repairing damage, 179-180
subterranean, 170
wood-polymer lumber, preventing wood rot, 160
woodwork repairs, 71

## X-Y-Z

yellow jackets, 244
IPM controls, 245-246
nests, 245-246
walls, 247
Yellow pages, professional help, 287

zappers, rodent reduction, 202

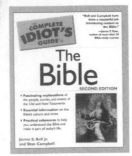

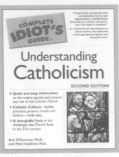